THE FAMILY
Handyman

1001
HOME
HINTS
&TIPS

THE FAMILY HANDYMAN 1001 TIPS

Editor in Chief: Ken Collier
Books Editor: Gary Wentz
Project Editor: Eric Smith
Designer: Diana Boger
Cover Design: Vern Johnson
Contributing Copy Editors: Judy Arginteanu, Donna Bierbach

The Reader's Digest Association, Inc.
President & Chief Executive Officer: Bonnie Kintzer
Vice President, Group Publisher: Russell S. Ellis

Warning: All do-it-yourself activities involve a degree of risk. Skills, materials, tools, and site conditions vary widely. Although the editors have made every effort to ensure accuracy, the reader remains responsible for the selection and use of tools, materials, and methods. Always obey local codes and laws, follow manufacturer's operating instructions, and observe safety precautions.

ISBN: 978-1-62145-224-9

Address any comments to:
Books Editor
2915 Commers Drive, Suite 700
Eagan, MN 55121

To order additional copies, visit shopthefamilyhandyman.com

For more Reader's Digest products and information,
visit our Web site at rd.com.
For more about The Family Handyman magazine,
visit familyhandyman.com.

Printed in the United States of America.
1 3 5 7 9 10 8 6 4 2

Contents

1 STORAGE AND ORGANIZATION

2 SAVING MONEY

3 TOOLS AND CARPENTRY SKILLS

4 KITCHENS AND BATHROOMS

5 PLUMBING AND HEATING

6 ELECTRICAL AND LIGHTING

7 BUILDING, REMODELING AND REPAIRS

8 SAFER HOME AND FAMILY

Instant fixes

9 CLEANING

10 PAINTING AND DECORATING

11 WORKSHOP

12 CARS, RVs AND YARD MACHINES

13 LAWN AND GARDEN

14 OUTDOOR REPAIRS AND IMPROVEMENTS

Chapter One

STORAGE AND ORGANIZATION

Basement, laundry and utility rooms

Basement junk

Junk takes many forms—luggage, camping gear, the ugly vase Aunt Martha gave you for your wedding…stuff you need to keep but don't use all the time. If your house has a set of stairs with a sloped closet underneath, you have a huge amount of space that's mostly wasted. Here's how to get the most out of that black hole. Build a custom rolling cart that fits perfectly in the closet. This one is built like a shelf unit and rides on fixed casters so it slides straight out to keep things organized and accessible. When Aunt Martha comes to visit, just roll it out, grab the vase and you're golden.

Keep paperwork on hand

Tired of ransacking the house to find paperwork related to your water heater, water softener and other mechanical systems? Use clear magnetic pouches sold at craft and office supply stores for manuals, receipts and other paperwork, and stick them right onto the water heater, fridge, washer and dryer, and furnace. No more digging around for important papers.

Hanger shelf

Sometimes you just need another place to hang clothes, like on the shelf over your washer and dryer. Turn the edge of that shelf into a hanger rack by predrilling some 3/4-in. plastic pipe and screwing it to the top of the shelf along the edge.

Laundry organizer

Make laundry day easier with this shelf for all your detergents, stain removers and other supplies. Build this simple organizer from 1x10 and 1x3 boards. If you have a basement laundry room, you may need to cut an access through the shelves for your dryer exhaust.

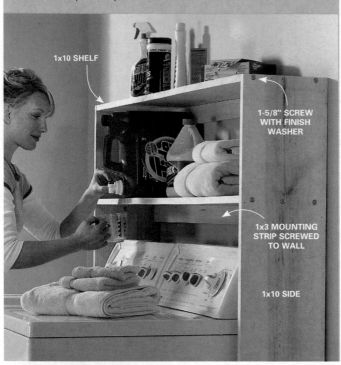

1x10 SHELF

1-5/8" SCREW WITH FINISH WASHER

1x3 MOUNTING STRIP SCREWED TO WALL

1x10 SIDE

No-slide laundry line

Tired of hanging your clothes on the line and having all the hangers slide to the center? Use plastic chain instead. No more sliding, and the links separate the clothes so they dry quicker. This works great in the laundry room or outside in the yard!

Skinny laundry room cart

A lot of laundry rooms have a narrow wasted space either next to or between the washing machine and dryer, and it's usually a hideout for socks and lint. To take advantage of this space, build a simple plywood cart on fixed casters to hold detergents and other laundry supplies.

Minimize liquid detergent mess

Dripless liquid detergent containers always drip just a little. Keep it under control with a special shelf on the corner of the laundry tub. Just cut a 1-1/2-in. aluminum angle long enough to support the front edge of the container, then glue it to the tub with silicone caulk. Rest the container on the ledge, and drips will just fall into the laundry tub instead of creating a gooey mess somewhere else.

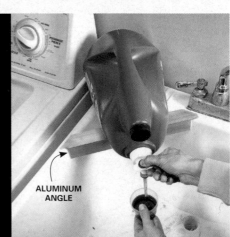

ALUMINUM ANGLE

Closets

Sliding tie and belt rack

If your closet needs a handy place to hang ties and belts, build a simple rack from plywood, dowels and a full-extension 12-in. drawer slide. Drill holes in the wood and pound in the dowels (use a dab of glue if they're loose). Attach the drawer slide to the side of the closet shelves and to the rack. If you need even more hanging room, add a block of wood to the side of your shelves to offset the slide, and attach dowels to both sides of the rack. The drawer slides come in pairs, so you might as well make another one for your wife to use for her belts and scarves.

Closet nook shelves

Salvage the hidden space at the recessed ends of your closets by adding a set of shelves. Wire shelves are available in a variety of widths at home centers. Measure the width and depth of the space. Then choose the correct shelving and ask the salesperson to cut the shelves to length for you. Subtract 3/8 in. from the actual width to determine the shelf length. Buy a pair of end mounting brackets and a pair of plastic clips for each shelf.

Wire shelving "corral"

If you store your gift wrap propped against the wall in the hall closet, some of the rolls can fall over and get lost behind other things or end up wrinkled or torn. Here's a better idea: Use plastic shelf clips and a small section of wire shelving to create a wrapping paper "corral." The rolls stay neatly organized and are easy to reach. You could corral other tall items too, like hockey sticks, bats and umbrellas.

Double-duty luggage

Put your luggage to use when it's not on vacation. Fill it with off-season clothes and stash it under the bed.

Garages

Vinyl gutter storage bins

Ten-foot lengths of vinyl gutter (sold at home centers) screwed to a 2x2 framework are a perfect place to store long items like hockey sticks, fishing rods, dowels, wood trim and corner bead. Items like these often end up leaning against a wall or taking over an entire corner only to tumble over or get wrecked because they're not really supposed to be stored on end.

Shorter sections of vinyl gutter and sturdy window box liners (sold at home and garden centers) attached the same way work well for storing hard-to-hang items like gloves, hose nozzles, fertilizer spikes and sprayers. And people who refuse to hang stuff back up on the wall can just toss it into the bin. If the gutter end caps don't fit snugly, apply PVC cement, silicone or gutter adhesive and press firmly.

Cut vinyl gutter sections to length with a miter saw. You can use a handsaw, but you'll need to mark the cut carefully to get it square.

Vinyl gutters are surprisingly sturdy—you can even store a few sections of rebar and metal pipe in them without a problem. Metal gutter is also an option. It's the same price, but it's harder to cut and too flimsy for heavier items.

Storage pockets for skinny things

Saw off short pieces of 1-1/2-, 2- or 3-in. PVC plumbing pipe with 45-degree angles on one end. Screw them to a board to hold paintbrushes, pencils, stir sticks and just about any other narrow paraphernalia in your garage. Mount them by drilling a 1/4-in. hole in the angled end, and then drive a 1-5/8-in. drywall screw through the hole into the board.

Handy hat hanger

Make space for your cap collection with this simple hanger. Take some clothes line, slip a bunch of clothespins over the line through the springs and then tie the line to a couple of eye hooks along one wall of your garage. It's a great way to store them and to let them air out after smoky hunting and camping trips.

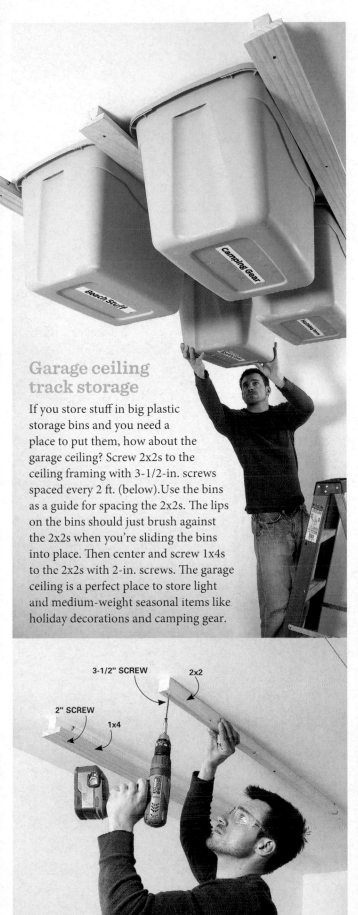

Garage ceiling track storage

If you store stuff in big plastic storage bins and you need a place to put them, how about the garage ceiling? Screw 2x2s to the ceiling framing with 3-1/2-in. screws spaced every 2 ft. (below).Use the bins as a guide for spacing the 2x2s. The lips on the bins should just brush against the 2x2s when you're sliding the bins into place. Then center and screw 1x4s to the 2x2s with 2-in. screws. The garage ceiling is a perfect place to store light and medium-weight seasonal items like holiday decorations and camping gear.

3-1/2" SCREW   2x2

2" SCREW   1x4

GIANT RESEALABLE PLASTIC BAG

Save your lawn products

Leave a bag of fertilizer or weed killer open for long and it'll soak up moisture from the air and won't go through a spreader. Even grass seed could use an extra layer of protection from a moisture-wicking concrete floor. Place opened bags of lawn products in large resealable plastic bags. The products will be free of clumps or pests when you need them.

Ski and pole organizer

Keep your skis up and easy to find with this simple 2x4 rack. Drill 3/4-in.-diameter holes spaced 3/4 in. apart. Glue 4-1/2-in. lengths of 3/4-in. dowel into the holes and then mount the 2x4 to the wall studs. Space the groupings about 8 in. apart to make room for ski bindings. Now you'll spend less time looking for your skis and more time on the trails.

Dustpan caddy

Keep a dustpan handy with an "unbreakable" wall file folder from an office supply store. Attach the file folder to the garbage can with 8-32 x 3/4-in. machine bolts and nuts. Position the screw heads inside the garbage can so the bag doesn't snag on the end of the bolt.

Fishing rod catcher

Cut an 8-ft. 1x4 in half and use 1-in. screws to mount 1-1/4-in. PVC caps on one 1x4 4 in. apart. On the second 1x4, equally space 1-1/4-in. PVC couplings. Screw the 1x4 with the caps to the wall a foot off the floor, and the one with couplings 6 ft. off the floor and directly above it. The rod tips slide up through the couplings and the handles rest in the caps.

Hoist your bike out of the way

When it comes to garages, there's no such thing as enough space. One product that will free up some floor space is a bicycle hoist. It's easy to install and very easy to use. When shopping for a hoist, beware of models that have undersized ropes. They can slip off the pulley wheels and jam. Look for one with a good, hefty rope. They're sold at a home centers.

Throughout the house

Mitten and shoe dryer

Drill pairs of 1/8-in. holes in a scrap of 2x4 and insert U-shaped pieces of galvanized 14-gauge wire sold at home centers. If you have forced-air heat, drill 1-in. holes between the pairs of 1/8-in. holes using a spade bit, and set the rack on a register for fast drying.

STIFF WIRE

2x4

Never-lose-it remote control

Tired of losing the bedside remote? Attach half a self-adhesive Velcro strip to the back of the remote and the other half to your headboard. You'll never have that remote slip between the mattress and the wall again.

Above-the-door shelves

The space above a doorway is an overlooked storage bonanza! It's the perfect spot for a cookbook cubby in the kitchen or a towel shelf in the bathroom. Consider adding a shelf or cubby over the doorways in your home office, laundry room and bedrooms too. You'll be surprised how many books, knickknacks and other items you can find room for in these valuable unused spaces.

Protect table leaves

When you're storing table leaves, protect the edges with pipe insulation. It will keep your dinner table picture perfect and free of scuffs.

Coat and hat rack

Organize your hallway or mudroom with this simple, attractive coat and hat rack. You just cut the boards to fit your space, paint them, outfit them with different kinds of hooks to suit your needs and then screw them to the wall. Shown are 6-ft.-long 1x4s, but use whatever length works for you and the space available.

Finish the boards first and then attach your hooks. Shown here are drawer pulls down the middle and a robe hook near the top to hold backpacks and larger items.

Attach the boards to studs, or to the drywall with screw-in drywall anchors. Drive three screws in each board: one at the top, one in the middle and one at the bottom.

MASKING TAPE FOR LAYOUT

FINISH WASHER

PROTRUDING TIP

2-1/2" SCREW

Drive your screws partway into each board so the screw tips poke out the back. Place the boards where you want them, and press hard to mark the spots for your drywall anchors.

Hanging shelves

Mark the tape, not the wall

The first step in any shelf-hanging project is to locate the studs so you can anchor the shelf to the studs if possible. Here's a tip that allows you to make marks that are clearly visible without the need to repaint the wall.

Use a level and draw a very light pencil line where you want the top of the shelf to be. The shelf will hide the line. Apply a strip of masking tape above the line. Use "delicate surface" masking tape to avoid any possibility of messing up the paint. Locate the studs and mark the centers on the tape. Electronic stud finders are the go-to tool for this task. Now you can plan your shelf-mounting project to hit as many studs as possible and use the tape as a guide for leveling and attaching the shelf.

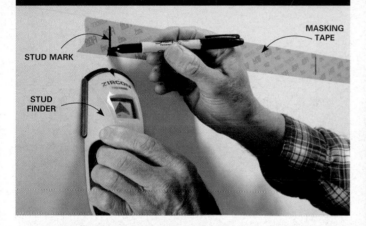

STUD MARK

MASKING TAPE

STUD FINDER

Super-sturdy closet shelves

Here's a fast, strong and easy way to install closet shelves. Paint a 1x4 to match your shelf. Then draw a level line and locate the studs or use our masking tape trick. Nail the 1x4 to the studs with 8d finish nails. Run the strip across the back and ends of the closet. Then put blocks in the locations where you want brackets. Now you have solid wood to attach the brackets and the closet pole sockets to. And the back of the shelf is fully supported to prevent sagging.

HOOK STRIP

Figure-eights simplify the job

These nifty little fasteners are actually designed to attach table and desktops to aprons (the vertical skirt around the perimeter), but they're also a handy solution for hanging shelves. You can buy a pack of eight at woodworking stores or online.

The only caveat is that the top of the figure-eight shows above the surface of the shelf, so it may be visible if you hang the shelf low. Try to position the figure-eights where there are studs if possible. You can use good-quality hollow-wall anchors if the studs don't line up with the figure-eights.

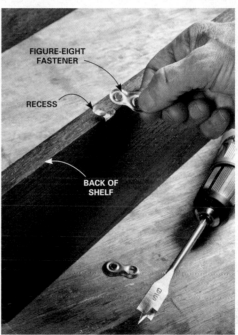

FIGURE-EIGHT FASTENER

RECESS

BACK OF SHELF

DRILL A RECESS FOR THE FIGURE-EIGHT
Use a spade bit or Forstner bit to drill a slight recess in the back of the shelf to accommodate the thickness of the figure-eight. Then chisel out the remaining wood until the figure-eight sits flush to the shelf. Attach the figure-eight with a screw.

SIMPLY SCREW IT ON
Mount the shelf by driving screws through the figure-eights either into hollow-wall anchors or into studs.

SHELF LEVEL

LASER LINE

SELF-LEVELING LASER

Dead-on leveling with a laser

Got a lot of shelves to level? A laser level is the perfect tool. We're using a self-leveling laser, but any laser that projects a horizontal level line will work. The tip is that you don't have to mess with getting the laser line at the height of your shelf. Just project it anywhere on the wall, and use it as a reference by measuring up from the line. This is especially handy if you're mounting several shelves at different heights, since you never need to reposition the laser. You can pick up a self-leveling laser for as little as $30 and use it for many other interior leveling tasks.

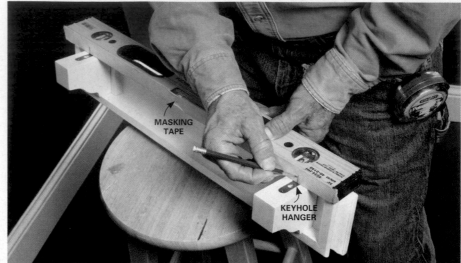

MASKING TAPE

KEYHOLE HANGER

MARK; DON'T MEASURE Place a strip of masking tape on one edge of your level and mark the center of each keyhole on the tape.

The key to keyholes

Keyhole slots on the back of shelves allow you to hang shelves or brackets on hidden screws, but you have to get the screws perfectly aligned or you'll have all kinds of trouble.

Here's one foolproof method for transferring a pair of keyhole locations to the wall for perfect screw placement. If you're lucky, you may be able to line up the screw locations with studs. Otherwise, use this method to mark the center of the hollow-wall anchors you'll need.

KEYHOLE LOCATIONS

TRANSFER TO THE WALL
Hold the level against the wall at the height you want the shelf. Remember that the top of the shelf will be above your marks. Adjust the level until the bubble is centered, and mark the keyhole locations on the wall. Then install anchors or drive the screws into the studs and hang the shelf.

Ditch those old-school toggle bolts

Of course it's always best to fasten heavy shelves to studs, but if you can't, there's an anchor that's almost as good. If you've used standard toggle bolts, you know they hold well. But they're a hassle to work with, and they leave an oversize hole that may show. And if you ever need to take the shelf down to paint, the toggle falls into the wall and you have to repeat the whole tedious process when you reinstall the shelf.

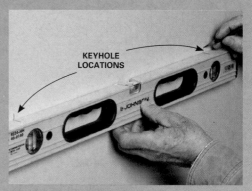

SNAP-TOGGLE ANCHOR

Snaptoggle anchors solve these problems. After installing the toggle according to the instructions, you'll have a threaded opening in the wall ready to receive

TOGGLE BOLT

the included bolt. You can simply screw the shelf to the captured toggle. And you can remove the bolt and the toggle will stay put, ready for you to reinstall the shelf. You'll find Snaptoggle anchors in hardware stores and home centers alongside the other wall anchors.

Throw away the free anchors

Most of the hollow-wall anchors included with shelves or shelf brackets aren't worth using. If you can't attach your shelf to studs and must use hollow-wall anchors, make sure to choose one that will support your shelf in the long run.

For light-duty shelves, we like the type of anchor shown here. You'll find them at any hardware store or home center. Make sure you know how thick your drywall or plaster is before you head to the store, though. Then match the anchor to the wall thickness.

To install the anchors, check the instructions and drill the right size hole. Then fold the wings so the anchor will fit and press it into the hole. You may have to tap it with a hammer until it's fully seated. Finish by pressing the included red tool through the hole to expand the wings behind the drywall or plaster. And make sure to use the screws included with the anchors, or ones that are the same diameter.

BETTER HOLLOW-WALL ANCHOR

LOOSE SCREW

SHELF STANDARD

Self-plumbing standards

The next time you install metal shelf standards, remember this tip. Rather than use a level to plumb the standards before you attach them, simply hang them loosely from the top with one of the screws and let gravity do the work. The standard will hang plumb, and all you have to do is press it to the wall and drive in the remaining screws. If you're using hollow-wall anchors, hang the standard from the top screw and use an awl to mark the screw locations. Then take the standard down and install the anchors.

French cleats for fast, solid hanging

Pairs of beveled strips that interlock to support shelves, cabinets or pictures are called French cleats. They're great for hanging any shelf or cabinet and have a few advantages in certain situations.

First, the cleats work well for heavy cabinets because you can easily mount the wall cleat and then simply lift the cabinet and "hook" it on. There's no need to support a heavy cabinet temporarily while you drive screws to anchor it.

Another common use for French cleats is to create a flexible system of shelves or cabinets. You can screw one or more lengths of wall cleats across the entire wall, and then easily relocate shelves, or add more shelves at a later date. Make cleats by ripping strips of 3/4-in. plywood with a 45-degree bevel on one edge. Screw one strip to the wall and the other to the back of the shelf or cabinet.

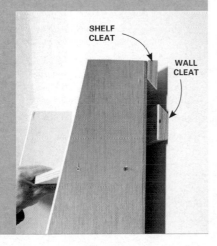

SHELF CLEAT

WALL CLEAT

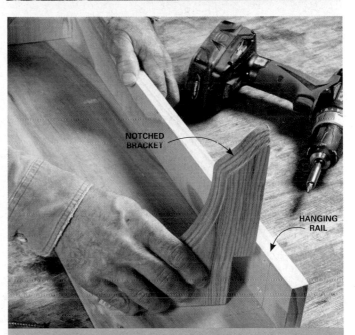

NOTCHED BRACKET

HANGING RAIL

Build in a hanging rail

Whether you're building a shelf or modifying a store-bought unit, including a hanging rail is a great way to add strength and allow for more flexible positioning while anchoring to studs. The rail strengthens the shelf and lets you anchor the shelf by driving screws anywhere along the length of the rail.

If the shelf isn't too heavy, you can hang it with finish-head screws that are easy to hide with wood putty. For heavier shelves, drill recesses for wood plugs to hide the screws.

Label everything!

Paint can reminder

Before you put that paint can away, draw a line on the side of the can to indicate how much paint is left. Then write the name of the room you painted and the date on the lid.

Organize tools by the job

Knowing exactly which tools you'll need for every job is next to impossible. Organize your toolboxes and storage bins according to the work that needs to be done—a box for plumbing tools, electrical, drywall, etc. No doubt this will lead to owning more than one of the same tool. But you won't believe how much time you'll save having all the proper tools on hand.

Instant labels for parts drawers

Plastic drawers let you see the nails or screws inside, but you can't always tell their size. Here's a simple solution: Cut the labels off fastener boxes and tape them inside the front of each drawer. You'll know exactly where everything is located at a glance.

Label maker mania

There should be a 12-step program for people who become addicted to their label makers. It starts when you innocently label tool cabinet drawers. Do the power strip next, and suddenly you just can't stop. The confusing light switches in the entryway—labeled. The kitchen items you take to potluck dinners—labeled with full names. File folders, the fuse box, pantry jars, tools the neighbors borrow, power adapters—stop before you label again!

EDITOR'S NOTE: Label makers are sold at office supply and discount stores.

Three-ring tool and appliance file

Store your appliance and tool manuals in three-ring binders so you can find them when you need them. Insert labeled dividers to organize them for quick reference.

I.D. bins the smart way

Before you start stacking plastic storage bins, think about how you'd like to identify the contents of each storage bin. Some people use adhesive labels or write with markers directly on the bins. The best system lets you make changes easily. We like the adhesive storage pouches that come with cardboard inserts (or you can just use index cards). Changing the label is as easy as slipping a new card into the pouch. Check office supply stores or find them online.

Printable magnetic labels

If you have terrible handwriting, try making magnetic labels with a home printer. Just create the labels on your computer, put the magnet sheets in your printer, hit "print" and cut them up. They're great on metal file drawers and tool chests. When you reorganize, just move the labels around or add new ones.

EDITOR'S NOTE:
Avery Magnet Sheets, which are compatible with ink-jet printers, are available in five-sheet packs at office supply stores and online retailers.

Easy label removal

It you love to reuse plastic containers for storing parts and fasteners, but have trouble getting the old label off, here's a tip. If you fill the container with hot water, the label will peel right off after a few minutes. If the water is hot enough from your tap, just fill the container, wait for the adhesive to soften and then peel the label. If you heat the water on the stove, don't boil it! Keep the water at about 160 degrees F—if it gets too much higher, your container can sag and lose its shape!

Headache remedy

Whenever you buy child-protected bottles of aspirin or ibuprofen, color both of the white arrows with red fingernail polish. That way, when you need some medicine, you can immediately see how the arrows line up and get the cap off fast.

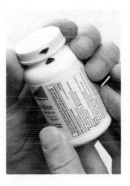

Moving tips

Get adjustable moving straps

Moving and lifting straps ("hump straps") make carrying heavy items easier on your back by relying on stronger muscle groups like your legs and shoulders. They also leave your hands free to maneuver awkward items like mattresses. However, they can be tricky to use on stairs because the weight shifts completely to the downhill mover.

Look for moving straps that can be adjusted for different length objects as well as for different-sized movers. Be careful not to trip on any slack from the straps. Since these straps are rarely padded, they can leave your shoulders sore (but that's better than your back!). Moving straps are available at home centers and online retailers.

Easier way to move boxes

If there's nowhere to grab it, moving a box can be awkward and put needless strain on your back. To make the task easier, cut a "V" in each end of the box and fold it in to make box handles.

HANDLES

No-scratch hand truck

Furniture and appliances scratch easily when you move them with a hand truck. You could struggle to protect the appliance with a piece of cardboard, carpet or a towel, but that's the hard way. Instead, slide some pipe insulation over the vertical rails of the hand truck and hold it in place with electrical tape.

Use plastic wrap, not tape, to secure items

Secure appliance doors, cords, tubing and other items with plastic wrap or moving bands rather than bungee cords or tape, which can leave a residue or damage the finish.

20 secret hiding places

The old hollowed-out book trick

We've all seen the hollowed-out book, but there's not much room in one of those. Instead, use several books with a plywood box attached to the back. If you have a band saw for cutting out the pages, great. If not, you can use a jigsaw. (After all, books are just a form of wood.)

If the sides of the books will be visible, fold back the covers of the books on the left and right sides of the assembly before cutting. Build a plywood box to fit the opening and glue the book parts to the box with construction adhesive. The disadvantage? You can see inside the box on low shelves, so you need to display it so the opening is above eye level.

②

Right out in the open

It doesn't have to be an old vacuum cleaner. Any common household item that has a cavity will work. Think old printers, computer towers, children's toys, etc. (Just be sure family members know about it so your valuables don't get donated or tossed!) For easy access, choose an item that opens instantly, like a vacuum cleaner bag compartment. For more security, choose an item with a cover that screws shut.

Air-return stash

Cut out a stud space opening to fit a return air grille. Cut off the grille screws and glue just the heads in place. Run four drywall screws into the corners of the opening so they fit just inside the rim of the grille. Then glue rare earth magnets to the back of the grille so they line up with the screw heads.

Buried treasure

Roll up some cash, stick it in a medicine bottle or any other watertight container, and bury it in a potted plant. For quicker access and to keep dirt from getting under your fingernails, place a stone or pine cone over it. Not many burglars are going to be excavating around your houseplants.

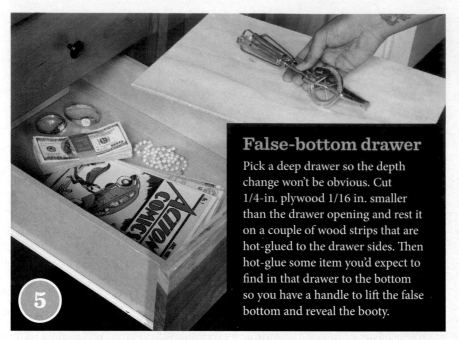

False-bottom drawer

Pick a deep drawer so the depth change won't be obvious. Cut 1/4-in. plywood 1/16 in. smaller than the drawer opening and rest it on a couple of wood strips that are hot-glued to the drawer sides. Then hot-glue some item you'd expect to find in that drawer to the bottom so you have a handle to lift the false bottom and reveal the booty.

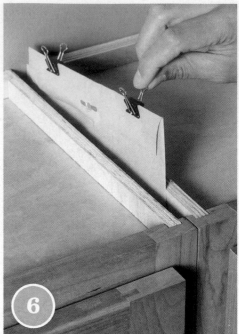

Cabinet hidey-hole

Between almost every pair of upper cabinets, there's a 1/2-in. gap. Take advantage of that gap by hanging a manila envelope containing, oh, I don't know, about two grand in hundred-dollar bills? Hang the cash with binder clips that are too wide to fall through the crack.

Toe-kick hideaway

There's an enormous 4-in.-tall cavity under all those kitchen cabinets behind the toe-kicks. It takes a few carpentry skills, but you can pull the toe-kicks free and make them removable. Most are 1/4-in. plywood held in place with 1-in. brads, and they're pretty easy to pull off. If you have a secondary 3/4-in. toe-kick, you'll have to cut it out at both ends. An oscillating tool works well for that task.

Stick both halves of round hook-and-loop self-adhesive tape to the toe-kick. Then push the toe-kick into place. The adhesive will stick to the cabinet base and leave half of the hook-and-loop tape in place when you pull it free. You can store approximately $2.4 million in gold bullion under two average-size cabinets—provided the floor is strong enough to support it.

Counterfeit containers

Go online and type in "secret hiding places" and you'll be amazed by how many brand-name phony containers are available. Comet, Coca-Cola, Bush Beans—whatever. But you can craft a homemade version too. This mayonnaise jar had its interior spray-painted with cream-colored paint for plastic.

The appliance caper

Fridges and dishwashers have a snap-off grille in the front. Well, there's a lot of secret storage space under there. Ask yourself this: How many burglars will be thinking about cleaning your refrigerator coils? But before you stuff treasures under a fridge, take a peek to see where the coils are. On some models, a stack of cash might block the airflow. That will make the fridge work harder and could even damage it.

11 Drill a hole in the top of any interior door. Size it to fit a cylinder such as an old film container or a cigar tube. Roll up some bills and keep them there.

If you want to do this trick on a hollow-core door, you have to stick close to the outside edges. Look at the door from the top and you'll see how wide the solid internal frame is.

10 Which paint can contains the gold?

12 It takes some effort, but you can sometimes free a tread from the stairs and attach a piano hinge to the back. It's almost invisible.

13 Whenever you build a piece of furniture, build in a stash spot. For instance, for a dresser, put a 1/4-in. sheet of plywood just above the top drawer and install a piano hinge on the top.

16 Put in a fake PVC pipe complete with a cleanout plug in your basement. Unscrew the plug and there are the goods.

14 Believe it or not, you can fit passports and a bit of cash underneath the shroud that covers the garage door opener.

15 Tape a stash on the underside of drawers in the kitchen.

17 ## Hide a key in plain sight

Say you want to hide a key—other than under the rug or over the door. How about mounting a phony plastic LB fitting. Screw it to the wall and run a bit of 1/2-in. conduit to the ground so it looks official. Cut the head off the bottom screw and glue it in place. That's it. Swing the cover aside and there's the key.

18 How many thieves are going to go through the dozens of pockets in your closet? Put cash in the pockets of your old pants and suit coats. Just be sure the clothes don't get donated!

19 The key is to use lots of hiding places. It's stupid to put all your eggs in one basket. Keep hundred-dollar bills between pages in books, tape an envelope behind your headboard and put cash behind the false panel in a dishwasher.

20 No burglar worth his salt looks in a kid's room for valuables. It's just full of useless junk. So find somewhere in there where the kid won't find it either.

Chapter Two

SAVING MONEY

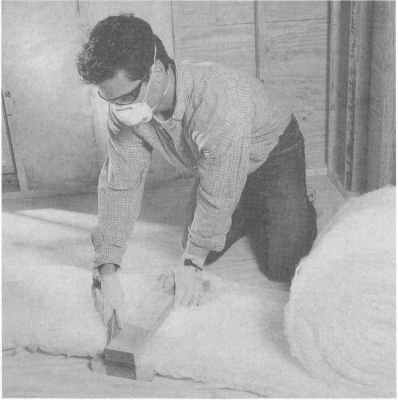

Spend less on gas

You see gas saving tips everywhere these days. But how much can you really save by following those tips? Actually the savings are pretty impressive.

Obviously no one will have all these car problems at the same time, so your savings will be substantially less than the full $2,000 shown in the following tips. But if you follow these tips, you will notice a difference in your fuel costs. The savings are based on driving 20,000 miles per year, in a car that gets 20 mpg, with gasoline priced at $3.75 a gallon.

Save $900 by keeping your tires at the right pressure

Surveys show that 50 percent of vehicles have underinflated tires. You can't "eyeball" tire pressure; you have to check it with a tire pressure gauge. It's worth your time to check tires monthly, because underinflated tires can cost you about $750 a year in wasted gas. Improper air pressure can wear out your tires twice as fast, costing you an additional $150 a year. The recommended air pressure for your vehicle's tires is on the decal pasted to the driver's door or pillar.

Change spark plugs before they're due

If your 100,000-mile spark plugs have 80,000 miles on them, they're 80 percent worn. Misfires and incomplete combustion occur more frequently during that last 20,000 miles, costing you almost $562.50 in wasted fuel. You have to replace your spark plugs anyway, so do it early and pocket the savings. Even if you have to replace the plugs one extra time over the life of your car, you'll still come out way ahead.

SPARK PLUGS

Save $307.50 by changing your air filter early and often

Your engine sucks 14 million gallons of air through the air filter every year. If it can't get enough air, the combustion efficiency will drop by at least 10 percent. Air filters are cheap and you can replace them yourself. Replace the filter at least every 10,000 miles or once a year, and even with that expense, still save $270.

Save $140 by keeping your car aligned

If your tires are bowed out of alignment by just .017 in., it's the equivalent of dragging your tire sideways for 102 miles for every 20,000 you drive. That'll cost you $187.50 a year in wasted gas. It will wear your tires faster, costing you $70 more a year. Here's an easy way to check your alignment without taking your car in to the shop. Buy a tread depth gauge and measure the tread depth on both edges of each tire (rear tires too). If one side of the tire is worn more than the other, your car needs to be aligned. An alignment costs about $80, so you'll still save $177.50 the first year alone.

Tread depth gauge, $2 at any auto parts store

WORN HERE

BUT NOT HERE

Uneven tread wear signals alignment problems

Brake drag can really sink your mileage

Brake calipers have a nasty habit of rusting, binding and dragging down your gas mileage. How can you tell if your brakes are dragging without having them checked at a shop? Easy! Buy an inexpensive noncontact infrared laser thermometer, remove the wheel cover (if equipped), and aim the laser at the wheel hub after a drive. Compare the readings from the right and left sides. If they vary by more than 20 percent, you've probably got a dragging brake or a wheel bearing problem, so take it in for repairs.

Lead foot = light wallet

Hard acceleration in stop-and-go driving costs you 20 percent in gas mileage. If you live your life in rush hour traffic and like to put the pedal to the metal, spend all your extra time at the next stoplight figuring out how you could have spent the $750 a year you're wasting.

Speed kills— your gas mileage and your wallet

Yes, you've heard it before, but how about some real-world numbers to drive the point home? Aerodynamic drag is a minor concern in city driving, but it really kills your gas mileage at speeds over 55 mph. In fact, increasing your speed to 65 increases drag by 36 percent! If you do a lot of highway driving, getting to your destination a few minutes early could cost you an extra $637.50 a year. Keep it closer to 55 mph and use your cruise control. It will pay off.

Replace your oxygen sensor(s) before the light goes on

Oxygen sensors monitor the efficiency of combustion by tracking the amount of oxygen remaining in the exhaust. But they degrade over time and that can cost you up to 15 percent in gas mileage. When they fail, the computer lights up your "service engine soon" light, forcing you to incur a diagnostic fee. On pre-1996 vehicles, replace your oxygen sensor every 60,000 miles to keep your mileage at its peak. On 1996 and newer vehicles, replace the sensors every 100,000 miles. Some vehicles have as many as four, but the sensors installed behind the catalytic converter rarely fail.

OXYGEN SENSOR

OXYGEN SENSOR SOCKET

Replace a broken or missing spoiler

The plastic air dam (aka "spoiler") that's broken or missing wasn't just for a sporty look. If your car had an air dam, driving without it or with a damaged one can reduce your gas mileage. The air dam literally "dams off" airflow to the under-carriage of your car, forcing the air up and over the hood. That helps your car cut through the air with less drag. It also increases airflow to the A/C condenser and radiator, reducing the load on your car's electrical system. Contact a junkyard or the dealer to get a replacement air dam.

Replace a failing thermostat

A thermostat that opens too quickly or stays open can dramatically lower the coolant temperature and put a mega-chill on your gas mileage. Remember the infrared thermometer you bought to check your brakes? Simply aim it at the thermostat housing. If your engine is warmed up and the thermometer reads less than 160 degrees F, you're wasting gas and it's time to replace the thermostat. (To reduce reflection errors, spray the thermostat housing with black paint prior to testing.) A new thermostat costs about $10.

THERMOSTAT HOUSING

Reduce energy costs

15 ENERGY-SAVING TIPS

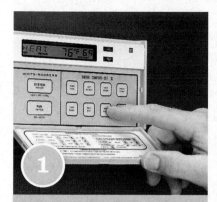

1 Install and use an automatic setback (programmable) thermostat. You can reduce your heating and cooling costs by 5 to 15 percent.

PIPE INSULATION

2 Insulate pipes, especially if they pass through an area you don't want heated or cooled. Have your air conditioner serviced to clean hard-to-reach evaporator coils and adjust coolant pressure to achieve maximum efficiency.

3 Clean the air conditioner condenser coils and fins when you see grass and airborne debris collected on them.

4 Change furnace filters every month, or more often if needed.

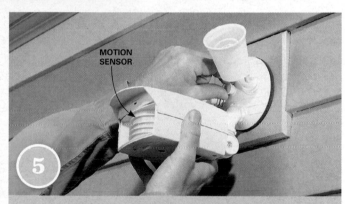

MOTION SENSOR

5 Install light controls like motion sensors, photocell switches and timers to shut off lights automatically when they're not needed.

6 Shade your windows with trees, awnings, overhangs, shutters or other devices to keep direct sunlight from entering your home.

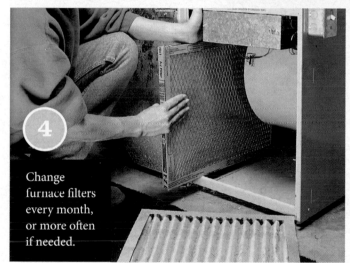

7 Replace lightbulbs used more than two hours per day with compact fluorescent bulbs. Fluorescent bulbs last longer and use only one-third as much energy as standard bulbs.

8 Replace recessed light fixtures with airtight models when you remodel.

9 Reduce hot water usage by replacing high-volume showerheads with low-flow heads (2 to 3 gallons per minute).

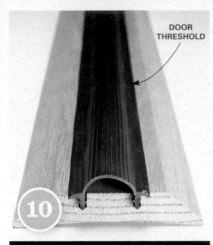

DOOR THRESHOLD

10 Replace worn-out thresholds and weather stripping around windows and doors.

11 Fix leaky faucets; dripping hot water is a waste of water, energy and money.

12 Have a furnace tuneup to clean and adjust burners and improve fuel-burning efficiency.

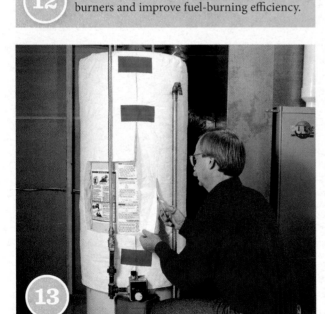

13 Wrap the tank of your gas-burning water heater in a special fiberglass blanket to decrease heat loss. Check your owner's manual to make sure a blanket is recommended for your model.

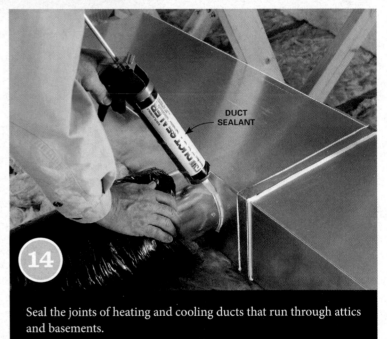

DUCT SEALANT

14 Seal the joints of heating and cooling ducts that run through attics and basements.

15 Buy gas stoves with electronic ignition. Install a reflector (shiny aluminum foil over cardboard will do) behind radiators to reduce heat driven into and through the wall. Save 5 percent.

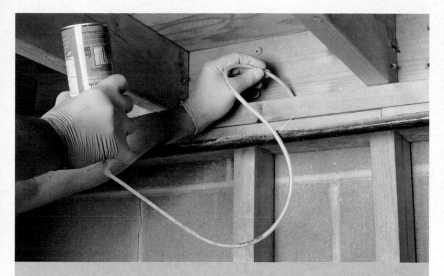

Spray-foam super tube

While sealing tiny openings around your home's foundation, it can be hard to position the inverted spray foam can just right. Try this solution. Fit some 1/4-in. clear flexible tubing on the end of the nozzle (you may need to run it under hot water to soften and expand it slightly). Now you can hold the can in a comfortable spot and then move the end of the tubing to fill the cracks with foam.

Finding air leaks

Locating air leaks can be tricky. They're often so small as to be hardly noticeable. To find them, follow a trail of smoke.

Close all the windows in the house, turn off all the fans and exhaust fans, and shut off the furnace. Light some incense and walk slowly around the outer walls of the house. Anywhere you notice the smoke blowing away from something or being sucked toward something, there's probably an air leak. Now that you've found it, seal it!

INCENSE STICK

Save on electric water heating

If you only use an electric water heater at certain times of the day, you're wasting electricity keeping the water hot 24/7. To solve that problem, install an electronic timer switch (Photo 1; sold at home centers). Timers are available for 120- and 240-volt heaters. They can be programmed for daily or weekly schedules so you only heat the water when you need it.

To make your water heater even more efficient, drain the tank and flush out the sediment at the bottom (Photo 2). Otherwise, you could be heating through inches of sediment before heating the water.

If your electric water heater is warm or hot to the touch, it's losing heat. Wrap it with an insulating blanket.

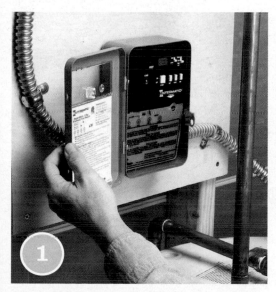

1

A timer turns on the water heater only when you need it, so you don't waste electricity heating and reheating water that sits in the tank.

SEDIMENT

2

Sediment lowers the efficiency of your water heater. Turn off the power, hook up a hose to the drain valve and drain the tank every 6 to 12 months.

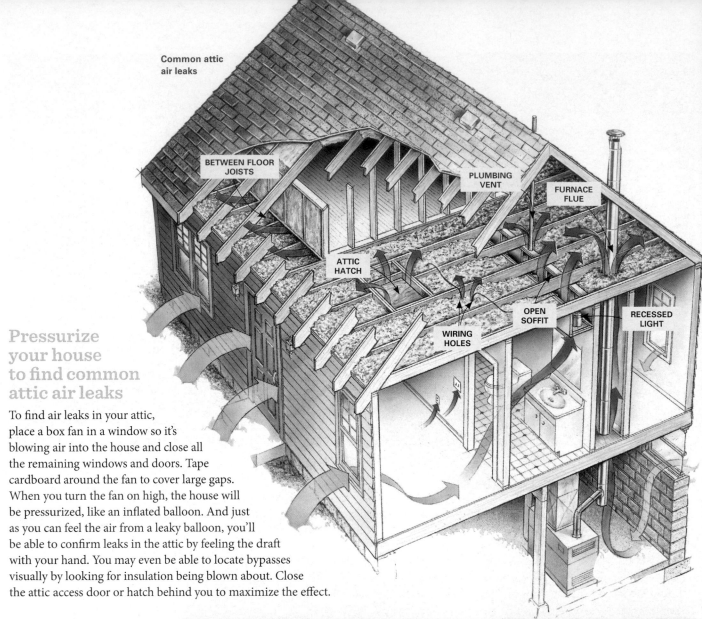

Common attic
air leaks

BETWEEN FLOOR
JOISTS

PLUMBING
VENT

FURNACE
FLUE

ATTIC
HATCH

WIRING
HOLES

OPEN
SOFFIT

RECESSED
LIGHT

Pressurize your house to find common attic air leaks

To find air leaks in your attic, place a box fan in a window so it's blowing air into the house and close all the remaining windows and doors. Tape cardboard around the fan to cover large gaps. When you turn the fan on high, the house will be pressurized, like an inflated balloon. And just as you can feel the air from a leaky balloon, you'll be able to confirm leaks in the attic by feeling the draft with your hand. You may even be able to locate bypasses visually by looking for insulation being blown about. Close the attic access door or hatch behind you to maximize the effect.

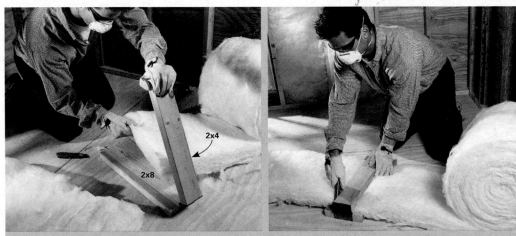

2x4

2x8

Insulation cutting jig

Cut wall insulation clean and fast with this jig made from two boards and an old door hinge. Cut a 2x4 and a 2x8 4 in. longer than the width of the insulation. Connect them with the hinge. Then open the jig and slide in the insulation. Press down on the 2x4 to compress the fiberglass and slice along the 2x4 with a utility knife. Clean cuts every time.

Recycle

Recycling zip ties

Whenever you buy something that's wrapped with zip ties, don't cut them off and toss them. Instead, remove the ties by inserting the tip of a pocketknife under the ratcheting mechanism of the ties and pulling the end out. You can reuse the ties and never worry about overtightening one because you can reposition it.

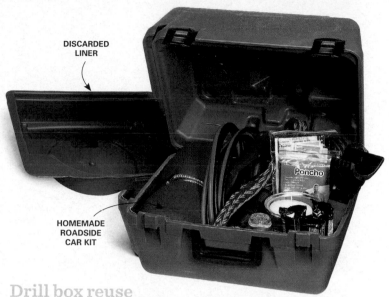

DISCARDED LINER

HOMEMADE ROADSIDE CAR KIT

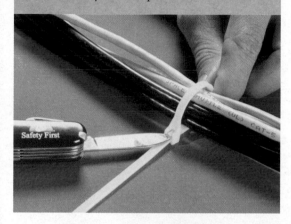

Drill box reuse

When that power tool finally gives up the ghost, give its carrying case a second life by carefully cutting out the liner with a utility knife. The case can be recycled into a roadside car kit or travel toolbox or holder for just about anything you can cram in there!

1/2" HOLE DRILLED FOR AIR

1/8" HOLES DRILLED FOR WATER

Laundry jug watering can

Instead of throwing away empty laundry detergent containers, rinse them out thoroughly and then recycle them for watering plants. Drill 1/8-in. holes in the top of the cap, and a 1/2-in. hole just above the handle to relieve pressure so the water flows freely.

Reduce, reuse, recycle

If you use a lot of paint thinner to clean brushes, check out this method of getting the most out of it. When you're through cleaning the brush, pour the used thinner back into a "slop" can and let the finish or paint settle to the bottom. The slop may eventually be one-third solids on the bottom, but the stuff on top is clear and reusable.

Free packing material

Line your packages with the recycled "shreddies" from your paper shredder. It cushions your parcels' contents, and with all the junk mail, you have a never-ending supply.

Pop bottle pillow

There's no need to strain your neck or get your hair dirty when you're working on your back under the sink or car. Take along an empty 2-liter plastic pop bottle for a pillow. You can let out air to adjust the comfort level, and even recycle it when you're done.

Easy-on-the-hands bucket handles

Don't throw away those old buckets with broken or missing plastic handles. Retrofit the buckets with new handles made from an old garden hose. Cut short lengths of hose, slit each one with a utility knife and slid them over the handles. If you can remove one side of the wire handle, you can just slide the hose grip on without slitting it. The handles work great and keep those buckets working hard!

Seedlings on the half shell

You don't have to buy seedling pots in the spring. Instead, make your own from eggshells, using the egg carton as a tray. Next time you use eggs, carefully crack them in half, rinse out the egg residue, then poke a drainage hole in the bottom of each half shell with sharp scissors or an ice pick. Fill the shells with a lightweight, sterile potting mix formulated for seed starting, and sow the seeds. When the seedlings are ready for transplanting, gently crush the eggshell with your fingers and plant them, eggshell and all. The shell will improve your soil as it decomposes.

Avoid expensive appliance repairs

1. Clean refrigerator coils

On the back or underside of your fridge, there are coils that dissipate the heat that's removed from the fridge (kind of like the radiator on your car). Dust buildup on these coils reduces airflow and wastes energy. Worse, it causes the compressor and condenser fan to run longer and hotter. That causes premature failure and a service call to install a new condenser fan. And a new compressor can be even more. That's quite an incentive to clean the coils. Cleaning the coils takes only a few minutes. See how at family-handyman.com. Just search for "refrigerator coils."

2. Don't block air vents

The freezer and refrigerator compartments require proper airflow to keep foods at the right temperature. So think twice before you buy warehouse-size packs of frozen food. Because if you jam them into the freezer and block the vents, you can cause cooling problems in the refrigerator and force the compressor and fans to run overtime. That'll result in premature fan and compressor failures. Replacing a fan usually runs about $150. But if the compressor fails, you're better off buying a new refrigerator.

3. Clean fridge gaskets

If you keep your refrigerator door gaskets clean, they'll seal properly and last the life of the fridge. But if you let sticky foods like syrup and jam build up on the door gasket, they'll glue the gasket to the frame. Pulling harder on a stuck door eventually tears the gasket, and that'll cost you (up to several hundred dollars on some brands). Plus, if the door doesn't seal properly, the fridge has to run longer, and that'll boost your electric bill. Clean the door gasket with warm water and a sponge. Don't use detergents; they can damage the gasket.

4. Don't overload your washer or dryer

You may think you're saving time, water or energy by cramming more clothes into your washer and dryer. But the manufacturers list a maximum load weight for a good reason. If you overload a top-loading washer, you can fry the drive belts or break the drive coupler. And, overloading can also cause socks and underwear to float over the basket. Then they get sucked into the pump and wreck it—another service call.

If you overload a front-loading washer or dryer, you can burn out the rear bearing or motor. That repair is so expensive that you'd be better off buying a new machine. In the dryer, the extra load weight not only takes longer to dry but also wears out drum support rollers and drive belts.

Weight limits range from as little as 6 lbs. to as much as 15 lbs. for top loaders and about 18 lbs. for front loaders. So consult your owner's manual and find the load limits for your machine. Then grab an armful of clothes and stand on a scale to get an idea of just how much your machine can handle.

6 Clean your dishwasher screen

If your dishwasher has a filtering screen under the bottom spray arm, clean it regularly. See how at familyhandyman.com. Just search for "dishwasher." If you don't, the stuck food particles degrade into slime that blocks water flow and reduces cleaning performance. So you'll pay a minimum service call just to have the filter cleaned. And while we're on the subject, cut back on the soap use too. You don't need more than a teaspoon to clean most loads. Excess soap builds up in the entire dishwasher and eventually reduces water flow, requiring another "cleaning" service call. To remove soap buildup, use a product like Dishwasher Magic, available at most hardware stores and home centers.

5 Don't slam the door

You can rationalize all you want about why you drop or slam the lid or door to your washer or dryer (your hands are full, you're in a hurry, etc.), but your appliances don't care. So forget the excuse and know this: If you continually drop or slam the lid to your washer or dryer (top or front load), you're going to break the lid/door switch. That'll cost you a few hundred. That's right—you can avoid this repair by lowering the lid and gently closing the door. Easy, huh?

7 Clean the lint filter

With a clogged lint filter, your clothes dry slower, and the machine works harder and wastes energy. But that's just the beginning of your troubles. Because the lint still has to go somewhere, it bypasses the filter, collects in the dryer's vent line, and reduces airflow even further.

At a certain point, the blockage gets so bad that the dryer overheats and the thermal fuse blows. The dryer will still start up, but it won't heat. The service call will run about $200 to replace the thermal fuse and clean the vent line (that charge will most likely include a lecture about cleaning the filter).

Avoid the entire lint and thermal fuse issue simply by cleaning the lint filter after each load. If you've neglected the lint filter and want to avoid a repair bill, clean out the vent line yourself. Find out how at familyhandyman.com. Just enter "lint" in the search box. Also, if you use dryer sheets, wash the lint filter with detergent every six months. Dryer sheets leave behind an invisible film, which blocks airflow.

8 Don't spray switches

Most people clean their stove and dishwasher knobs and touch-control panels with spray cleaners. But those liquids can easily work their way into the switches and behind the control panels and short them out. Spray just a little liquid cleaner onto a rag or sponge and then clean the knobs and touch-control panel. That'll prevent shorting.

9 Don't drag clothes out of the washer

Nobody likes lifting a heavy bundle of clothes in or out of a front-loading washing machine. But it's a mistake to drag them over the door ledge. That may save your back, but zippers and buttons gradually tear up the rubber door gasket. Replacing that gasket requires a lot of disassembly, and that'll cost you. So lift out the wet clothes.

10 Change the furnace filter

A dirty furnace filter can actually damage your furnace. The clogged filter restricts airflow so much that the area around the heat exchanger reaches an unsafe temperature and the burners shut down. Once the furnace cools down, it'll fire up again. But if the overheat/shutdown cycle repeats enough times, the furnace controls will shut it down for good. Hello, emergency service call. If you're lucky, the repairperson will just replace the filter and reset the computer. But repeat overheat cycles can also damage the temperature sensor, and that'll add to the service call.

The dirt level in every home is different, so you can't rely on a weekly or monthly schedule for filter changes. Instead of guessing when to replace the filter, install an air filter gauge (sold online).

Fix computerized appliances yourself

Many newer appliances include computerized touch pads and control boards. You may think they're too complicated to repair yourself. Wrong. They're actually easier to work on because the computer does all the diagnostic work for you. Once the computer detects a problem, it stores a fault code in memory. All you have to do is put the computer into readout mode and consult the fault code chart to discover which part failed. Fortunately, most manufacturers pack the code retrieval procedure and code translation information right inside the machine.

The trick is to find them. The diagrams here show typical locations. Remove the cover panel and look for the fault code instructions in a plastic bag. Follow the instructions to put the computer into code retrieval mode, then count the blinks or read the fault code from the display. Once you learn which part failed, copy the model and serial number off the tag and buy a replacement part.

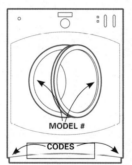

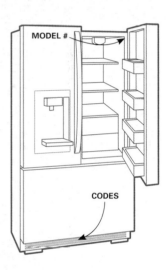

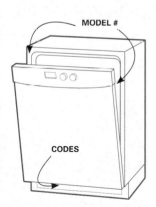

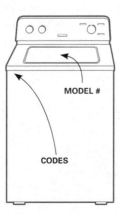

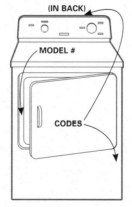

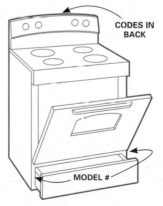

FIND THE MODEL NUMBER AND THE FAULT CODE SHEET Here are the typical locations on various appliances. (You may need to remove a cover panel to find them.) With the fault codes, the appliance diagnoses itself!

Chapter Three

TOOLS AND CARPENTRY SKILLS

Circular saw tips

SCRAP SIDE OF BOARD   "V" MARK

CHALK LINE

Sharper chalk lines

The fastest way to make straight cutting lines on plywood is to use a chalk line. But before you lay the line on the plywood, give it a quick midair twang. That first twang will get rid of excess chalk, and your mark will be less fuzzy and easier to follow. This is an especially important step to do right after filling your chalk line.

Start with accurate marks

To get an accurate cut, you have to start with an accurate mark. Stretch out your tape measure, place your pencil at the correct measurement and make two marks that form a "V," with the tip of the "V" pointing at the exact measurement. A "V" is more accurate than a single line, which can stray slightly to the right or left and throw off your cut mark.

Using a square, mark your cutting line over the tip of the "V." Finally, put an "X" on the "scrap" side of the board; that's the side of the line you want to cut along. Cutting on the wrong side of your line can make a 1/8-in. difference in the length of your board; sometimes this is a big deal, sometimes not.

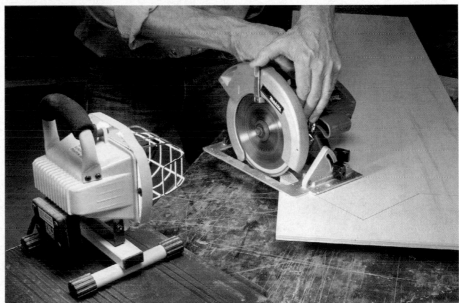

Light up the cut

A perfect cutting line won't do you any good if you can't see it. So before you pull the trigger, take two seconds to check the lighting. Even in the best-lit workshops or the sunny outdoors, you or your saw can cast shadows that make it hard to see your mark. Change the angle of the board or reposition your work light so the line won't disappear into the shadows as you cut.

Tape before you mark

When cutting dark wood or laminate, mark your cutting line on masking tape rather than directly on the workpiece. You'll be able to see your line easier, and in some cases—like when you're cutting hardwood plywood— the masking tape can minimize splintering.

MASKING TAPE

Watch the blade, not the guides

Every saw has notches or marks on the front of the shoe to indicate where the blade is going to cut. Unfortunately, they can get covered with sawdust or the whole shoe gets bent out of whack, which throws off the guide.

Many carpenters prefer to watch the actual blade and line as they cut. The problem, of course, is that sawdust covers the line. Some saws have built-in blowers to clear away dust. If your saw doesn't, use your own built-in blower—your mouth. All it takes is a light puff every few seconds to keep your view clear and open.

Clamp before cutting angles

Blade guards tend to hang up when they contact a board at anything other than a 90-degree angle. Since you need one hand to push the saw and the other to retract the guard, clamp your workpiece down so it doesn't move around—even if that clamp happens to be your knee. When I cut angles or bevels, I keep my left thumb on the blade guard retracting lever and start retracting the guard when I feel the saw hesitate a little.

Safe = accurate

What do earmuffs, safety glasses and dust masks have to do with cutting accurately? Well, it's tough to watch the cutting line with your eyes squinting and blinking through a storm of sawdust. And let's face it: Protection against noise, dust and splinters will make you more comfortable and more patient—and less likely to make a sloppy rush through the cut.

Shoulder the cord

On most saws, the electrical plug is perfectly engineered to snag on the edge of plywood. And that will throw off your cut. To prevent snags, drape the cord over your shoulder. This trick will also reduce your cord-cutting rate by 90 percent!

CLEAT

FENCE

Quick, identical cuts

When you need to cut dozens of boards the same length, don't measure and mark them one at a time. Instead, make a simple jig. This one takes less than five minutes to build and guarantees that all your cuts are exactly the same length.

To make one, screw a fence to a long scrap of plywood and run your saw along the fence to trim off the excess plywood. Then measure back from the cut end and screw on a cleat. The cleat location determines the length of the cut, and the fence guides your saw for perfectly square cuts every time.

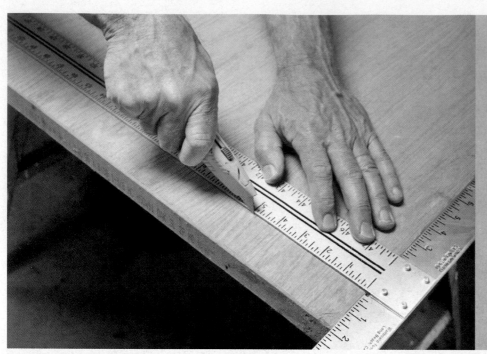

Score a clean cut

Circular saws usually splinter the wood that's facing up and cut cleanly on the side that's facing down. So when you're cutting veneered plywood, always position the material "good side down" so the teeth of the blade are pushing the veneer up against the core rather than ripping it away. Pushing your saw more slowly than normal also helps reduce splintering. If you need both sides splinter-free, mark your cut by scoring the veneer with a sharp utility knife, then cut just a hair to the "waste side" of the line. Any splintering will occur on the waste piece. A quick swipe with sandpaper will clean up any little fuzzies left behind.

Plywood cutting pad

Only NBA players have arms long enough to push a saw across an entire sheet of plywood. It's easier to lay the plywood on a sheet of extruded foam, then crawl on your knees while making the cut. You don't have to reach as far and you'll have better sight lines. Cut the foam into two or three pieces and rejoin them with duct tape. The tape creates hinges, which allow you to fold up the foam and stash it away when not in use.

When to retire your saw

There comes a time when you should throw your circular saw a retirement party—or at least assign it a new job. Most saws cut accurately out of the box, but after years of hard use, the bearings become sloppy, the blade and motor vibrate, the shoe gets bent, and the blade guard becomes stubborn. It all adds up to a saw that just won't cut as accurately or cleanly as a new model. So as your saw enters old age, use it for rougher tasks like demolition or cutting concrete. Then invest in a new one.

DUCT TAPE "HINGE"

3/4" FOAM INSULATION

Clamp your work for precise bevel cuts

You can make crisp, accurate bevel or miter cuts with a circular saw but it's tricky. The blade guard can stick, making it tough to get started. And because the blade is angled, it's more difficult to follow a line accurately without twisting the saw and possibly binding the blade.

Two things will help you get a good cut safely. The first is to clamp the board you're cutting. Clamping allows you to use one hand to lift the blade guard out of the way until the cut is started. The second is to use a straightedge guide, like the giant Speed square shown. It allows you to concentrate on moving the saw steadily forward without having to worry about following the line. If possible, cut with the wider part of the bed on the "keeper" side of the board for better control and more accurate bevels. Near the end of the cut, concentrate on a straight-ahead follow-through.

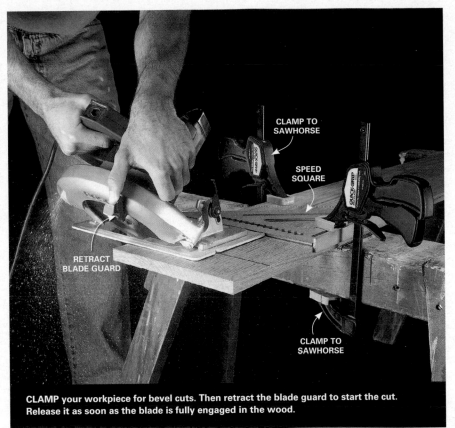

CLAMP TO SAWHORSE

SPEED SQUARE

RETRACT BLADE GUARD

CLAMP TO SAWHORSE

CLAMP your workpiece for bevel cuts. Then retract the blade guard to start the cut. Release it as soon as the blade is fully engaged in the wood.

Safety tip for circular saws

Your circular saw is one of the most dangerous tools in the shop. Accidents happen quickly and without warning and injuries are usually severe. Binding the blade in a cut is probably the most common and scariest mistake because the saw blade will jump up and run back toward you. It usually happens when you're cutting a long board or large sheet of plywood in half without proper support. To avoid it, make sure the cutoff piece is free to drop or move away from the blade. This will eliminate any chance of binding and make all of your cuts safer.

Scratch-free sawing

Here's how to cut an inch off a nicely finished door or workpiece when you don't want to risk dinging up the surface with that scratched-up shoe on your circular saw. Apply painter's masking tape to the shoe and you'll saw scratch-free every time.

Jigsaw essentials

MASKING TAPE

Protect the work surface

When making a cut, you need to firmly hold down the saw to keep the blade from chattering, and even then, it may vibrate a bit. The combination of downward force and vibration is tough on the work surface. Reduce marring by applying a layer or two of masking tape to the base of the jigsaw. Remove the tape when you're done so it doesn't leave a sticky residue on the base.

Find the SPM "sweet spot"

Typically, there's an SPM (strokes per minute) "sweet spot" where the saw cuts the fastest and cleanest and with the least vibration. Try different speeds by changing pressure on the trigger. Once you find the best speed, set the adjustable speed dial so you can pull the trigger all the way while maintaining the desired SPM.

Let the tool do the work

Pushing as hard as you can on the saw doesn't necessarily make it cut faster; sometimes the exact opposite is true. And pushing too hard into a curve can cause you to veer off your line, burn the material or break a blade. Ease off on the pressure until the saw cuts smoothly with little vibration.

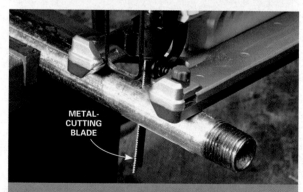

METAL-CUTTING BLADE

Cut anything

The main mission of a jigsaw is to cut curves in wood, and it's easy to overlook its other abilities. Instead of slaving away with your hacksaw, grab your jigsaw to quickly cut steel, copper or any metal. You can also cut plastics and tougher stuff like ceramic tile and fiber cement siding. The key to success is to match the blade to the material (more on that later).

Get the right saw for you

It's helpful to think of jigsaws in three categories: For $50 or less, you'll get a jigsaw that will do its job just fine, but you'll probably sacrifice features and power. For most DIYers, a saw in the $50 to $100 range is a good choice. It will have some special features and adequate power. Saws that cost over $100 will have large motors and all the best features.

Our favorite features are toolless blade change, toolless base plate bevel and oscillating control. Bonus features include an LED light, a blower to blow away dust, a larger base plate and a speed control dial.

If you'll be cutting a lot of material that's 1 in. or thicker, look for a saw with a higher amp rating (listed in the specifications). Smaller saws draw 5 amps or less; larger models go up to 7 amps. Larger motors also add a little "heft" to the saw, which helps cut vibration.

Some jigsaws have handles; some don't. Many pros like the no-handle "barrel-grip" style. They feel they have better control with their hands closer to the action. Folks with smaller hands often complain about the barrel being too large to grab.

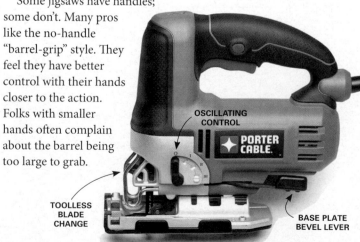

OSCILLATING CONTROL

PORTER CABLE

TOOLLESS BLADE CHANGE

BASE PLATE BEVEL LEVER

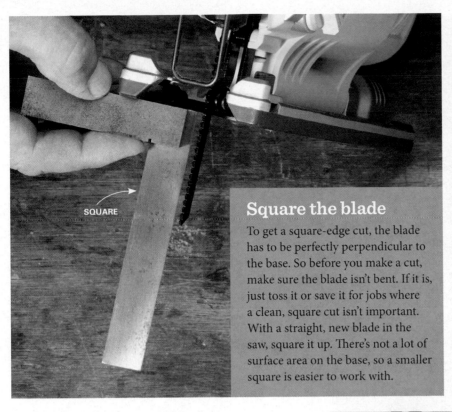

SQUARE

Oscillation education

Most jigsaws offer oscillating action: While the blade moves up and down, it also lunges forward with each stroke. Typically, you can turn off the oscillation or select from three levels of oscillation. The higher the setting, the faster you cut.

But faster isn't always better. More oscillation means rougher, less-accurate cuts. So turn the oscillation way down or off when you need clean or precise cuts or when you're working with delicate materials like veneers. Turn the oscillating feature off when you're cutting metal. Practice on a scrap to find the best setting for the material.

Square the blade

To get a square-edge cut, the blade has to be perfectly perpendicular to the base. So before you make a cut, make sure the blade isn't bent. If it is, just toss it or save it for jobs where a clean, square cut isn't important. With a straight, new blade in the saw, square it up. There's not a lot of surface area on the base, so a smaller square is easier to work with.

Make a metal sandwich

Jigsaws are great at cutting sheet metal, but it's difficult to clamp the material down so the saw blade doesn't just rattle the material up and down instead of cutting through it. One way to solve this problem is to sandwich the metal between two sheets of 1/4-in. plywood. Once the plywood is clamped down, the metal has nowhere to go, so you get a fast, easy, clean cut. You don't have to spend a bunch of money on plywood either; inexpensive 1/4-in. underlayment works fine.

TEAR-OUT

TOP-SIDE TEAR-OUT

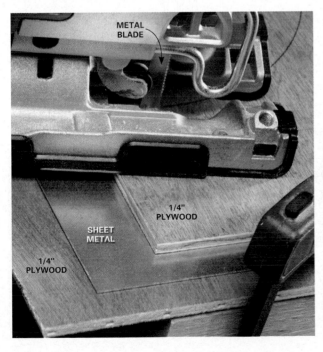

METAL BLADE

1/4" PLYWOOD

SHEET METAL

1/4" PLYWOOD

Cut with the "good" side down

Most jigsaw blades cut on the upstroke, so chips and splinters occur mostly on the top of the wood. So if you value one side of a board more than the other, make sure you keep the good side face down, and mark and cut the less important side.

You can buy "reverse cut" or "down cut" blades that do cut on the down stroke. These blades are used when you want as little tear-out on the top surface as possible. Cutting out a sink hole in a laminate countertop is one common use for reverse-cut blades.

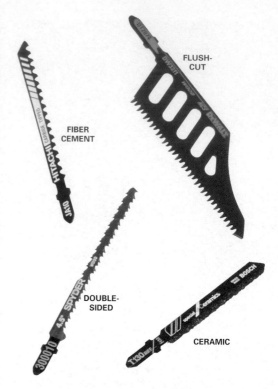

Make relief cuts for sharp turns

There's a limit on how sharp a curve a jigsaw can cut, and that depends on the blade—the narrower the blade, the sharper the turns it can make. If you try to force the blade into a turn tighter than it's capable of, you'll either veer off your line or break the blade.

If you're not sure about a particular shape, mark it out on a scrap and practice on that. If you have a curve you know is too tight, make relief cuts. The sharper the curve, the more relief cuts you'll need. And be sure you don't cut past your line. Play it safe and leave at least a blade's width of material between the relief cut and your pencil mark.

A blade for every occasion

There are a couple of basic things to know about blades: The larger the teeth, the more aggressive and rougher the cut. And the narrower the blade, the tighter the turns it can make. Narrow, double-sided blades are especially well suited for sharp turns because the teeth on the back side widen the kerf as you turn.

Match the type of blade with the material you're cutting—don't use a wood blade to cut metal. Most manufacturers have taken the guesswork out of blade selection—the description of the blade and what it does is usually written on the blade itself. Buy a combo pack and you'll be ready for most jobs. A 15-pack of quality blades doesn't cost much, and you'll avoid making a special trip to the store.

There are also specialty blades designed for very specific jobs: blades for cutting tile and fiber cement, and flush-cut blades that extend the cut right up to the front of the base. Specialty blades are usually sold individually and can cost more.

Drill starter holes

If you need to cut out a hole in the center of the work surface—like a hole for a heat register in a sheet of bead board wainscoting—drill a hole slightly bigger than your jigsaw blade in two opposite corners. That way, you can make four neat cuts starting from the two holes.

Smart starting and stopping

Be sure the blade is up to speed before you start your cut. If you start the saw with the blade touching your material, it can grab hold and rattle the material, possibly damaging it. And let the saw come to a complete stop when you pull it from the material mid-cut. If you don't, you might experience the dreaded "woodpecker effect," when a moving blade bounces off the surface, leaving behind pockmarks and a bent blade.

Miter saws

SCRAPS

Boost crosscut capacity

If your miter saw can't quite cut the full width of a board, lay the board on a stack of scraps. That will give you an extra inch or so of crosscut capacity. If that's not enough, try this: Cut the board as far as possible, then flip it over to complete the cut. But don't expect a perfect cut. Aligning the two cuts precisely is surprisingly difficult.

Bump and shave

When you need to trim just a smidgen off a board or molding, try this: Lower the blade of your miter saw and press the end of the workpiece against it. Then raise the blade, pull the trigger and cut. Depending on how hard you pushed against the blade, you'll shave off from 1/16 to 1/32 in. Once you get the feel of it, you'll be able to adjust the pressure and the width of the shave.

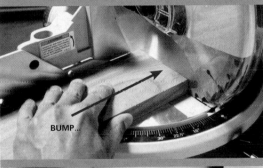

BUMP...

...THEN SHAVE

DIY dust collector

If your shop vacuum hose is a little too big to attach to your miter saw's exhaust port, try this simple but effective DIY adapter. Cut a 3/4-in.-nap paint roller cover in half and duct-tape it to the saw's exhaust port. The shop vacuum hose fits perfectly over the roller cover, creating a tight seal that allows almost all of the sawdust to be captured. The thicker the nap, the tighter the seal. Works great!

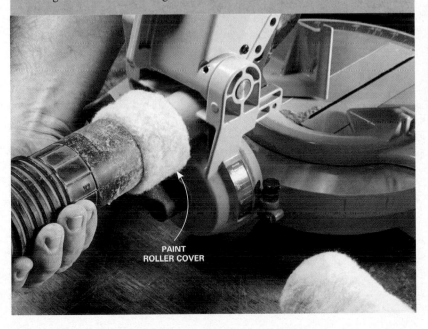

PAINT ROLLER COVER

Clamp short pieces in the "no hands" zone

As a reminder to keep hands well away from the blade, most new miter saws have red lines indicating the "no hands" zone. But what if you need to cut a piece that's shorter than the 7- or 8-in. hands-free area? The best solution is to cut short lengths from longer boards whenever possible. However, when you have to trim a short piece of molding, use clamps to hold it in place. The auxiliary fence comes in handy for this task by providing a better clamping surface. You'll get better quality miters because the molding can't slide away from the blade. And you'll be assured safer, hands-free cutting.

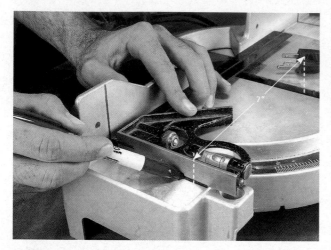

NO HANDS THIS SIDE OF LINE

AUXILIARY FENCE

1 DRAW red lines on the bed and fence of your saw to indicate the "no hands" zone. Draw the lines 7 in. from 10-in. blades and 8 in. from 12-in. blades.

2 CLAMP short pieces of molding. Use strong spring clamps or C-clamps.

Throw together a miter saw bench

Whether you're working in your garage, out in the backyard building a shed or up at the in-laws' cabin building a deck, take a few minutes and cobble together a miter saw bench. With a little creativity, you can use just about any materials you have on hand. The only custom work you'll need to do is to rip some spacer boards to make the outfeed support the same height as the saw table. It sure beats kneeling on the grass or perching the miter saw on horses. And the bench does double duty as a super-convenient work surface too.

Table saws

Cut dust, save time

A great addition to any woodworking shop is a basic, low-cost dust collection system. It keeps the air clean, but it's also a time-saving tool. It drastically cuts cleanup time—you don't have to sweep off every surface and tool after cutting wood all day.

A dust collector is basically a big vacuum, but it sucks in a lot more air (and dust!) than the most powerful shop vacuums.

Complete with hoses and fittings, a small-scale dust collection system costs around $300.

Some home centers carry dust collectors, but the best place to browse is online. Just search for "dust collector."

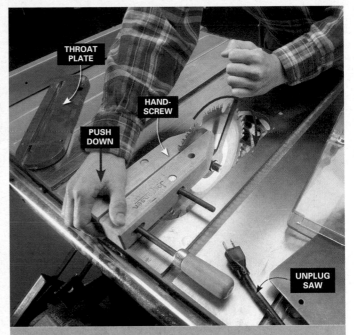

THROAT PLATE

HAND-SCREW

PUSH DOWN

UNPLUG SAW

Painless blade removal

Ever wondered how to remove a table saw blade without scratching your hand and fingers when you loosen the arbor nut? Here's the elegant and safe solution. Unplug the saw, lift out the throat plate and clamp the cranked-up blade in a handscrew. Now you can hold the handscrew—not the blade!—while untightening the arbor nut. The wood jaw surfaces can't ding up the blade. This method works just as well for tightening the blade on the saw.

The right blade for the job

A blade designed specifically for the job—whether it's ripping or crosscutting—will give you much better cuts. "Combination" blades are OK, but they can't match the performance of dedicated ripping or crosscut blades.

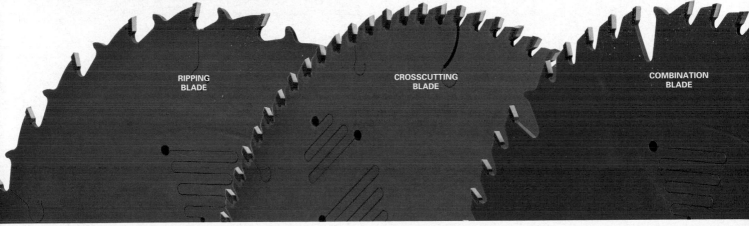

RIPPING BLADE

CROSSCUTTING BLADE

COMBINATION BLADE

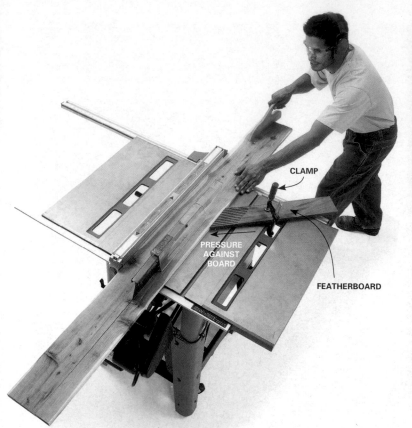

CLAMP

PRESSURE
AGAINST
BOARD

FEATHERBOARD

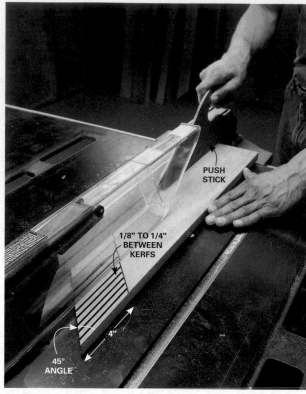

PUSH
STICK

1/8" TO 1/4"
BETWEEN
KERFS

4"

45°
ANGLE

Use featherboards for an extra set of hands

When it's tough to keep a board aligned with the fence, pull out a featherboard for smooth, straight cuts. Featherboards have a series of wooden "fingers" that hold wood tightly against the saw fence. The fingers are slightly flexible and are cut at an angle, so they allow you to push the wood through while maintaining firm, even presure. They also dig in and hold wood in place if it starts to kick back. They're a great "third hand" when you want the perfect rip. Just push the featherboard firmly against the piece of wood

1 to 3 in. before the saw blade, then clamp it tightly to the saw table. It should be fairly easy to push the wood forward but hard to pull it back. And when you're ripping large boards, add a second clamp for extra-firm pressure.

Make your own featherboards from a 2-ft. length of knot-free 1x4. Cut one end at 45 degrees. Then cut a series of 4-in.-long kerfs every 1/8 to 1/4 in. (narrower on stiff hardwoods, wider on softwoods)—thin enough so the long fingers flex slightly.

Cut narrow strips with a sliding jig

To make a series of identical narrow strips for shelf edging, you don't need to remove the blade guard or move the fence for every cut. Just attach a short strip of wood slightly thinner than the width of the rip cut to the end of a 4-ft. 1x6. Then hold the board against it and push the jig through. The jig keeps your hands well away from the blade, and you can rip as many pieces as you need without ever moving the fence.

To make the jig, attach a 5-in.-long strip of wood, 1/16 in. narrower than the width of the desired rip, to the end of a 1x6 as shown. Basically you're creating a horizontal push stick. Add a handle near the end of the jig to give yourself better control as you run the jig through the saw.

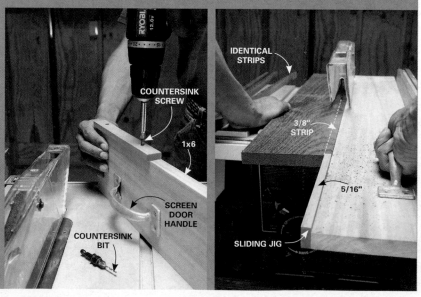

COUNTERSINK
SCREW

1x6

SCREEN
DOOR
HANDLE

COUNTERSINK
BIT

IDENTICAL
STRIPS

3/8"
STRIP

5/16"

SLIDING JIG

Trim crooked boards with a plywood straightedge

The prettiest pieces of wood at the lumberyard aren't always straight and smooth. But cleaning up those rough edges isn't difficult. To straighten out a crooked board (with minimum waste), simply screw it solidly to a straight strip of plywood. Then run the board through the saw with the plywood against the fence. Your board will now have a straight, smooth side to hold against the fence when you're ripping it to width.

Plywood straightedges are also handy for ripping tapers. Simply mark the desired taper on your board, align it with the edge of the plywood, screw it in place, and cut.

Make the sliding plywood straightedge from a 1-ft. x 8-ft. strip of 3/4-in. plywood. Attach the rough board to the plywood with screws driven (predrilled) through a waste section. If there's not enough waste area, screw up through the plywood into the rough board and fill the small holes later. Or consider using special surface-mounted hold-down clamps, available from woodworking stores.

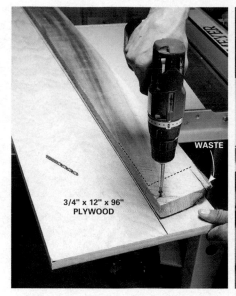

3/4" x 12" x 96" PLYWOOD

WASTE

PLYWOOD STRAIGHT-EDGE

ALIGNMENT MARK

Clamp on a long fence for long boards

Keeping a long, heavy board or a full sheet of plywood tight against a short fence is a challenge, especially when you work alone. It's all too easy for the wood to wander away from the fence, ruining the cut or causing the blade to bind and leave burn marks along the edge. To avoid these problems, clamp a long level or a long, straight board to the fence. The longer the fence, the easier it is to keep the wood firmly against it.

TABLE SAW FENCE

4' LEVEL

Pencil lube for miter slots

When the miter gauge on your saw or sander starts to stick, grab a pencil and lubricate the miter slot with a few quick strokes of the pencil lead (which is really graphite, a great dry lubricant that won't attract dust). You'll find this lube job helpful for any sliding metal parts that get tacky from lack of use.

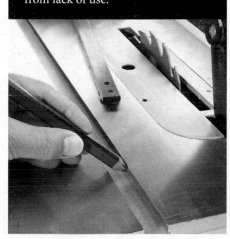

Slick table saw

A good way to protect a cast-iron table saw top is to occasionally rub on a coat of paste wax. This makes a nice, slick top for easier material feeding, and if you drip glue on the surface, it won't stick. It also helps prevent surface rust when the air is humid.

A word about blade guards

Get together with any group of woodworkers and carpenters and invariably you'll hear gruesome stories about table saw injuries. All the accidents have one thing in common: The blade guard was removed. There is a persistent myth in the carpentry world that blade guards are difficult to work with, but in our experience, it's simply not true. They slide up easily as the wood goes through, and the blade is clearly visible through the plastic. And they save fingers.

Save your fingers with push sticks

If you find your hand within a foot of the table saw blade, it's time to reach for a push stick. This essential table saw accessory is notched to hook solidly over the end of the board. You can then push it on through and hold it down firmly at the same time. It allows you to complete a perfectly straight cut while keeping your hands well away from the blade.

It's best to keep at least these two styles handy (see photo). Use the long, narrow push stick for smaller, lighter boards and for narrower cuts. And use the broad, flat push stick for wider, heavier boards when you need to apply more downward pressure.

1/2" PLYWOOD

10"

1/2"-DEEP NOTCH

12"

1/2"-DEEP NOTCH

As a rule, use 1/2-in. plywood for general-purpose push sticks. It's light and tough and won't split as easily as most solid wood. But don't hesitate to make several different thicknesses and styles to use in special situations. Customize your push sticks with different handles, shallower notches (for 1/4-in. plywood, for instance), or strips of rubber or sandpaper for better grab.

PUSH STICK

PUSH STICK

Drilling and fastening

Got a light?

Got a small keychain flashlight just gathering dust in your shop? Blow the dust off the flashlight and glue a small magnet on with epoxy. Then attach them to your drill, or any other tool that needs extra light.

Drill clearance holes

Have you ever screwed two boards together but not been able to pull the two pieces tight together? This happens when the screw threads engage in both pieces of wood while there's still a gap between them. One solution is to clamp or nail the boards together before making the permanent screw connection. If you don't want to mess with clamps or nailing, you can drill a clearance hole through the first board to solve the problem. Choose a clearance hole bit that's large enough to allow the screw to spin freely. Even cupped or twisted boards are easily drawn tight with this method.

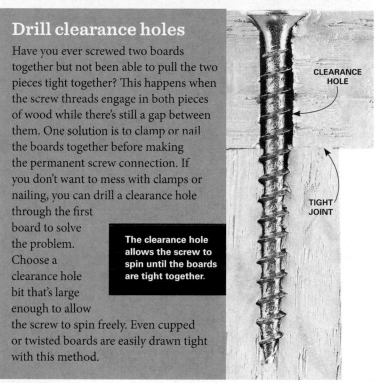

CLEARANCE HOLE

TIGHT JOINT

The clearance hole allows the screw to spin until the boards are tight together.

One handy drill bit

There's nothing better than a step bit for drilling through thinner metal. It's designed to drill incrementally larger holes the deeper you drive the bit, so you can drill several size holes with one bit. It creates a nice clean hole and doesn't catch and kick back like a twist bit.

Electricians use step bits all the time to drill electrical boxes and circuit panels. You can also use them to prep storm door hardware and drill large starter holes in gutters so you can cut out a downspout hole with a tin snips. A good-quality 1/8-in. to 1/2-in. 13-hole step drill bit costs about $20. One that creates a 1-in. hole will cost more. You can save money by buying them in a set.

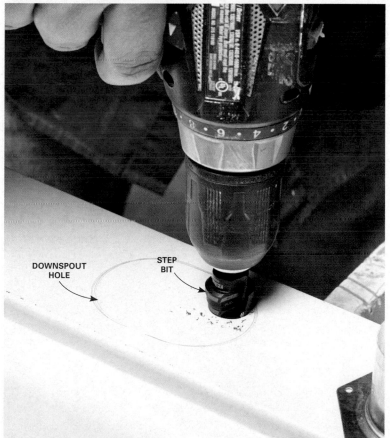

DOWNSPOUT HOLE

STEP BIT

STEP BITS

Two great drill press jigs

Adjustable fence

Add an adjustable fence to your drill press to make it a lot handier for woodworking projects! A fence is especially useful for drilling rows of precisely placed holes. Also, boring holes in a small workpiece is a snap—just clamp the piece to the fence at any angle and drill the hole. You won't struggle with holding small pieces in place while you drill. (That's also dangerous!)

1. Attach a 2-ft. x 1-ft. scrap of plywood or particleboard to the drill press table with countersunk 1/4-in. flat head machine screws, fender washers and nuts. (Run the screws through the slots in the metal table. The fender washers will span the slots.)

2. Create the fence from a 2 ft. x 4-in. x 1-in. board bolted to a 2-ft. piece of 3-in. x 1/8-in. aluminum angle iron. Again, countersink the holes in the board before bolting the board to the angle iron.

Vertical drilling jig

If you've ever tried to drill a perfectly straight and centered deep hole in the end of a board, you know that it's nearly impossible with a handheld drill. But add a drill press and a jig and the job becomes very doable. Make this jig from two 8-in. x 12-in. pieces of 3/4-in. plywood or medium-density fiberboard (MDF). Just screw the pieces together to form a "T" and reinforce the jig with a couple of triangles.

To use the jig, clamp it to the drill press table and the workpiece to the jig. Draw an "X" across the corners to find the exact center of the piece. You'll have to adjust the height of the table and pivot it until you line everything up, but after that, drilling a straight, centered hole is a cinch. This trick will work for rectangular or square boards.

3" ALUMINUM ANGLE IRON

1x4 FENCE

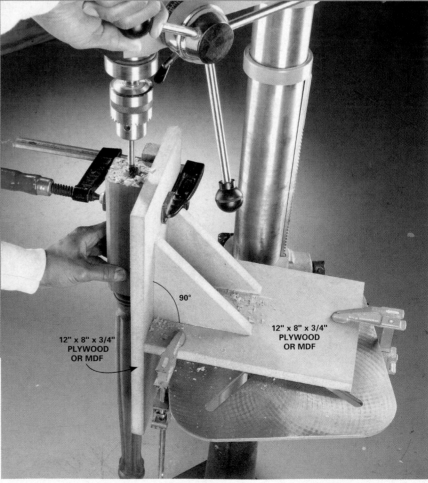

12" x 8" x 3/4" PLYWOOD OR MDF

90°

12" x 8" x 3/4" PLYWOOD OR MDF

SELF-CENTERING BIT

Use a self-centering bit when mounting hardware

Even with a steady hand and a sharp eye, it's tough to drill a perfectly centered pilot hole for hardware installation. And if the hole is off-center, the screw won't seat properly. But there's an easy solution. Self-centering bits drill a centered pilot hole, resulting in perfectly centered screws. There are several sizes of self-centering bits available. Choose one to match the size of screw you're using.

SELF-CENTERING BIT

Use the clutch

At times, drills can provide too much power, causing screw heads to snap off or strip, especially with small brass or aluminum screws. Most newer cordless drills are equipped with a clutch, which can eliminate this problem. Set the clutch by twisting the ring near the chuck to the smallest number. Try driving a screw. If the clutch releases (you'll hear a ratcheting noise) before the screw is fully driven, move the setting to a higher number. Choose a setting that drives the screw fully before the clutch releases.

Tip: Using square or star-drive screws and bits reduces the tendency for the bit to slip off the screw head.

CLUTCH ADJUSTER

Don't mount the bit directly in the chuck

Magnetic bit holders are so handy that it's surprising they're not included as a standard accessory with every cordless drill. Bit holders are readily available wherever cordless drills are sold. Some have a sliding sleeve that keeps your fingers safer by allowing you to drive long screws without holding the screw shank. Here are a few other advantages of using a bit holder:

■ Driver bits are easier to install and remove.
■ The extra length allows better visibility and makes it easier to keep the bit aligned with the screw.
■ Long bit holders allow easy access to hard-to-reach areas.
■ You can stack two bit holders for an extra-long reach.

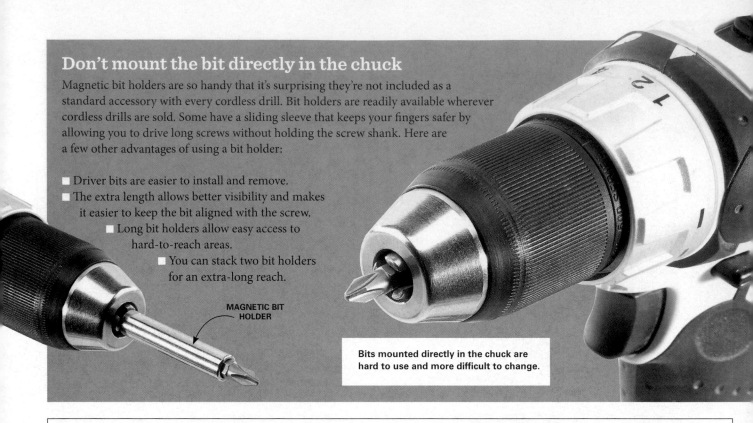

MAGNETIC BIT HOLDER

Bits mounted directly in the chuck are hard to use and more difficult to change.

Drill pilot holes for toe screws

Driving screws at an angle (toe-screwing) is a common technique for making right-angle connections. But if you simply angle the screw in the desired direction, it will usually just slip down the board. The key to successfully driving screws at an angle is to use this two-step process to create an angled pilot hole. Choose a drill bit with a diameter equal to the screw shank, not including the threads. First, estimate the entry point based on the length of the screw. Then start the bit at a right angle to the wood at this point (below left). As soon as the drill bit engages the wood, tilt the bit to the desired angle and finish drilling the pilot hole (below right). Now drive the screw into the angled pilot hole to complete the job.

STRAIGHT STARTER HOLE

1 Start the bit at a right angle to the piece you're fastening.

ANGLED PILOT HOLE

2 Tip it to the correct angle and drill the hole.

BIT AND
SCREW
ALIGNED

Line it up and push hard

Driving screws with a drill can be tricky until you master the technique. The most common mistake beginners make is applying too little pressure. Coupled with bad alignment, this spells trouble. If the bit is skipping out of the screw head and you already know that the bit isn't worn, then improving your technique will help. First, be sure the driver bit is aligned with the screw shank. If the bit's sitting crooked in the screw, it won't engage firmly and will slip. Then, with the bit firmly seated, start the drill slowly (assuming you have a variable-speed drill) while pushing hard against the screw. Apply extra pressure with a hand on the back of the drill body. The combination of correct alignment, pressure and slow speed will ensure that the screw goes in without bit slippage, which can damage the screw head and driver bit.

Use a countersinking drill bit

Countersinking bugle head screws so they are flush or slightly recessed leaves a neat appearance. You can drill a pilot hole and a countersink in one step with a combination countersink and drill bit. For straight-shank screws, the less expensive straight-bit design works fine. For tapered-shank wood screws, use a countersink fitted with a tapered-shank bit.

Countersink bits are available with or without stop collars. An adjustable stop collar lets you set the maximum depth of the countersink for more consistent results. Also, you can hide the screw by drilling a deep countersink, called a counterbore, and gluing a plug into the hole. Countersink drill bits are available in sizes to match screw sizes. If you're an avid woodworker, it's worth buying a full set. Otherwise, a No. 7 or No. 8 will cover the most common screw sizes.

STRAIGHT-
SHANK
COUNTERSINK
BIT

TAPERED-
SHANK
COUNTERSINK
BIT

Don't use a worn bit

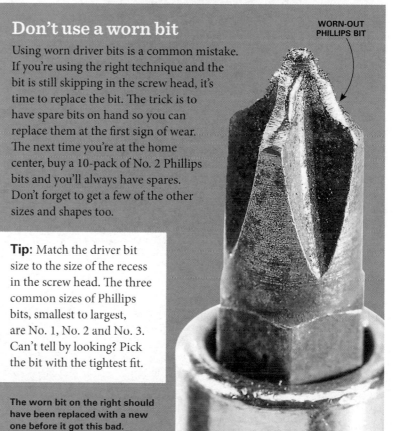

WORN-OUT
PHILLIPS BIT

Using worn driver bits is a common mistake. If you're using the right technique and the bit is still skipping in the screw head, it's time to replace the bit. The trick is to have spare bits on hand so you can replace them at the first sign of wear. The next time you're at the home center, buy a 10-pack of No. 2 Phillips bits and you'll always have spares. Don't forget to get a few of the other sizes and shapes too.

Tip: Match the driver bit size to the size of the recess in the screw head. The three common sizes of Phillips bits, smallest to largest, are No. 1, No. 2 and No. 3. Can't tell by looking? Pick the bit with the tightest fit.

The worn bit on the right should have been replaced with a new one before it got this bad.

Routers and other power tools

FIXED BASE

PLUNGE BASE

Buying advice for routers: fixed-base or plunge?

A fixed base is simple: You just set the depth of cut and rout. You can do the same thing with a plunge base by locking in the depth. Or of course you can plunge. The legs on a plunge router are kind of like shock absorbers: Push down and the legs compress. That means you can lower the bit while it spins. And that allows you to start your cut in the middle of a surface, rather than only along an edge.

This power to plunge lets you do things you couldn't (or shouldn't) do with a fixed base: cut stopped flutes or dadoes, mortises or engravings. Despite that extra versatility, most router aces told us their plunge routers mostly sit on the shelf. One pro woodworker summed it up this way: "My fixed-base routers are simpler, easier to set up and adjust. So I only use a plunge when I have to—and that's about once a year."

Two collets are better than one

Router bit shanks come in 1/4- and 1/2-in. diameters. (There are also 3/8-in. shanks, but they're very rare.) Usually, you can get the same bit with a shaft of either size. But some small bits are available only with 1/4-in. shafts, while some large bits require 1/2-in. shafts. Most routers on the market today come with collets to handle both sizes.

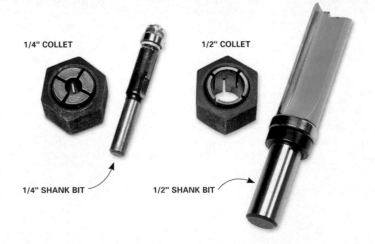

1/4" COLLET

1/2" COLLET

1/4" SHANK BIT

1/2" SHANK BIT

Variable speed is essential for big router bits

Variable speed is a feature that's pointless most of the time, but mandatory at other times. In most cases, you want the bit spinning as fast as the router can go, and adjusting the speed wouldn't make sense. With large-diameter bits, however, full speed isn't safe (check the rpm restrictions on the label). So if your plans include big bits, choose a variable-speed router.

Some routers also offer constant speed, which keeps the rpm stable under load. When you're running at full speed, this feature isn't much of an advantage. But when you dial down the rpm to use a large bit, the router senses the load and feeds more power to maintain the speed set on the dial. It's not essential, but it's a nice feature that prevents running at slower speeds than you intended.

VARIABLE-SPEED DIAL

MOTOR

PLUNGE BASE

FIXED BASE

Beware of horsepower ratings

Take the horsepower rating on any power tool with a grain of salt. It's not that the manufacturer is lying—it's just that there are no consistent industry standards for determining horsepower. So it's better to squint at the specifications and find the amp rating. The amp rating isn't a perfect indicator either, but it's more reliable than horsepower.

Consider a combo kit

Can't decide between fixed-base and plunge? You don't have to. Most manufacturers now offer "combo kits" that give you one motor along with both a fixed and a plunge base. You truly get the best of both worlds. But do the math before you buy. In some cases, the extra cost of a combo kit is more than the cost of a second good-quality router.

Single-stage plywood cutting

To avoid wrestling heavy sheets across a table saw, many of us perform a two-act play: We rough-cut with a circular saw, then make finish cuts on a table saw. With a track saw, you can skip the second act. The first cuts will be your final cuts—every bit as straight, smooth and accurate as you'll get on a table saw.

Soft shoe for recip saws

To reduce vibration and protect surfaces while using a reciprocating saw, take a piece of 3/4-in. foam pipe insulation and cut it to about 4 in. Open the split side and slide the insulation over the blade to cover the saw shoe. The split will naturally squeeze the shoe, holding it in place. The insulation eliminates scratches and marks on finished surfaces.

Chip-swallowing router fence

This made-from-scraps router fence—along with your shop vacuum—collects wood chips while you work.

On a table saw, cut a straight piece of 2x4 to 2-1/4 in. wide for the fence's height, being sure the vertical face and bottom edge of the fence form a 90-degree angle.

Saw a "mouse hole" in the center of the fence to fit over the router bit, then screw together a plywood box with a hole in the top to fit your shop vacuum hose (1-1/4 in. or 2-1/4 in. diameter).

It's noisy to run a router and vacuum at the same time, so wear hearing protection!

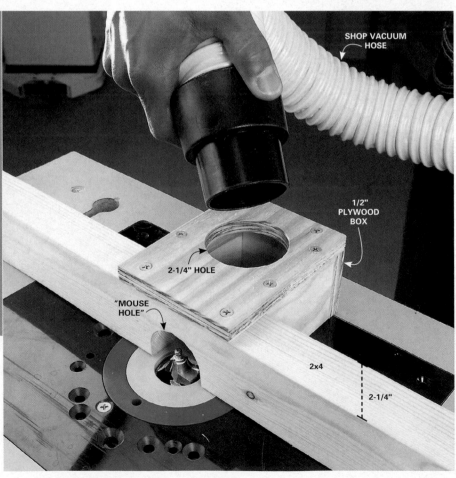

SHOP VACUUM HOSE

1/2" PLYWOOD BOX

2-1/4" HOLE

"MOUSE HOLE"

2x4

2-1/4"

A 4-1/2-in. grinder for fine woodworking

For the sheer pleasure of working wood, nothing compares to sculpting and shaping wood by eye and feel.

A 4-1/2-in. disc grinder is perfect for shaping gently curved projects. Equipped with a 24- to 36-grit sanding disc, the grinder is aggressive enough for most projects. You can get a grinder for about $40, but spend more if you plan to use it a lot. It'll last longer and be more comfortable to handle. Do final sculpting with 100- to 120-grit, which also leaves a surface smooth enough to finish-sand with a random orbital sander. This Windsor chair seat took about an hour to carve with the grinder.

Versatile angle grinder cuts almost anything fast

An angle grinder excels at grinding down metal or masonry, but it's a must-have tool because it can do so much more.

One great use for an angle grinder is as a tile saw. Fitted with a diamond blade, it'll cut just about any stone or ceramic tile. And the relatively small blade is perfect for the intricate cuts needed for outlet openings or the curved holes around a shower faucet.

Grinders cut metal fast too—all you need is a metal cutting wheel. With wire wheels and brushes, you can strip paint from metal or remove rust from wrought iron. For occasional use, an inexpensive angle grinder will work fine for all these jobs.

Trim nailer tips

Use a block to push baseboard

When baseboard—or the floor—isn't straight, force the trim down with a 2x4 block. The block gives you a broad surface to push against and lets you apply a lot more pressure. This trick also works with uncooperative crown molding.

Use nails before screws

It's difficult to keep parts aligned when screwing cabinets together, but a couple of shots with a finish nailer or brad nailer will keep the parts aligned while you drill pilot holes and drive screws for strong joints.

Tongue-and-groove the easy way

With a trim nailer, you can install tongue-and-groove paneling in a fraction of the time. Some carpenters use a finish nailer for this, but it's easier to use a smaller, lighter 18-gauge brad nailer, especially on ceilings. Brads don't have the holding power of 15- or 16-gauge nails, of course, but you can make up for that by shooting two brads into every stud or joist.

A pinner means no splitting

A 23-gauge pinner almost never splits wood, even on very small parts. In most situations, it's a good idea to dab on a little wood glue to give the joint more strength than pins alone can provide.

Prefinish parts

One of the best things about trim nailers is that you don't have to worry about beating up the wood, unlike with a hammer. That means you can finish parts before assembly or finish trim before installation, which gives you better results in less time. Just be sure that the soft rubber tip that came with your nailer is actually on the gun before you shoot.

Invisible nail holes with a pinner

Pins are tiny and headless, so they're hard to see even before you fill them. Afterward, nobody but you will know they're there.

Tight spot? Use a pinner

The working end of most pinners is just over 6 in. long and goes where no other nailers fit.

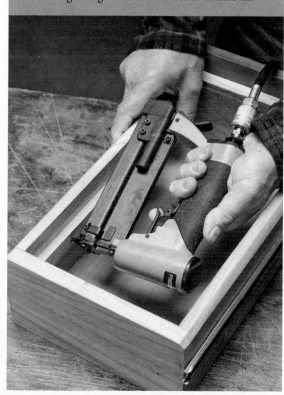

Nail before you clamp

With a coat of slippery glue, parts will slide out of alignment while you're desperately trying to clamp them. A good solution is to tack the parts together with a couple of nails. That keeps the parts aligned while you apply serious pressure with clamps.

Extend your reach

Starting a nail with a hammer takes both hands—and that limits your reach. A trim nailer, on the other hand, lets you reach way over to shoot a nail. And using a bench, rather than a ladder, lets you nail off even the longest runs in only two or three moves.

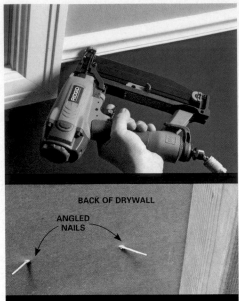

BACK OF DRYWALL

ANGLED NAILS

No stud? No problem

Studs aren't always located where we need them. When you need to nail trim where there's no stud, dab some construction adhesive on the back of the trim and then drive nails into the drywall at 45-degree angles. That holds the trim tight against the wall while the adhesive cures. This "trap nailing" technique works fine with brad nailers and even better with finish nailers.

Convenient compressor drain

Most compressor manufacturers recommend draining the tank after every use. And most compressor owners ignore that advice without serious consequences. Still, draining the tank is important, and the more often you do it, the better. As a compressor runs, water condenses inside the tank. That means rust. In extreme cases, you can even lose tank capacity. We've heard stories of tanks that held only half as much air because they were half full of water.

The twist-open drains on most compressors are pretty lousy. They're hard to turn and easily plug up with rusty gunk until they can't open or close properly. But for about $10, you can install a drain that's fast, easy and reliable. Go to the compressor aisle at a home center and look for a ball-valve drain kit. If you don't find one, go to the plumbing aisle to pick up a 1/4-in. ball valve, plus any 1/4-in. nipples and elbows you'll need.

BALL VALVE

NIPPLE

ELBOW

OLD VALVE

Easy on old walls

Hammering nails through old plaster walls is a recipe for cracks. A trim nailer, on the other hand, drives nails instantly, without the repeated blows that can cause cracks. Use a 15-gauge nailer for these jobs; the nails are stout enough to push through the hard plaster and long enough to bite into the framing behind it.

Pinners are perfect for crafts

A pinner is the go-to tool for delicate assemblies like this.

WHICH NAILER DO YOU NEED?

23-gauge pinner

These tiny pins don't have enough holding strength for most jobs. But there are times when pins are perfect, especially to nail small parts. Most pinners shoot pins ranging from 1/2 to 1 in. long. That's long enough for most jobs, but models are available that can handle pins up to 2 in. long.

Trim nailers are categorized by the thickness or "gauge" of the nails they shoot: The bigger the gauge number, the smaller the nail (seems backward, doesn't it?). Nailers that shoot the biggest trim nails—15 and 16 gauge—are usually called "finish nailers." Midsize 18-gauge nailers are called "brad nailers." The smallest nailer, the 23-gauge, is usually called a "pinner" or "micro pinner."

15-gauge finish nailer

This is the gun for nailing large 3/4-in.-thick baseboard and trim. It's also a good choice for more demanding jobs like nailing doorjambs or stair treads. These nailers have a large piston, and because of the extra bulk, often have angled magazines so you can get into tight spots. Most 15-gauge nailers handle nail lengths up to 2-1/2 in.

23-GAUGE

15-GAUGE

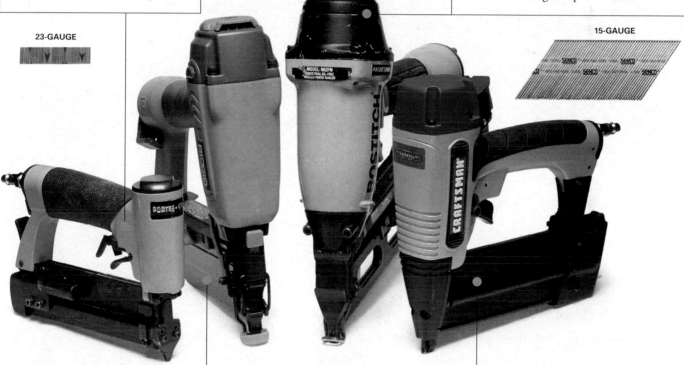

16-gauge finish nailer

Like 15-gauge nailers, most 16-gauge guns shoot nails up to 2-1/2 in. long and are suitable for thick trim. The main advantage of a 16-gauge gun is that it's smaller and lighter. If you're shopping for a finish nailer, we recommend the larger 15-gauge gun, simply because the fatter nails provide more holding power. But some carpenters disagree with this, and really there's not that big a difference.

16-GAUGE

18-GAUGE

18-gauge brad nailer

If you plan to buy only one trim nailer, this is the size to get. Most carpenters use this one more than all the others combined. It's perfect for standard trim, furniture making and odd jobs around the shop. Models that shoot brads up to 1-1/4-in. are common, but we strongly recommend spending a few bucks more for a gun that can handle brads up to 2 in. long.

Hand tools

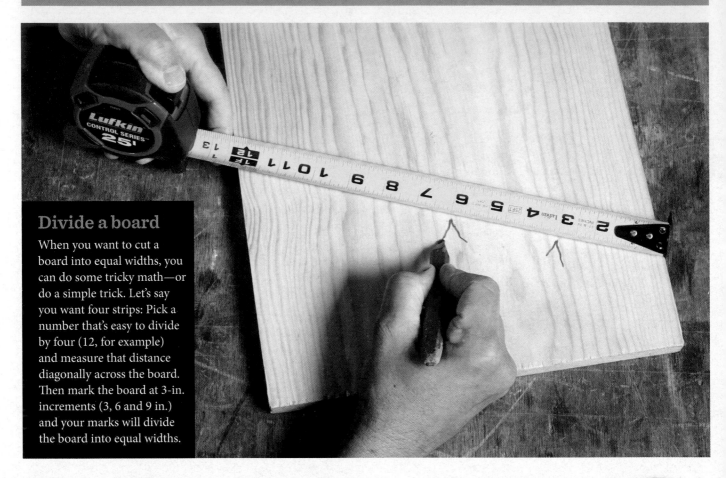

Divide a board

When you want to cut a board into equal widths, you can do some tricky math—or do a simple trick. Let's say you want four strips: Pick a number that's easy to divide by four (12, for example) and measure that distance diagonally across the board. Then mark the board at 3-in. increments (3, 6 and 9 in.) and your marks will divide the board into equal widths.

Built-in nut drivers

Combination screwdrivers have two Phillips head sizes and two slotted head drivers, but many people are not aware that when these drivers are pulled out, the two ends that hold the driver heads will drive 1/4-in. and 5/16-in. bolt heads as well. This makes them perfect nut drivers for tightening and loosening hose clamps as well as appliance fasteners.

Easy-to-read tool markings

Stamped-in tool markings can be tough to read. To solve this, buy some white fingernail polish, brush it on the tool and quickly wipe it with a clean cloth. The white polish stays in the grooves, and the numbers are easy to read at a glance. You can use lacquer thinner to wipe it if the polish dries too quickly.

Measuring reminder

Place a self-adhesive label on the side of your tape measure for jotting down measurements when you're on a ladder or roof or at the hardware store. The label can be easily erased or replaced as needed.

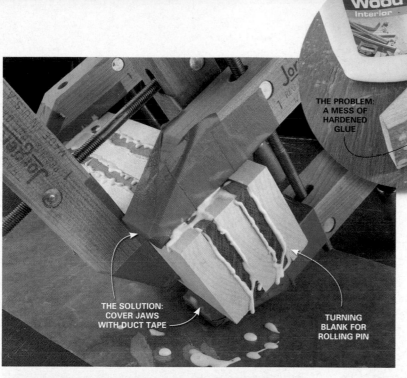

THE PROBLEM: A MESS OF HARDENED GLUE

THE SOLUTION: COVER JAWS WITH DUCT TAPE

TURNING BLANK FOR ROLLING PIN

No glue on your handscrews!

Handscrews are the pros' choice for clamping face-glued boards and laminates. The only drawback is that the handscrew jaws can load up with glue, and if you're not careful, they could become a permanent part of the project! Besides, dried glue on the jaws will dent your projects.

Here's the solution.

1. Wrap duct tape or clear packaging tape around the handscrew jaws to keep glue from penetrating and adhering to the clamps.

2. Remove the clamps once the glue is set but still pliable. Use a moist rag to clean the glue off the taped handscrews, or strip off the tape and apply new tape before your next messy job.

Prevent rusty tools

Maybe you've got some nice tools. But if you're like many of us, you have to store them in the garage or shed where heat and humidity can take their toll. You can prevent them from rusting if you store them with vapor corrosion inhibitor (VCI) products. VCI products (capsules, mesh liners and zipper bags) are infused with rust-inhibiting compounds that vaporize and attach to tools' metal surfaces. The vapor molecules form an anticorrosive coating on tools to prevent rust.

Some home centers carry VCI products. If yours doesn't, check online. There are a few manufacturers that sell directly to consumers without a huge minimum order.

■ Line your toolbox or chest drawers with anti-corrosion nonslip mesh liner. The anti-corrosion feature lasts five years, but the nonslip feature lasts much longer.

■ Add a VCI capsule to your toolbox or your power tool's carrying case to keep the tool in pristine condition. The VC2-1 capsule lasts one year, and the VC2-2 lasts two years.

■ Slide critical measuring tools like micrometers and calipers inside a VCI zipper bag for five-year protection. This 9 x 12-in. bag only costs $1. Other sizes are available.

ANTI-CORROSION NONSLIP MESH LINER

VCI CAPSULE

VCI ZIPPER BAG

Mini tools from concrete nails

Need a nail punch or skinny chisel or tiny screwdriver RIGHT NOW? It's only as far away as a box of 3-in. concrete nails. These nails are made extra hard for pounding through stone, concrete and thick layers of stucco, and they're easy to grind into the mini tool you need. Be sure to hold the nail in a locking pliers for safe grinding, and dip it in water frequently to preserve its temper.

CHISEL

CENTER PUNCH OR NAIL SET

GRINDING A MINI CHISEL

SCREWDRIVER

Get a beefy bench vise

A wimpy $30 vise may satisfy your wallet, but you'll regret buying one the first time you have to crank the bolts off a really big part. So skip the cheapies and invest in a heavy-duty vise. You want a vise with at least 5-1/2-in. jaws, a pipe clamping area, dual swivel locks and a large anvil area. They're more expensive, but worth the price. You can also find great deals on good used vises on Craigslist or at neighborhood garage sales.

The best tape for any kind of job

Shop work

For woodworking and tinkering in the shop, there's rarely any reason to go bigger than a 16-ft. tape. It's small and light, and it slips comfortably into a pocket or shop apron.

Big projects

A tape in the 16- to 30-ft. range is best for remodeling jobs. Most of us prefer the upscale versions with wider blades, better standout and a bigger hook.

Long-distance measuring

An "open reel" tape is perfect for long measurements. There's no spring or enclosure, so it won't get choked with dirt or sand. Unlike metal blades, the fiberglass tape won't kink or break when you step on it. And the big crank winds in the tape fast.

Using laser levels

CEILING MARK

THREE-POINT LASER

FLOOR MARK

Lay out on the floor first

With a point-type laser level, you can lay out your ceiling box and light fixture locations on the floor, where it's easy to measure, and then use the laser to transfer them to the ceiling. This technique is especially useful for vaulted or sloped ceilings, where locating light fixtures would require a plumb bob.

Start by marking the light fixture locations on the floor with masking tape. Then elevate the laser and line up the downward pointing beam with the center of the fixture. Now you can mark where the upward pointing beam hits the ceiling.

Working in bright light? Use special glasses

Laser beams are hard to see in bright light. But you can improve the visibility of the line or dot with special red glasses. Don't expect miracles, but the glasses definitely make the beam easier to see, and they're worth buying if you're working outside or in a brightly lit space. You'll find laser-enhancement glasses at some home centers or online.

No-fuss square layout lines

All kinds of remodeling projects require square layout lines. Tiling—floors or walls—is a perfect use for a laser-level square. The only function of this special type of laser level is to project a pair of perpendicular lines, like crosshairs. A laser square is great for planning your layout: You can set it on the floor and measure from the lines to see how your tile layout will work. And it's perfect for actually setting tile too, because the lines won't get covered by the thin-set or mastic. You'll find laser squares at home centers and online.

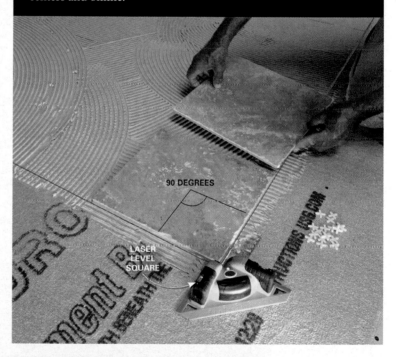

90 DEGREES

LASER LEVEL SQUARE

Working outdoors? Try dusk or dawn

Lasers don't show up well in sunlight. A rotary laser with a laser detector works in daylight, but this setup is too expensive for most DIYers. If you have a lot of outdoor leveling to do, consider renting a rotary laser and detector. But if you already own a laser level, try this tip first. Do your laser-leveling work at dusk or dawn, when the light is dim. Or if you're a night owl, you could level your deck posts in the dark.

Self-leveling is a great feature

Adjusting a bubble-vial laser until it's level in two directions is time consuming and error-prone. Self-leveling lasers are quick and easy to set up, and accurate. The only caveat is that you have to set up self-leveling lasers so they're within about 5 degrees of level for the self-leveling feature to work. If the level isn't within the required range, it will flash or shut off to indicate that it's not working.

CROSS-LINE LASER

PLUMB LASER LINE

STUD MARK

Transfer stud locations with a laser

If you've ever installed kitchen cabinets, you know how time consuming it is to mark the stud locations inside the cabinet to position the mounting screws. With a laser level that projects a plumb line, it's easy. You still have to locate the studs and mark the centers. But once this is done, you can simply align the vertical beam with the stud mark and drive your screw on the laser line. This tip will work for cabinets, shelves or any other installation that requires you to anchor to studs.

Mount it on a tripod

Most laser levels have a threaded hole on the bottom that accepts a standard 1/4-in. tripod mount. Some laser levels come with a tripod. But if yours doesn't, it's worth buying one. A tripod allows you to easily adjust the laser to the best height and level it on uneven ground.

But you don't need a tripod that's designed for lasers. If you already have a camera tripod, it'll probably work just fine with your laser since the threads are usually the same size. Or buy one wherever cameras are sold.

BELT LINE

LEVEL REFERENCE LINE

CROSS-LINE LASER

Measure from a level reference line

A common misconception about using a laser is that you have to get the beam lined up exactly where you want the line to be. In most cases, it's easier to simply project a laser line somewhere on the wall, and use it as a reference. Just measure up or down from the line the desired amount and mark the wall. When you use this method, it's a good idea to mark the wall at the laser line, too. Then if the laser gets bumped, or you move it, you can reestablish the same reference line by lining up the laser with your mark. You can also use a point-type laser as a reference. You'll just have to swivel it to make marks in other locations.

Tips for choosing a laser

Buy an inexpensive torpedo laser level for occasional use around the house, or if you want a compact level for your tool belt. As with traditional levels, you'll have to manually align the bubble with the center of the vial. Then the laser will project a level or plumb laser line or dot.

For tile layout and for laying out 90-degree corners for decks or sheds, a laser level square is handy. It will project a pair of perpendicular lines.

Consider a self-leveling, cross-line laser for ease of use and the greatest versatility. Cross-line lasers project a level line, a plumb line or both. They're great for all kinds of leveling and plumbing tasks.

Choose a three- or five-point self-leveling laser if you need to transfer points from the floor to the ceiling. You can also mount a point-type laser on a tripod and swivel it to mark the ends of a level line. Point-type lasers don't project lines, but work great as a quick and accurate substitute for a plumb bob.

Rent an auto-leveling rotary laser for large outdoor projects like setting elevations for foundation footings or leveling posts on a large deck. The kit will include a tripod, an elevation rod and a laser detector. The laser detector allows you to use the laser in bright sunlight.

Find the high and low spots in a floor

When you start a kitchen cabinet installation or tile a wall, you need to know whether the floor is level and how much variation there is from the high and low spots. It's easy to figure out with a laser level.

Just set the laser on a few scraps of wood or a paint can in a spot that will project a beam across the floor. Make a quick sketch of the floor plan. Then pick a spot and extend a tape measure to the floor. Note the measurement where the laser beam crosses the tape, and mark this on your sketch. Then check other areas of the floor and jot down these measurements. The location with the smallest dimension is the highest spot, and the difference between the largest and the smallest dimensions tells you how much the floor is out of level.

LEVEL LINE

TOP PLATE LINE

WALL LINE

CROSS-LINE LASER

BOTTOM PLATE LINE

Build walls with laser lines

Here's a huge time-saver if you're building walls in an existing space. Normally you would have to snap a chalk line on the floor, then use a plumb bob or a level with a long straight-edge to transfer the floor marks to the ceiling. With a laser that projects a vertical beam, you can skip all these steps.

Just line up the laser where you want the wall to be, and you'll see lines on the ceiling and floor. You can leave the laser in place and build to the laser lines, or you can use the lines to make marks for the top and bottom wall plates. Either way, it's much faster and easier with a laser. A self-leveling cross-line laser works great for this. You can buy one at home centers or online.

Working with ladders

PALMS TOUCH RUNG

EXTEND ARMS

LADDER AT CORRECT ANGLE

TOUCH TOES TO LADDER BASE

Set your ladder at the correct angle. Put your toes against the ladder's feet. Stand straight up and extend your arms. The palms of your hands should just reach the ladder's rung.

Get the angle right

Setting the ladder at the correct angle is one of the most important steps to a safe ladder setup. Too steep and it could tip over backward. Too much angle and it could bend or the bottom could slide out. The photo shows how to get the angle just right. If an obstacle prevents you from setting the ladder at the correct angle, don't take chances—consider using scaffolding instead.

Ladder pouch

There's no need to load up your tool belt when you're working from a ladder. Any type of hook, pouch or pocket made for a tool belt works just as well when mounted on a ladder.

SWIM NOODLE

Ladder guards

Protect your gutters from dents and scratches with ladder protectors made out of an old swim noodle (foam pipe insulation would work too). Cut 2-ft. sections of the foam noodle, slit them with a razor knife and stuck them on the sides of the ladder. They make the perfect cushions. If the foam doesn't stay put, tape it on.

A round of protection

To prevent your ladder from marring your home's exterior, slip golf club covers on the ends of the ladder. It may also motivate you to get your household chores done and get you out on the links.

Fasteners

Stay-tight bolts

If you have a loose bolt and you're out of thread sealant, here's a quick solution. Coat the bolt threads with fingernail polish and screw the bolt into place. The bolt will stay tight.

Choose 3/16-in. screws for most light- to medium-duty tasks

Home centers and hardware stores stock concrete screws in two diameters: 3/16 in. and 1/4 in. The 3/16-in. diameter screws are plenty strong for most home tasks like installing furring strips, screwing down walls to concrete floors, and attaching hardware to block or brick. And since they're a little cheaper and the smaller hole is easier to drill, the 3/16-in. size is usually the better choice. If you're having trouble with the 3/16-in. screws snapping off because the concrete is too hard, switch to stronger 1/4-in.-diameter screws instead. You could also keep some 1/4-in. screws handy in case you strip out the hole for a 3/16-in. screw. Switch to 1/4-in. screws for heavy-duty work like securing a wall cabinet to a concrete or block wall, or supporting shelving that will hold a lot of weight.

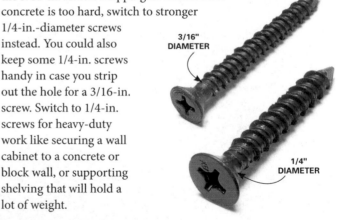

3/16" DIAMETER

1/4" DIAMETER

Cake-pan hardware sorter

You won't have to waste time sorting through your fastener jar for the right bolt or nut with this timesaving device from an old baking pan. Using a bimetal hole saw, drill a hole slightly smaller than the jar opening. Carefully file and then sand the sharp edges around the cut edge. Now you can pour the contents into the pan, find what you need and then rake the contents through the hole back into the jar!

SCREW EXTRACTOR

Stripped screws, no problem

A stripped screw can turn a 10-minute fix into a two-hour nightmare. One of the best investments you can make is a screw extraction kit. One side of the extractor bit reams a hole into the screw, and the other side has reverse threads that dig into the screw as you turn it out. Kits are sold that include different size bits.

REAMING END

REMOVER END

Keep a handful of plastic anchors in case of strip-out

Occasionally the threads of a screw won't grip and the screw will spin in the hole. Usually you can just abandon this hole and drive another screw a short distance away. But if relocating the screw isn't a good option, simply enlarge the hole and slip in a plastic anchor. Then drive the concrete screw into the anchor.

PLASTIC ANCHOR

1/4" HEX DRIVER

Faster concrete fastening

A concrete screw installation tool allows you to use one tool without having to switch between a masonry bit and a screw-driving bit. Just drill the hole and slip the driver shaft over the masonry bit and then sink the screw. If you have a bunch of concrete fasteners to install, it's definitely worth the money. The version shown here is one of several brands.

Nail drill bit

Drilling pilot holes in your latest project but can't find your itty-bitty drill bit? A nail will do the job. Cut off the nailhead with a wire cutter, then tighten the nail in the drill chuck and go to work. The chiseled tip on the end of the nail drills clean holes fast, especially in softer woods and plywood.

NO. 4 FINISH NAIL— REMOVE HEAD TO FIT IN DRILL CHUCK

Cutting threaded rod

When you're shortening a bolt or threaded rod with a hacksaw, you always mangle the threads at the sawn end, making it difficult to get a nut threaded onto it. This tip produces a much better ending. Thread two nuts onto the bolt at the cutoff spot, tighten them against each other, then saw against the shoulder to create a clean right-angled cut. Next, loosen the nuts and file a slight bevel around the end to clear burrs created by sawing. Then spin off the nuts to clean and realign the threads. Your shorter bolt will work just like a new one from the box.

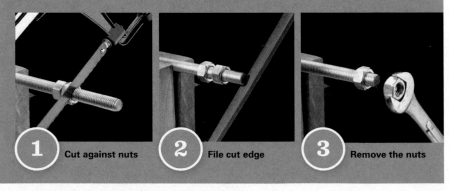

1 Cut against nuts   **2** File cut edge   **3** Remove the nuts

Faster fastening with better screws

Premium construction screws have a few big advantages over the drywall screws we've all been using for years.

For starters, most have improved head designs—hex, Torx or Spider, for example—that eliminate slipping and stripped screws. Premium construction screws are also less brittle than drywall screws, so they won't break off as easily, and they're coated to resist corrosion. Special self-drilling thread designs coupled with a thin shank means you rarely need to drill a pilot hole. Large structural screws can replace lag screws, and the smaller ones are better than drywall screws for woodworking and framing projects.

There are several brands. You'll find GRK screws online and at contractor-oriented lumberyards. Spax and FastenMaster screws are readily available at home centers and hardware stores. Like any premium products, they cost a little more.

Keep track of screw bits

It's common now for a box of screws to include a bit—for star or Torx heads, for example. However, it can drive you crazy when you can't find that bit when you need it. Here's a solution: When you buy a box of screws, store them in a glass jar and glue a magnet to the inside of the lid. The magnet holds the bit, and you don't have to dump out all the screws to find it.

Spin-cut a bolt

When you need to shorten a bolt, let your drill do the work. Put two nuts on the bolt and tighten them against each other. Then stick the bolt in a drill and hold a hacksaw against the spinning bolt. The nuts help to steady the saw blade and remove burrs when you take them off the bolt.

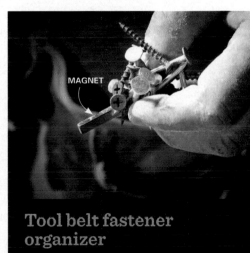

MAGNET

Tool belt fastener organizer

While you're working on projects, your tool belt fills up with random screws, washers, nails, and other odds and ends. And when you want to find something in your belt, you have to take your gloves off and rummage around in all that mess.

Here's a simple but helpful timesaver: Toss a magnet into your tool belt. Every small fastener will stick to it, and all you need to do is grab the magnet and pick off whatever you need. You don't even have to take off your gloves. Awesome!

Chapter Four

KITCHENS AND BATHROOMS

Cabinets and countertops

Super-glue knobs

Oblong and rectangular knobs that fasten with a single screw are notorious for twisting over time. Thread sealant will keep a screw from coming loose from the knob, but it won't necessarily stop the knob from twisting. For that, add a drop of superglue to the back of the knob before installing it.

No room for an island? Try a cart instead

Kitchen islands are more popular than ever, but because you need at least 36 in. all around an island for walking space, they just don't fit in most small kitchens. A rolling kitchen cart will give you many of the benefits of an island and is more versatile. You can move it into the center of the kitchen for food prep or use it as a buffet table when guests arrive. Then just roll it out of the way when you don't need it. In new kitchens you can leave a spot under the countertop for the cart. Commercially made carts are available with cutting board tops, shelves and hooks on the sides for utensils. Search online for "kitchen cart."

JOHN BOOS & CO.

Get an extra hand from jack

Hanging cabinets solo is slow, frustrating work. A car jack, boosted by scrap wood, can hold a cabinet steady for as long as needed and without a complaint.

Replace worn-out drawer slides

If you find that slides are bent, rollers are broken or rollers won't turn even after lubricating, replacement is the best solution. To keep the project simple, buy new slides that are identical (or almost identical) to the old ones. That way, replacement is an easy matter of unscrewing the old and screwing on the new. Remove a drawer track and a cabinet track and take them shopping with you. Whether you have pairs of side-mounted slides (as shown here) or single, center-mount slides, there's a good chance you'll find very similar slides at a home center. If you can't find them, check with a cabinet materials supplier or search online for "cabinet equipment and supplies."

DRAWER TRACK

CABINET TRACK

A zillion questions equals the best kitchen

Before designers break out the drawing board, they sit down with the clients and go through a six-page questionnaire. Are they right- or left-handed? Do they buy in bulk? Are there special physical or sight considerations? Finding out more about the clients—right down to where they like to store the dog food—helps create a more efficient, user-friendly (and user-loved) kitchen.

Corner appliance cabinet

A corner appliance cabinet hides coffeemakers, toasters and other small appliances while making efficient use of often-wasted corner space.

Fix squeaky drawers

Vanity drawers can develop squeaks over time, but the wrong lubricant can leave graphite stains or sticky residues that attract dust and dirt, and can even drip onto flooring or cabinet interiors.

For lubing drawer slides, door hinges, overhead fans and other sticky or squeaky things inside the house without causing stains or odor, use a dry lubricant that contains PFTE (commonly known as Teflon). It dries fast and leaves a durable, light-colored lubricating film right where you spray it.

Three common brands are Liquid Wrench Dry Lubricant, DuPont Teflon and Blaster Dry Lube, which are available at home centers and hardware stores.

Sideways rollout

To build a kitchen rollout like this, you'll need to perform major surgery. Remove the cabinet's back panel, then move it forward after you rip the shelves down. Next, cut a hole in the side and build the slide-out shelf. The shelf rides on fixed casters and is guided by full-extension drawer slides (two at the bottom and one on the top).

← ROLLOUT DOOR

Closed
This rollout is a solution to big, overloaded shelves and useless space at the back of a deep pantry cabinet.

Open

Adjust hinges on misaligned doors

If your cabinet doors are out of whack and you have European-style hinges, you're in luck. Euro hinges are designed for easy adjustment. Don't let their complex look scare you; all you have to do is turn a few screws, and any mistakes you make are easy to correct. The Euro hinge shown here adjusts in three directions. Others adjust in two directions. Either way, it's a trial-and-error process: You make adjustments, close the door to check the fit, then adjust again until it's right.

First . . .

If the door isn't flush with the doors next to it, adjust the depth screw. This screw moves the door in or out. Some depth screws move the door as you turn them. But with most, you have to loosen the screw, nudge the door in or out and then tighten the screw. If your hinges don't have depth screws, start with the side screws.

Second . . .

If the door is crooked—not standing parallel to adjacent doors or square with the cabinet—adjust the side screw. This moves the door from side to side. In some cases, you have to loosen the depth screw slightly to adjust the side screw.

Third . . .

If the door is flush and parallel with other doors but too high or low, use the mounting screws to raise or lower the mounting plates. Loosen the screws at both hinges, slide the door up or down and tighten the screws. Some mounting plates adjust by turning a single screw.

MOUNTING SCREW
DOOR SCREW
DEPTH SCREW
SIDE SCREW

Tighten the door screws and the mounting screws before you make any adjustments. Then adjust the depth screw and side screw.

Check the fit of the door after each adjustment. With double doors like these, perfect the fit of one door first, then align the other door.

Thyme saver

If your spices are jammed into a drawer with only the tops visible, this nifty rack that slips neatly into the drawer will solve the problem. And it only takes an hour to build. Make it with scraps of 1/4-in. and 1/2-in. plywood.

1/4" PLYWOOD

1/2" PLYWOOD

Storage tips

VERTICAL PLYWOOD PANEL

CUT SHELF TO NEW LENGTH

DRILL HOLES FOR SHELF PINS

Cookware organizer

Most kitchen base cabinets lack vertical storage space for big, flat cookware like cookie sheets and pizza pans. To provide it, just remove the lower shelf, cut a vertical panel of plywood and fasten it at the cabinet bottom with furniture braces and at the top with a strip of wood. Drill holes for the adjusting pins to match the original locations and trim the shelf to length.

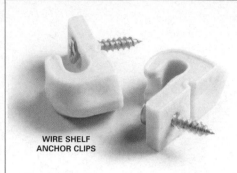

WIRE SHELF ANCHOR CLIPS

Swinging trash

Here's a space-saving solution to the bathroom wastebasket problem. Screw wire shelf anchor clips to the inside of the door and hook the lip of a small wastebasket right on the hooks. It's easy to use, it hides unattractive trash, and it frees up precious bathroom floor space.

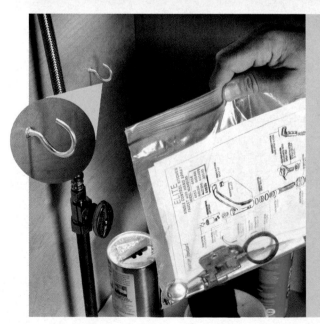

Under-sink archives

Don't file away the manuals for your kitchen and bath fixtures. Instead, slip them into a zip-top plastic bag and hang the bag in the cabinet under the sink. They'll always be right where you need them. Toss in paint samples and spare cabinet hardware too.

Triple your bathroom storage with new shelving

Bathrooms never have enough storage or shelf space. There's hardly enough room to display knickknacks, let alone store unsightly items like extra toilet paper, blow dryers, curling irons, cans, soaps and bottles. Once the vanity is filled, there's really no more storage in a small bathroom.

2 Add glass shelving to the unused space over the toilet.

1 Replace that tiny medicine cabinet or mirror with a larger, surface-mounted cabinet.

3 Steal space from an adjoining room or closet by insetting kitchen pantry cabinets (or tall utility cabinets) into the wall.

EASYCLOSETS.COM

Pantry cabinet in a closet

Moving some of your bulkier or seldom-used items out of the kitchen and into a nearby pantry can free up a lot of space. Look around. You may have extra space in a nearby closet or hallway where pantry shelves would fit. A pantry could be as simple as adjustable shelves on wall standards or a more elaborate built-in cabinet. Build your own or search online for "closet shelves."

Plastic bag holder

An empty rectangular tissue box makes a convenient holder for small garbage bags, plastic grocery bags and small rags. Simply thumbtack it to the inside of a cabinet door.

Get more storage space—without remodeling

Lower cabinets offer the biggest storage spaces in most kitchens. But according to kitchen designers, the back half of this space is usually wasted—it's packed with long-forgotten junk or left unused because stored items are out of view and hard to reach. Rollout bins let you see and use the whole space. Search "rollouts" at familyhandyman.com for more information.

Add a shower shelf

On new tile walls, the correct way to install a ceramic corner shelf is to set it directly into the thin-set mortar during tile installation. But you can add a corner shelf (or another soap dish) on existing tile.

Stop by a tile shop and pick up a "flatback" corner shelf unit. Then buy soap scum remover, double-face foam tape and a tube of silicone caulk. Clean off all the soap scum or the bond might fail.

Apply a strip of foam tape on each mounting flange, stopping 1 in. short of the ends. Test-fit the shelf before you remove the wax liner paper from the tape. Shim any gaps with additional layers of foam tape. Once the shelf fits squarely into the corner, apply the silicone caulk (Photo 1).

Locate a spot in the middle of a row of tiles (no horizontal grout lines running through the caulk). Then remove the liner, square up the shelf and press it against the tile (Photo 2). Once the tape grabs, let go, wipe off the excess caulk and then tool the joint with a damp fingertip. If you blow the placement, you'll have to muscle off the shelf, completely clean off the back and reapply fresh tape, so be careful.

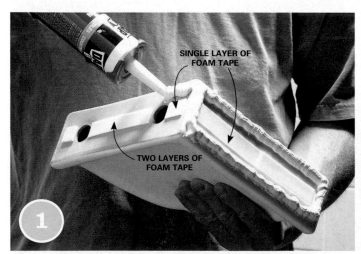

Tape, shim and caulk. Add extra layers of foam tape to compensate for an "out-of-square" corner. Then lay a thick bead of caulk around the entire perimeter.

SINGLE LAYER OF FOAM TAPE

TWO LAYERS OF FOAM TAPE

MOUNT IN CENTER OF TILE

Double-check before you stick. Make final adjustments before driving it home—you only get one shot at placement. Once the foam tape touches the wall, you're done.

Bathroom fixes

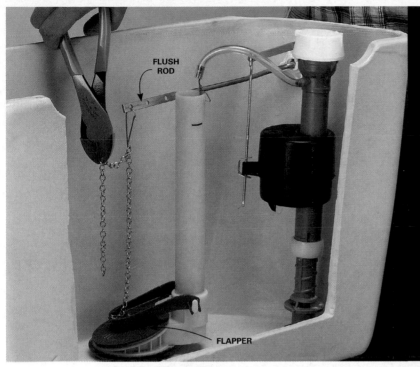

FLUSH ROD

FLAPPER

Adjust a flush handle/ flapper chain

A chain that's too short or tangled won't allow the flapper to close and water will continue to leak into the bowl. This causes the fill valve to cycle on and off to refill the tank. A chain that's too long, or a flush rod that hits the tank lid, won't open the flapper wide enough to stay open for the full flush. You'll find yourself having to hold the lever to complete a good flush.

To avoid these problems, adjust the linkage in the chain to leave only a slight bit of slack when closed. Cut the chain at the rod to leave only about an inch extra to reduce the potential for tangles.

Adjust the chain to leave a little slack with the flapper closed. Then cut off the excess, leaving about an inch.

Then put the tank lid back on and make sure the flush rod doesn't strike the lid when you press the lever. If it does, bend it down slightly and readjust the chain.

1

Loosen the retaining nut. Grab the nut with pliers and turn to the left to loosen.

2

Install the new handle. Slide the new handle into place. Then thread on the retaining nut. Tighten by turning to the right.

Foam a loose showerhead

Have a wobbly shower arm? Before you tear into the wall and refasten the plumbing, try this fix. Shield the wall with plastic and inject a few shots of expanding foam. The foam encases the pipes in the wall and eliminates the wobble.

TRIM RING

Replace a broken or corroded toilet flush handle

There's no trick to replacing a toilet flush handle—as long as you remember that the retaining nut inside the tank is a reverse thread. So, if you're in front of the toilet, turn the nut to the left (Photo 1). Remove the old handle and lever and install the new one (Photo 2).

Don't overtighten the water connections

Do yourself a favor and buy a flexible water supply line when you install a toilet or other fixture. They're a lot easier to install than stiff metal or plastic tubing. Be sure to get one that's covered with stainless steel mesh. For a good seal, hold the hose so it aims straight into the shutoff or fill valve while you're screwing on the connectors. Make them hand-tight, then add another quarter turn with pliers. Connections that are too tight can actually cause leaks or spin the fill valve inside the tank. Check for leaks and tighten them a bit more if needed.

A quiet bath fan

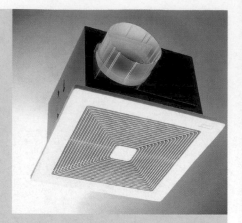

You might be tempted to leave your noisy bath fan off. But don't. Humidity from hot showers feeds mildew, causes condensation and can support rot inside your walls. Instead, upgrade to a quiet fan.

Fan noise is measured in "sones." The lower the number, the quieter the fan. "Quiet" fans usually hum at 1.5 sones or less; some are as low as .3 sones. If a fan doesn't carry a sone rating, it's probably loud (3 to 5 sones). Quiet fans are more expensive, but worth it.

Replacing a fan and ductwork takes one day. But usually you can connect a quiet fan to existing ductwork—or even just replace the motor and leave the housing in place—and save hours of work. Most quiet fans require duct that's at least 4 in. in diameter. To determine the size of your existing duct, pull off the fan's grille and motor and look inside. Find the manufacturer and model number, then go online and see if the manufacturer sells a quieter replacement motor—most major brands do. If not, remove the housing and install a new fan with the same size duct.

To remove moisture from your home, it's best to let a fan run for 15 to 30 minutes after you shower or bathe. So consider replacing the fan's switch with a timer. Rotary timers work well but make a buzzing sound. For silent operation, get an electronic timer. Another option is to install a fan that switches on when humidity levels rise.

CLEANER

BUFFER/POLISHER

1,000-GRIT SANDPAPER

Renew a scratched cultured marble countertop

I've got a cultured marble countertop in my bathroom that's quite scratched up and shabby looking. Can I do anything to make it look like new?

Cultured tops are made of polyester resin with a clear topcoat (called the gel coat). This is the same material that's used with fiberglass and it buffs out beautifully. Removing the faucet makes it easier to buff the top.

First wet-sand with 1,000-grit paper (available at auto parts stores) to remove small, shallow scratches and surface stains. Don't try to remove deep scratches or deep stains. You'll risk sanding right through the gel coat. Rinse and dry the top.

Next, buff with medium-cut cleaner (available at auto parts stores). The buffing can be done by hand, but a small power buffer is much easier. Finally, protect the restored finish with a coat of cultured marble polish (available at home centers and bath specialty stores). Follow the label directions.

Faucets, drains and fixtures

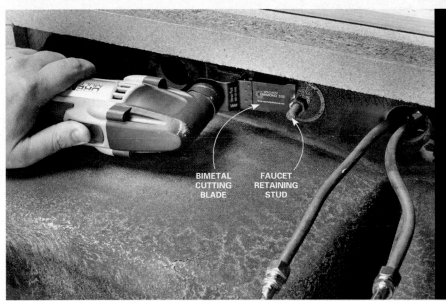

BIMETAL CUTTING BLADE

FAUCET RETAINING STUD

Cut rusted faucet nuts with an oscillating tool

Sometimes you just can't muscle off rusted-in-place faucet nuts with even the best basin wrench. And you can forget about using a reciprocating saw under the sink deck—there simply isn't enough room.

But you may be able to pull off the impossible by using an oscillating tool equipped with a high-quality bimetal cutting blade.

Angle the tool against the nut and start it off at slow speed until it cuts a groove. Then increase the speed and keep sawing until you're about three-quarters of the way through. Then break off the remaining portion with pliers.

Stop sink-sprayer hang-ups

If you have to jiggle the hose as you pull out your kitchen sink sprayer, chances are the hose is catching on the shutoff valves. For smooth operation, slip 1/2-in. foam pipe insulation over the pipes and shutoff handles. Tape it if it won't stay put. Get the insulation at home centers and hardware stores.

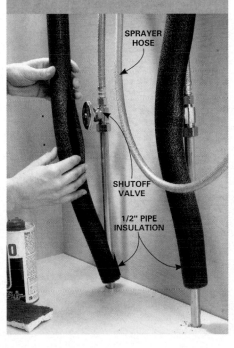

SPRAYER HOSE

SHUTOFF VALVE

1/2" PIPE INSULATION

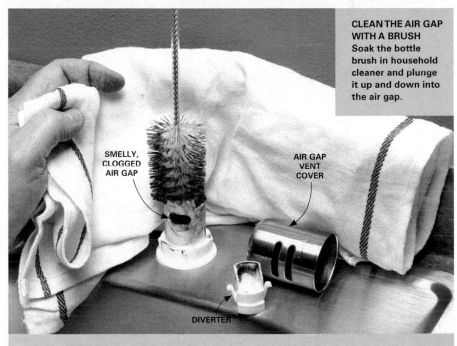

CLEAN THE AIR GAP WITH A BRUSH
Soak the bottle brush in household cleaner and plunge it up and down into the air gap.

SMELLY, CLOGGED AIR GAP

AIR GAP VENT COVER

DIVERTER

Clear a clogged air gap

An air gap prevents dirty dishwater from backflowing into fresh water lines. But over time, ground-up food and grease can build up inside the air gap and form a clog. If water squirts out the air gap's vent holes or you notice a foul smell coming from it, it's time to clean it. All you need is a bottle brush and some household disinfecting cleaner.

Yank the cover off the air gap and remove the snap-in or screw-on diverter. Remove any loose food particles, then clean with the bottle brush as shown. If you still have a water leak after cleaning the air gap, clean the drain line where it meets the garbage disposer or drain wye (aka "Y").

Fix an erratic sink sprayer

Inside your faucet, there's a diverter valve, which stops the water flow to the spout and sends it to the sprayer when you press the spray head's trigger. Here are the symptoms of diverter trouble:

• Very little water, or none at all, comes out of the sprayer when you press the trigger. A bad sprayer head can cause this, but more often the diverter is the culprit. To check this, remove the spray head and turn on the faucet. If the water flow out of the hose is weak, the diverter is to blame.

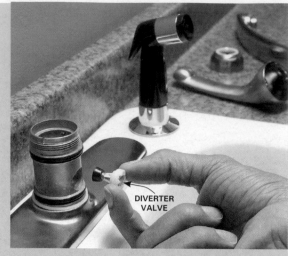

Disassemble the faucet to access the diverter. Clean or replace the diverter and reassemble the faucet.

• The sprayer pulsates like a machine gun.

• Water continues to flow out of the faucet spout when you're using the sprayer.

Often, a misbehaving diverter needs only light scrubbing with a toothbrush and a good rinse. But since removing a diverter usually requires major faucet disassembly, it's best to simply replace the diverter rather than risk taking it apart again.

Diverter styles and removal procedures differ widely. Some are small valves like the one shown here. Others are larger cylinders that don't look like valves at all. Some newer diverters aren't inside the faucet, but are instead connected to the sprayer hose below. So the first step in diverter repair is finding a diagram of your faucet. If you can't find your owner's manual, do an online search. Type in the manufacturer of your faucet followed by "faucet parts diagram." With a little searching, you'll find an illustration showing your faucet's internal parts. You'll also find several sources for replacement parts online.

Restore free flow to a faucet

Kitchen or bathroom faucets sometimes lose pressure because of a dirty aerator screen. Luckily, cleaning a screen is an easy job. Start by closing the drain plug (so you don't drop parts down the drain). Then remove the aerator using a rag or masking tape so you don't mar the finish with your pliers.

To remove the sand and other deposits, soak the aerator in vinegar, then scrub it with a toothbrush. This usually solves the problem. If you have to disassemble the aerator to clean it, lay out the parts in the order you removed them so you can reassemble them correctly.

Tighten a floppy faucet handle

If you have a loose valve handle— on a shower, bathroom or kitchen faucet—tighten the screw that holds the handle in place. With some faucets, you'll have to pry off the metal button at the center of the handle. With others, you'll find a setscrew near the base of the handle. Setscrews usually require a hex (or Allen) wrench. If tightening doesn't work, the stem inside the handle may be worn, especially if it's plastic. Here's a trick to tighten worn stems on most types of faucets: Wrap the stem tightly with pipe-thread tape and slip the handle back over the stem. In most cases, a single wrap creates a snug fit.

Tiling and grouting

HOT-MELT GLUE

Hot glue for tile accessories

Most tile setters use masking tape to support ceramic soap dishes and shelves while the tile adhesive cures. Here's a better way: Apply a small bead of hot-melt glue along the seam. Hold the item in place for just a few seconds while the hot glue stiffens. The glue creates a strong seal, so there's little chance of slipping or breakage. Once the permanent adhesive sets, just peel away the bead of glue.

No-slide knee pads

Knee pads that slip down your shins every time you stand up are a huge nuisance. Avoid the slide by strapping on a pair of hockey or baseball catcher's shin guards instead. You get comfortable knee pads that stay put, and shin protection, too. You can try a secondhand sports store or get a pair online.

Grout squeeze bottle

Grouting ornate tile borders is a challenge because of the raised details. Instead of using a grout float, try a clean, empty mustard bottle. Just fill it up and squeeze the grout between the tiles. You can cut the tip to get a better angle or increase the volume. P.S. It also works great for porous stone because it doesn't fill the pores with grout.

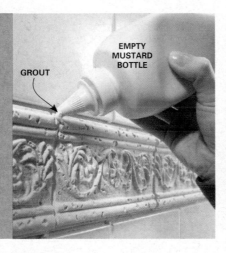

EMPTY MUSTARD BOTTLE

GROUT

Better tub caulking

Here's an old plumber's trick to try before you caulk the seal between your tub and the tile wall. Step inside the tub. If it flexes or you feel any movement at all, fill the tub with water and stand in it while you caulk (make sure to use silicone). Let the caulk dry before you drain the water. The weight of the water (and you) will settle the tub slightly downward or outward. This will help the caulk seal last longer because it won't stretch when you use the tub.

Brush-on waterproofer

A top-notch tiling job in wet areas like showers and around tubs requires a waterproof membrane under the tile. The easiest type is liquid waterproofing that you apply with a brush, trowel or roller. When dry, it forms a flexible membrane that's perfect to tile over.

This handy waterproofing makes the installation of a watertight tile job as simple as a brushstroke. Once the tile substrate is securely installed and seams are taped, all you need to do is apply a coat of the pudding-like liquid to the surface, let it dry, and it's waterproofed. This makes waterproofing shower curbs, benches, tub decks and steam showers a breeze.

You'll find brush-on waterproofing at home centers, tile stores and online.

Level the floor

Tiling a wavy floor is a nightmare. You push and pry to get each tile flush with its neighbors and you still end up with "lippage" (edges that protrude above adjoining tiles, usually at corners). So before you tile, check the floor with a 4-ft. straightedge. If you find low spots more than 1/4 in. deep, screed thin-set over them to create a flat surface.

For really bad floors, self-leveling compound (also called "self-leveling underlayment") is a lifesaver. You just mix the powder with water and pour to create a flat, smooth surface. Some products require metal or plastic lath; some don't. (You can also use self-leveling compound under floating wood and laminate floors.)

Self-leveling compound is almost goof-proof, but there are two big pitfalls. First, it will slowly seep into the tiniest crack or hole, leaving a crater in the surface. So before you put down the lath, grab a caulk gun and fill every little gap—even small nail holes. Second, you have to work fast. Most compounds begin to harden in about 30 minutes. To get the whole floor poured in that time frame, you need at least one helper to mix the compound while you pour. And even with help, you'll have to move quickly.

PLASTIC LATH

SELF-LEVELING COMPOUND

HEATING CABLE

POUR A PERFECT FLOOR
Self-leveling compound gives you a flat, smooth base for tile. It's also a fast way to embed in-floor heating mats or cables.

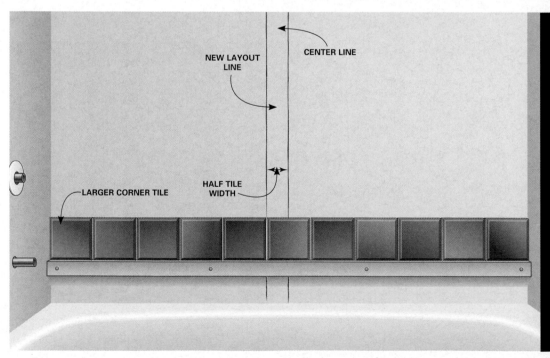

NEW LAYOUT LINE

CENTER LINE

LARGER CORNER TILE

HALF TILE WIDTH

Laying out wall tile

Locate the starting plumb line to leave the widest possible same-sized tiles at each corner. Lay out the tile on the floor and use the back wall measurement to determine how wide the corner tiles will be. If starting with the edge of a full tile in the center of the back wall leaves a skinny strip in the corner, shift the plumb line by half the width of the tile. This will increase the size of the corner tiles.

Kitchen appliances

Sparkling dishwasher

Add a cup of vinegar to your empty dishwasher and let it run a full cycle once a month or so. Your kitchen may smell a bit like a pickle jar for a few hours, but hard-water lime buildup will be rinsed away, making your spray arm and other dishwasher parts work better.

VINEGAR

Clean your refrigerator coils

If your refrigerator conks out on a hot day and you have a cat or a dog, immediately check the coils for pet hair. Service pros find this problem on half of their refrigerator calls. The coils are the black tube-and-wire grid that cools the fluid in the compressor. A buildup of hair will cause the compressor to overheat and trigger the overload switch. On many fridges, you get to the coils by opening the grille at the bottom of the refrigerator. Then push a coil cleaning brush (sold at home centers) into the coils, pull it back and vacuum it clean.

If the coils are located on the back, pull out your fridge (it's often on rollers) and brush them off. Bonus: The clean coils will cool more efficiently and save you money on your electricity bill.

TIP: Once the overload switch is tripped, you may have to wait a few hours for it to cool. It will reset itself and turn the refrigerator back on.

COIL CLEANING BRUSH

Pull out a fridge without wrecking the floor

Lay down a cardboard runway before dragging out your fridge. For the ultimate floor protection, use 1/8-in. hardboard (sold at home centers). A pair of shims create a ramp for easier pulling.

1/8" HARDBOARD

SHIM

Pro tip: Dirty igniters are the most common problem. It takes only a minute to clean them.

IGNITER

Gas stove

If your stove burner won't come on, the likely culprit is the spaghetti sauce that boiled over a few days ago. Use a toothbrush to clean off food spills from the igniter. On an electronic ignition stove, it's a little ceramic nub located either on the stovetop or under the ceramic seal strike plate. Also make sure that the round ceramic seal strike plate is properly seated on the burner.

BURNER PRONG

Electric range

If your electric stove burner won't heat, turn the burner off and pull it out from its socket. Then plug it in again and wiggle it around. If it feels loose, remove the burner again and gently bend the burner prongs slightly outward for a tighter connection. Easy does it. You could end up pushing the whole socket out of its bracket.

TUBE

PILOT HOLE

Standing pilot gas range

To access the ignition system in an older-style standard gas range, pop the lid. It's usually hinged on the back side. If the pilot flame is out, poke a needle into the pilot hole to clean out soot (be careful not to ream it wider). Brush off any debris and clean the tube that leads from the pilot to the burner. Then relight the pilot.

Clean a stinky garbage disposer

Even if you run your garbage disposer until the last shred of food is gone, and you let the water run the recommended time, you can still wind up with an out-of-control science experiment that stinks up your kitchen. Face it; some food is going to stick to the inside of the grinding chamber, and it's going to decay. You can clean the chamber by grinding ice and lemon rinds, adding baking soda or rinsing with vinegar and water. Or you can add commercial cleaners, which are available at discount stores and most home centers.

However, if you don't clean the underside of the splash guard, you haven't finished the job and may still wind up with a stinker. Cleaning the splash guard is easier than you think. You don't even have to remove it. Just clean it with a toothbrush and cleaner as shown.

GREASE AND FOOD

SPLASH GUARD

BRUSH OFF THE CRUD AND RINSE
Dip an old toothbrush in antibacterial grease-cutting kitchen cleaner and lift up one corner of the splash guard. Scrub off the crud and rinse with cold water. Repeat with each flap until it's totally clean and rinsed.

USING AND STORING CAULK

Reusable caulk tube

How often do you have dry caulk stuck in the tip of the tube but know that there's a lot of fresh stuff behind it? Get to the fresh stuff by first cutting two slits along the tube, on opposite sides, with a sharp utility knife. Pry out the dried plug of caulk. Then wrap the tip with duct tape, put the tube back in the gun and use up that caulk.

Cut tips off straight

You probably learned to cut the tip at an angle. That works OK in some situations, but an angled tip limits the position the caulking gun has to be in. With a straight tip, you can swivel the gun out of the way of obstacles, and you'll be able to caulk right up to an inside corner. And if you have various-size gaps to fill, cut the tip small and do the small gaps first, then cut it bigger for the larger gaps. We guarantee it won't work the other way around.

Airtight caulk tube seal

Done with the caulking job but the tube's only one-third empty? Dip the nozzle into a can of rubber coating (sold at home centers). You'll create an airtight seal that's easy to peel off when the next job calls.

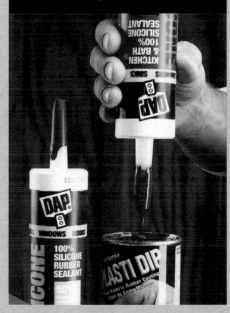

Caulk tube organizer

Tired of having your caulk tubes lying all over the workbench or your shelves? Make this organizer from a scrap of 2x8 and a piece of 1/4-in. plywood. Just lay out a pattern for your 2-in. hole saw to follow and drill holes through the 2x8. Then glue the plywood to the bottom. Now you can set it on a shelf and easily identify the tube you're looking for.

Choose the right caulk for the job

The selection in the caulk aisle at home centers is mind-boggling, but actually choosing the right one is pretty simple. Most of the caulk on store shelves is basically one of four types: elastomeric, polyurethane, latex or silicone. Here's how to make the right choice:

1 **Siding, windows and doors:** Polyurethane is a hands-down favorite. It's paintable. It doesn't shrink. It stays flexible. It adheres better than silicone, and it doesn't attract dust and dirt the way silicone does.

2 **Roofing:** Use an elastomeric or rubberized product. This stuff won't dry out in extreme conditions, and it sticks to everything.

3 **Interior trim:** If you're sealing gaps and nail holes in trim that's going to be painted, use latex. It cleans up easily and dries fast. It's also easy to tool—and cheap.

4 **Kitchen and bath:** This is where silicone products shine. Silicone tools well. It can be purchased with antimicrobial additives, and can be removed and replaced when it gets grungy.

The after-mess

Some tubes have air in them and "burp" at the worst possible moment. Some continue to run after you set them aside. The bottom line: There's going to be cleanup. Use mineral spirits to clean up elastomeric and polyurethane. Latex cleans up great with just a wet rag. Silicone is another story. It seems to get on everything. The only tip for cleaning up silicone is that when it does get all over your gloves (and it will), just consider the waterproofing it provides as a bonus.

Push, don't pull

Always try to push the caulk into the gap rather than drag it over the gap. This greatly increases the odds the caulk will adhere to both surfaces because it forces caulk into the gap—pulling doesn't. One exception to this rule is when both surfaces are flush. When caulking flush surfaces, if you try to push the tip too hard, it will skate all over the place, and you'll have a big mess on your hands.

Tooling tips

It's best to try to get the bead right the first time. But sometimes tooling is a necessary evil. Elastomeric and polyurethanes don't tool well—a finger dipped in soapy water is your best bet. Latex is easily tooled, and even if you screw it up, you can wipe it off with a wet rag and start over. However, tape off the area when using a silicone product.

If you don't want to use your finger for tooling the silicone, use a caulk tooling kit. The one shown above is available at home centers. If you get your bead close to the way you want it, the best advice is to leave it alone. It seems the more you mess with a bead, the uglier it gets.

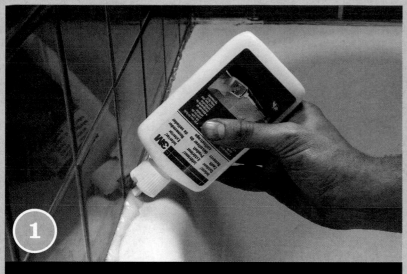

1

Spread a wide bead of caulk remover along the caulk line, covering it completely.

2

Remove the loosened caulk with a putty knife, pulling it out from the gap between the tile and the tub.

Remove old caulk the easy way

Scraping out moldy caulk from around a bathtub is a tough, tedious job. And if you get too aggressive, you'll chip a tile or mar the tub finish. Make the job a lot easier by first softening the caulk with a caulk remover.

Application is simple. Just squeeze the remover onto the caulk, making sure it covers the edges (Photo 1). Let it sit for several hours (or as directed on the package). Then start scraping out the old caulk (Photo 2). The caulk remover works by destroying the bond between the caulk and the tub or tile, so that instead of chipping at the caulk with a razor blade, you just pull away big chunks of it with a putty knife. Most removers work on both silicone and acrylic latex caulks.

Clean off the residue with soap and water, let dry and then recaulk.

Ride the smooth side

When one of the surfaces you're caulking is rougher than the other, always try to ride the tip on the smoother surface (the brick mold in this case). If you ride the middle or the rough surface (siding), the caulking will duplicate the bumps, sometimes in an exaggerated way.

Finish projects ... now

Don't learn to live with incomplete projects. If you do, the last couple of pieces of trim can linger for years!

Chapter Five

PLUMBING AND HEATING

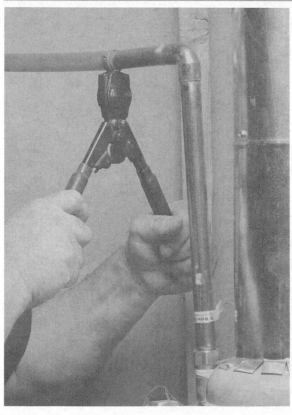

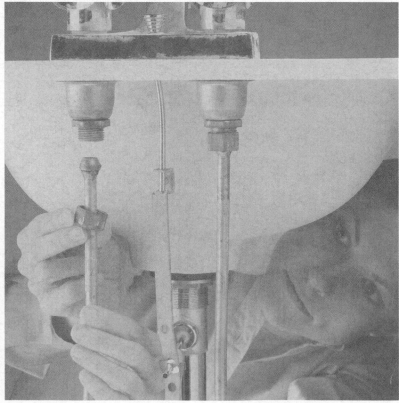

Plumbing know-how

Strap your water heater if you live in an earthquake-prone region

Earth tremors can tip water heaters and break the gas lines that lead to them, causing either water damage, or worse, an explosion and fire. Water heater straps can prevent this disaster. (They're required in California and other regions.) In earthquake-prone regions, you can find them at home centers and hardware stores. Otherwise, order them online.

WATER HEATER STRAP

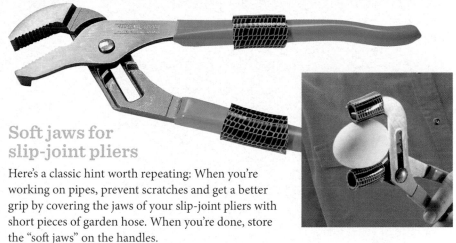

Soft jaws for slip-joint pliers

Here's a classic hint worth repeating: When you're working on pipes, prevent scratches and get a better grip by covering the jaws of your slip-joint pliers with short pieces of garden hose. When you're done, store the "soft jaws" on the handles.

Bucket flush

You don't have to run to the neighbor's bathroom during a plumbing project. Before you turn off the water supply, fill 2-gallon buckets with water. Flush the toilet by dumping the water in the bowl. You'll get one flush per bucket. Works just as well as the usual method, although it won't refill the bowl.

Old gas valves can leak

GREASE-PACK VALVE

BALL VALVE

VEER (RF)

The "grease-pack" valves found in older homes tend to leak as they age. Even if your local code doesn't require replacement, you should install a ball-type gas valve instead. Replacement isn't difficult; you just unscrew the old valve and screw on the new one. But you will have to turn off the main gas valve and later relight pilot lights. If you don't know how to handle these tasks, call in a professional plumber.

Buy extra plumbing parts!

No matter how carefully you plan, it seems like you always need another elbow or extra length of pipe. Save yourself a trip to the store and buy extra the first time. Then return what you don't use.

ABS vs. PVC

Most professional plumbers prefer ABS black pipe and rarely use white PVC. It's all about the glue. Gluing ABS is a one-step process, which makes it faster to work with than PVC. Purple PVC primer is messy, emits noxious fumes, and it's just ugly.

ABS cement lasts longer in the can and dries clear, making it more forgiving if you get a drip or two on the floor. ABS cement also dries faster, which reduces the risk of connections pushing apart before they set up. In most cases the labor saved by using ABS more than makes up for the extra money spent on pipe and fittings. ABS is also lighter and more flexible, which makes it easier to flex for bending it into tight spaces.

The only downside—retailers don't always carry ABS.

Turn off the water supply before going on vacation

Water damage from undetected plumbing leaks will quickly ruin ceilings, floors and walls, leading to repair bills in the thousands. This is especially true if you're away on vacation. Yes, such a leak is unlikely, but insurance companies report hundreds of these incidents every year. Look for the main valve near the water meter and turn it clockwise to close it. If it's stuck, leaks or doesn't turn on again, hire a plumber to replace it. The ice maker in your refrigerator may freeze up while you're gone, so shut it off too or thaw it with a hair dryer when you return.

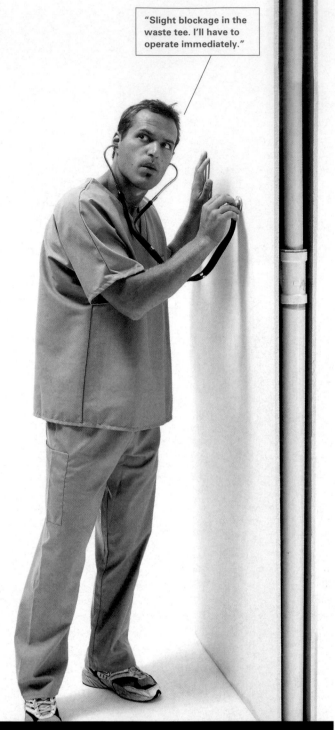

"Slight blockage in the waste tee. I'll have to operate immediately."

MAIN WATER SHUTOFF

Pipe-finding prescription

A stethoscope (sold at drugstores) lets you locate plumbing lines inside walls when you're planning a remodeling project. You need a steady flow of water, so turn on faucets full blast to find supply lines. To locate waste lines, have a helper flush toilets or fill sinks and let them drain. You'll hear the flow from several feet away, and the sound will get noticeably louder as you get closer. You'll be able to locate pipes within a foot or so. A stethoscope also lets you hear the hiss of larger leaks in supply lines.

Waste and vent lines

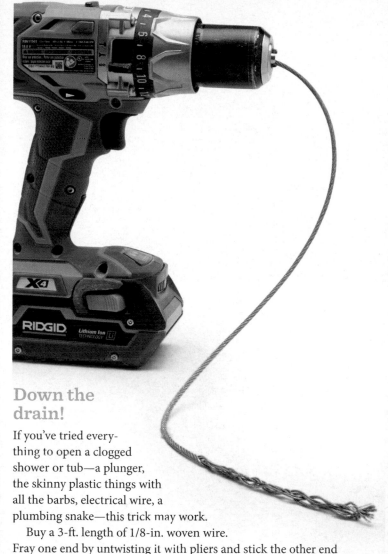

Mark pipe before gluing

When you're working with PVC pipe, dry-fit the fittings and the pipe to make sure they're in the correct position. Use a level where appropriate. Then mark the pipe and fitting so you can get them back in exactly the same position when you're gluing the joint. PVC cement sets quickly!

Down the drain!

If you've tried everything to open a clogged shower or tub—a plunger, the skinny plastic things with all the barbs, electrical wire, a plumbing snake—this trick may work.

Buy a 3-ft. length of 1/8-in. woven wire. Fray one end by untwisting it with pliers and stick the other end into your cordless drill chuck. Push into the drain as you pull the trigger on the drill. It should find its way past the trap and into the clog. Then just pull out the mess and clean up.

FOAM CORE

Seal the ends!

Most ABS pipes have either a cellular or a foam core that air will actually pass right through. If you don't believe it, wrap your lips around the pipe wall and blow through it. If you don't seal pipe ends with cement, air will escape into the porous center core and find its way out of the plumbing system and you'll fail a pressure test every time. Can you even imagine that disaster? You'd have to replumb everything!

Plum-wonderful plumbing shortcut

Most municipalities (but not all, so check) allow engineered air admittance valves (AAVs). You can use an AAV instead of running a vent up through the roof or connecting to an existing vent pipe. A HUGE time and labor saver.

The only downside is that an AAV needs to be located in free air space, meaning you can't completely enclose it in a wall or joist space. But you can buy a recessed box with a grille that makes it look like a heating vent. You can find AAVs at some home centers and online.

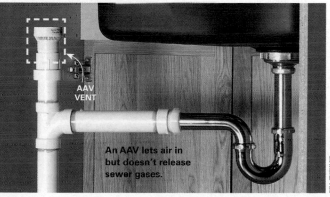

AAV VENT

An AAV lets air in but doesn't release sewer gases.

BILL ZUEHLKE

Slope pipes with a shim

The next time you need to put a consistent slope on pipes, concrete formwork or landscaping projects, try this hint. Tape a shim to one end of your level to establish the desired slope—say, 1/4 in. per foot for a drain. Center the bubble and your project will be perfectly sloped. Calculate the thickness of the shim by multiplying the length of your level in feet by the desired slope (inches per foot). We wanted 1/4-in.-per-foot slope on this drainpipe, so for our 2-ft. level we needed a 1/2-in.-thick shim. If it's more convenient to set the level on top of your project, tape the shim to the bottom instead.

PIPE SLOPED 1/4" PER FOOT

1/2" SPACER

2' LEVEL

Tape a shim to one end of your level and use it to set the slope of plumbing pipes.

String saw pipe cutter

Amaze your friends and mystify your neighbors by cutting PVC pipe with a string. It's a great trick to know if you have to cut pipe that's buried in a wall or some other tight spot. We used a mason's line to saw through 2-in. PVC pipe in less than a minute.

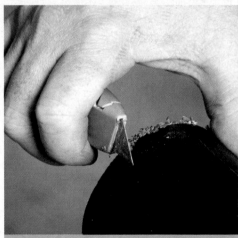

Deburr for leak-free connections

Leftover burrs on the end of a pipe will create channels in the cement when you push the fitting onto the pipe—and then stay there like little canals. That's when you'll get leaks or flunk a pressure test. Always scrape away burrs with a utility knife before joining the pipes.

Don't glue yourself into a corner

In many assemblies, there are pipes that move and pipes that don't. If you start gluing fittings together willy-nilly, you may end up in a situation where you're unable to attach the last fitting because one or both of the pipes don't move enough to slide the fitting on.

The last fitting to be glued should be the one on a pipe that has a little wiggle room. That's usually where a vertical run meets a horizontal one so you can snug on an elbow or a tee from two directions.

MOVABLE PIPE

Align slip joints precisely for a tight seal

The rubber slip-joint washers on the joints of chrome trap assemblies often leak. If you're reassembling a chrome trap, buy new slip joint washers and nuts. However, new washers sometimes stick to the pipe, causing them to twist or distort as you push them tight with the slip joint nut. To avoid this, lubricate the drain tubing and slip joint with a little pipe joint compound (Photo 1). The compound helps the washer slide smoothly and creates a tighter seal.

Start the slip joint nut by hand, and twist it on until the threads are engaged correctly. Hand-tighten all joints first (Photo 2). Then adjust the trap parts until they're aligned and pitched slightly for drainage. This is key; a misaligned joint will leak, even with new washers. Finally, use a large slip joint pliers to tighten the nuts an additional half turn.

Plastic trap parts use hard plastic slip joint washers for a seal. Make sure the flat part is against the nut with the tapered side facing the fitting.

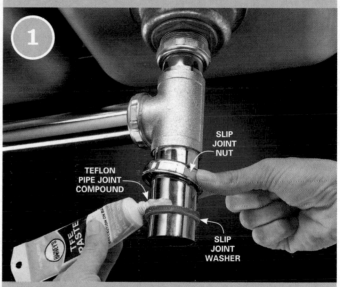

1

SLIP JOINT NUT

TEFLON PIPE JOINT COMPOUND

SLIP JOINT WASHER

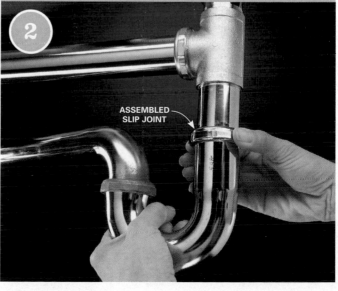

2

ASSEMBLED SLIP JOINT

Use the right elbow

LONG SWEEP

SHORT SWEEP

VENT ONLY

For pipes under 3 in., there are three basic types of 90-degree elbows: vent, short sweep and long sweep. Vent elbows are easily identified by their drastic bend and can only be used on a vent run that carries air, not water.

Here's a good system to remember when to use the other two types of elbows. If water is speeding up as it turns the corner (usually going from horizontal to vertical), use a short sweep. If water is slowing down (usually from vertical to horizontal), use a long sweep.

Toilet tips

Tip for caulking the toilet to the floor

Toilets should be caulked to the floor to prevent side-to-side movement that can break the wax seal (and to prevent splashes or overflows from puddling under the toilet and rotting the floor). DIYers often set the toilet and then apply a tiny bead of caulk along the outside edge. That doesn't always provide a good enough bond to the floor, and it leaves a prominent caulk line. There's an easier way to secure the toilet and provide a cleaner caulk line.

First set the toilet in place (without the wax ring) and square it up to the wall. Then make an outline of the toilet on the floor with masking tape. Remove the toilet and turn it on its side. Measure the depth and width of the gluing edge of the bowl. Next, move your caulk gun to the inset depth you just measured and apply caulk directly to the floor, maintaining the inset depth as you follow the tape (photo right). Install the wax ring and lower the toilet onto the flange. Stand on the toilet to compress the wax ring and ensure good contact with the caulk. Then use paper towels to clean up any caulk that oozed out.

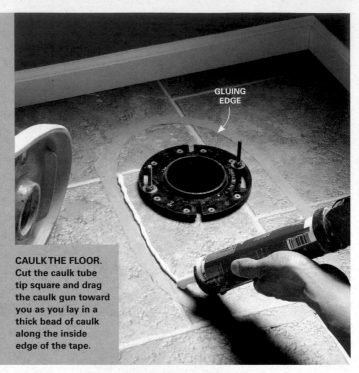

GLUING EDGE

CAULK THE FLOOR. Cut the caulk tube tip square and drag the caulk gun toward you as you lay in a thick bead of caulk along the inside edge of the tape.

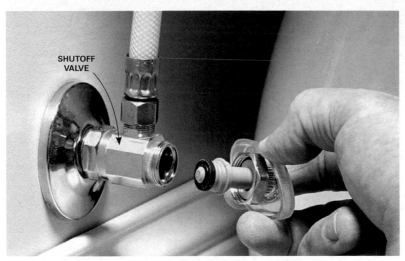

SHUTOFF VALVE

Fix a shutoff valve

There's nothing worse than starting a sink or toilet repair only to find that the shutoff valve won't shut off. Some shutoff valves are easy to replace. For those that aren't, turn off the main water valve, remove the packing nut, and then unscrew the stem and take it to the hardware store to find a replacement washer. Clean any grit out of the valve body and pop on the new washer. The valve will work like new.

PACKING NUT

STEM

NEW WASHER

WASHER

Flush without hang-ups

Here's a tip for fixing toilet chain hangups: Cover the flapper chain with a plastic straw. Just remove the chain from the arm attachment and slide the straw over it, covering about two-thirds of the chain. Then reattach the chain to the arm. It's that simple, and you'll never have a running toilet caused by a kinked chain again.

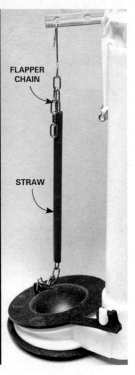

FLAPPER CHAIN

STRAW

Troubleshoot toilet tank problems

When you flush a toilet, a carefully balanced series of events takes place in the tank. As you push the flush handle, the tank-stopper ball is lifted from its valve seat, allowing water to flow from the tank into the bowl. When the tank is nearly empty, the tank ball falls back into the valve seat, cutting off the flow.

As the tank's water level falls, so does the float, opening up the supply, or ballcock, valve just as the tank ball seals the tank. The tank then refills through the tank fill tube, and the bowl and trap refill from the bowl fill tube, directing water down the overflow tube. As the float rises, it shuts off the ballcock valve and the toilet is ready for action once again. When any part of this balancing act is out of whack, you'll need to make one of the repairs shown in the chart below.

If your toilet tank or bowl develops a leak, check all pipes and connections. If a pipe or tube is corroded or the tank or bowl is cracked, replace it. If the leak appears near a joint, clean away any corrosion, replace any gaskets or washers and tighten the connection. Be careful when tightening bolts and nuts mounted to porcelain—the porcelain may crack and ruin the toilet.

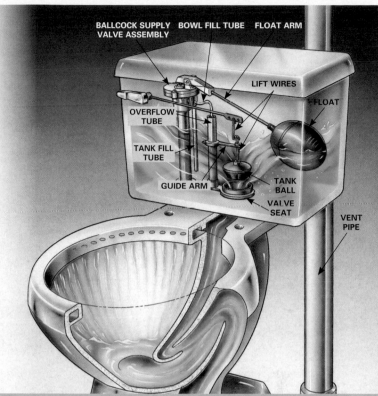

Problem	Solution
Water runs continuously.	Adjust lift wires or chain to align the tank ball. Clean valve seat.
Water spills into overflow tube.	Bend the float arm down.
Water runs after flushing.	Bend the float arm. Clean the valve seat. If the float is waterlogged, replace it. Replace tank ball or flapper.
Whistling sounds occur.	Put new washers in the ballcock-valve plunger. Replace ballcock assembly.
Splashing sounds are heard.	Reposition the refill tube to eject directly into overflow tube. Put new washers in the ballcock-valve assembly.
Tank flushes partially.	Shorten the lift wires or chain to make the tank ball rise higher. Bend the float arm upward to raise the water level.
Tank sweats.	Insulate the tank by lining it with sheets of polystyrene or foam rubber. Have plumber install tempering valve to warm the water in the tank.
Tank leaks.	Tighten connections to the water supply line. Check gaskets and washers around discharge pipe and mounting bolts to the bowl.
Toilet leaks at base.	Tighten bolts at base of bowl. Disconnect the toilet from the floor and replace the wax seal under the bowl.

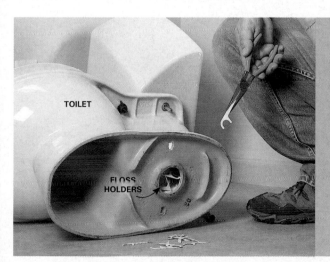

Your toilet's not a garbage can

One of our plumbing consulatants got a call to unplug a toilet he had recently installed. He was surprised because he had put in a toilet that he knew was almost impossible to clog. After repeated attempts with a plunger and a toilet auger, he gave up and removed the toilet to look in from the bottom. The outlet was completely clogged with a tangled web of plastic dental floss holders, which had to be removed one at a time with a needle-nose pliers. Save yourself a service call. Use the wastebasket for garbage.

Water lines

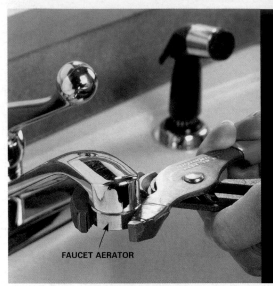

FAUCET AERATOR

Low water pressure at the faucet?

Over time, aerators get clogged with minerals or other bits of stuff that break loose from the inside of the pipes. Remove the aerator by turning it clockwise when you're looking down on it. You may have to grip it with pliers to unscrew it. Once it's off, you can take the parts out of the aerator and clean them, but it's usually better to simply replace it. Take it along to the hardware store to find an exact thread match.

Too-easy pipe fittings

Just push the fitting onto the pipe. That's it. Done. The first time you do this, you'll worry. A connection that easy just can't be reliable. But experience—and years of testing by plumbing industry organizations—proves that it is. Push-in fittings are now accepted by most plumbing codes for most kinds of water supply pipe (copper, plastic, PEX). Find them in various shapes and sizes at home centers.

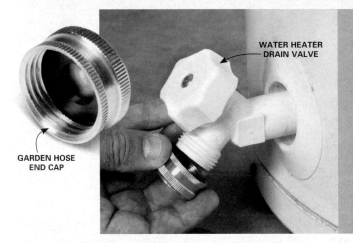

WATER HEATER DRAIN VALVE

GARDEN HOSE END CAP

Stop a water heater drain valve leak

You're supposed to flush your water heater regularly to remove sediment from the bottom of the tank. But many homeowners don't do it until they hear rumbling from the tank. After the flush, they discover that the drain valve leaks. If the drain valve is brass, you can usually replace the washer. It's a fairly easy but time-consuming fix because you have to shut off the water and drain the tank. If you have a plastic drain valve, your best bet is to replace the entire valve. You guessed it; you'll have to drain the tank for that fix, too. So how do you stop the drip until you get around to fixing the valve? Simple—buy a brass garden hose end cap and screw it onto the valve threads.

Ball-type shutoff valves won't fail when you need them

If you're remodeling your kitchen or adding a bathroom, here's some advice you'll thank us for later: Choose ball-type shutoff valves instead of standard stop valves. Shutoff valves go unused for years. Standard valves have rubber washers that harden with time and other fussy parts that become caked with mineral deposits. Then—when the time comes to replace the faucet or fix the toilet—the valve won't seal off the water flow.

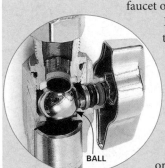

BALL

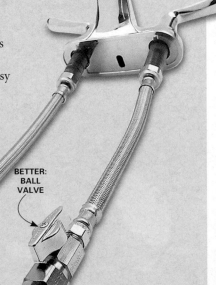

GOOD: STANDARD VALVE

BETTER: BALL VALVE

Ball valves are simpler inside. A ball with a hole through it opens and closes with a quarter turn. Fewer complex parts, fewer things to go wrong. Ball valves almost never let you down. This reliability costs a few bucks more than standard valves. Ball valves are sometimes labeled "quarter turn" valves. You'll find them at any home center or hardware store.

Stop a leaky valve

Plumbers say that leaks are one of the most common complaints they get. Valves are one of the main culprits because they have moving parts and seals that can wear out. The next time you see a suspicious puddle of water, look for a leaky valve before you call the plumber. Look at the valve to see if water is leaking out around the valve stem. If it is, try turning the packing nut about an eighth turn with a wrench. You'll know if you overtighten the nut because the valve will be hard to turn. If tightening the nut doesn't stop the leak, the fix is a little tougher. You'll have to shut off the main water valve, remove the handle and nut, and add to or replace the packing material—still a pretty easy fix.

Torch caddy

Here's a caddy that holds hot torches steady and works as a third hand when you're soldering pipes. Mount a toilet flange to a 1-ft. square plywood base with 1-in. wood screws. Cut an 8-in. piece of 3-in.-dia. pipe and glue it into the flange.

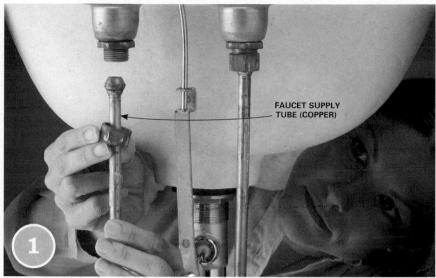

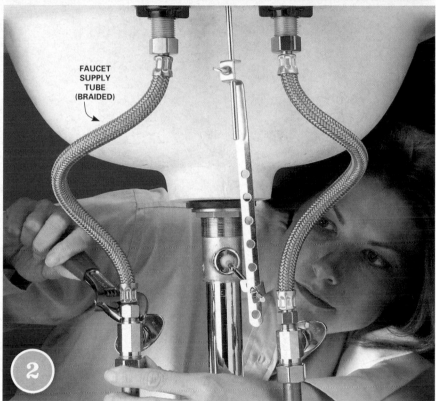

Choose flexible supply tubes

The skinny copper or chrome supply tubes used to connect faucets and toilets (Photo 1) are tricky to cut, bend and align. But you don't have to put up with them. When you're replacing a faucet or toilet, use flexible supply hoses with a braided covering instead (Photo 2). They have rubber gaskets at each end and don't require much force to seal. They're available in many lengths and are flexible enough to fit almost any configuration. The only trick is buying a connector with the correct size nuts on the ends. Take your old tubing and the nuts on each end along with you to the store to be sure of an exact match.

Start the nuts carefully and hand-tighten. Then tighten an additional half turn (Photo 2). Avoid overtightening. It's easy to tighten the nuts a little more if the joint leaks.

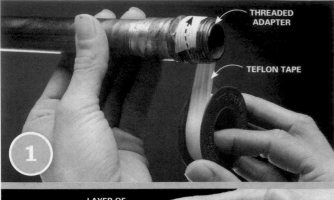

THREADED ADAPTER

TEFLON TAPE

①

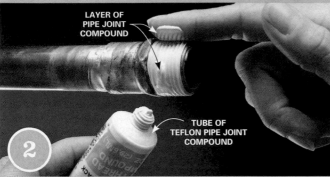

LAYER OF PIPE JOINT COMPOUND

TUBE OF TEFLON PIPE JOINT COMPOUND

②

TEFLON TAPE PLUS PIPE JOINT COMPOUND

③

Use two types of Teflon on threaded joints

Connections that rely on threaded pipes and fittings are prone to leaks if they're not sealed with either Teflon tape or Teflon pipe joint compound. Careful plumbers use both on every joint for extra security. They don't want to come back.

Start by wrapping the male threads with Teflon tape (Photo 1). With the end of the threaded pipe facing you as shown, wrap the tape clockwise. Usually three layers is enough. Once in a while, you'll run into a loose fitting that requires four or five wraps. Stretch and tear the tape to complete the wrap.

Spread a thin layer of Teflon pipe joint compound over the tape (Photo 2). If you're working with plastic pipe, choose compatible Teflon pipe joint compound. Then start the threads by hand before tightening the connection with wrenches (Photo 3). Wipe away the excess.

Lubricate the ferrule on compression joints

Compression joints are most common on shutoff valves, although you find them on other fittings as well. They have a brass or plastic ring (ferrule) that's compressed into a recess when you tighten the nut, forming a seal. Lubricating the pipe and the ferrule with a bit of Teflon pipe joint compound (Photo 1) helps the ferrule slide along the pipe and squeeze tightly into the recessed fitting with less wrench pressure (Photo 2). Tighten compression fittings firmly with two wrenches to crimp the ferrule onto the pipe (Photo 3). Also make sure the pipe or tube goes straight into the fitting. Misalignment will cause a leak. If the fitting leaks after you turn on the water, try tightening the nut an additional one-quarter turn. This usually stops the leak.

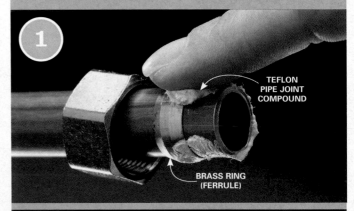

①

TEFLON PIPE JOINT COMPOUND

BRASS RING (FERRULE)

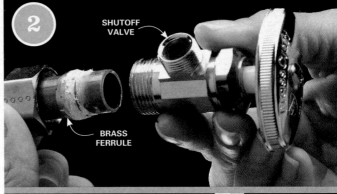

②

SHUTOFF VALVE

BRASS FERRULE

③

Working with PEX

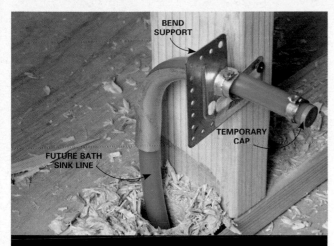

BEND SUPPORT

TEMPORARY CAP

FUTURE BATH SINK LINE

Install PEX directly to the fixtures

It's best to run PEX directly to the fixtures so you won't have to bury fittings behind the walls. It's hard to keep PEX perfectly straight when it exits the wall, so another option is to use a 90-degree copper stub-out when you run a line to a toilet or other fixture where your shutoff valve will be visible.

ABRASION CLIP

PIPE INSULATION

Protect your PEX

PEX expands and contracts with changes in temperature, which causes the pipes to move back and forth. Several years of even the slightest movement can wear a hole in PEX pipes, especially if they're rubbing against something abrasive.

ABRASION/ SUSPENSION CLIPS

If your pipe is in contact with a joist, duct, electrical box or steel stud, or it is passing through a block wall or concrete slab, it needs to be protected. You can protect your pipe with abrasion clips, cover the pipe with inexpensive pipe insulation, or enclose it with a larger pipe. Pipes that are encased in concrete (for in-floor heating, for example) are OK because the concrete holds them in place. And pipes running straight through wood studs and joists are fine too—just protect the pipe in areas where it bends as it passes through.

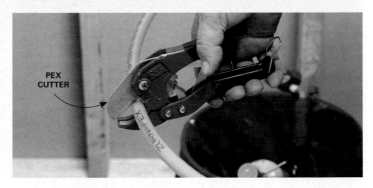

PEX CUTTER

Cut it straight

There's no reason to spend a bunch of money on a fancy PEX cutting tool. The one shown costs about $12. Whether you use a $100 cutter or just a utility knife, the most important thing is to cut straight. A pipe that is cut at an angle won't fit properly against fittings, and that increases the risk of leaks.

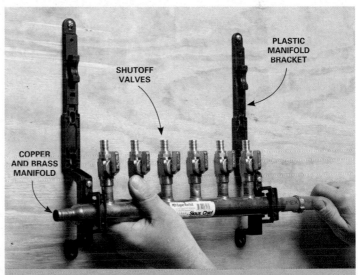

PLASTIC MANIFOLD BRACKET

SHUTOFF VALVES

COPPER AND BRASS MANIFOLD

Home runs are best

You can install PEX with main lines and branches to each fixture, but "home runs" are better. A home run is one line that runs directly to a fixture, starting at a manifold (above). Home runs require more piping but deliver a stronger and more consistent water flow. Also, installing home runs is fast and requires only two connections (one at the manifold and another at the fixture end), which reduces leaks.

You can also use a hybrid system where you run 3/4-in. hot and cold lines to a set of fixtures—for example, in a bathroom—and install a smaller manifold behind an access panel. Then make short runs of 1/2-in. lines to each fixture. Another cool thing about home runs is that each fitting has its own shutoff at the manifold. That means you can shut off just that fitting to do some work—you don't have to shut off the water to the whole house.

ELASTIC CORDS

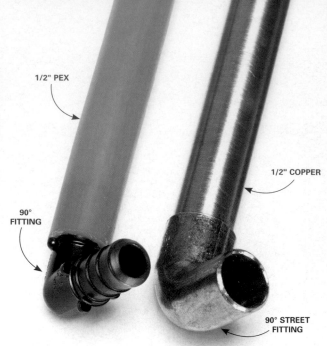

1/2" PEX

90°
FITTING

1/2" COPPER

90° STREET
FITTING

Control your coil with an elastic cord

One complaint about working with PEX is that the coils have a mind of their own. As soon as the banding is removed from the coils, they tend to explode out in every direction. A good tip is to use bungee cords to help keep your coils in check. Leave the cords on and unroll just the amount you need. If your coil comes wrapped in plastic, don't remove it. Sometimes you can just feed out pipe from the innermost section of the coil. If you have just a few smaller runs or short lengths to install, buy sections of straight pipe—it's a lot easier to work with.

Upsize to avoid poor pressure

The inside diameter of 1/2-in. PEX is smaller than that of 1/2-in. copper (and even smaller with fittings). If you're tearing out copper and replacing it with the same size PEX pipe, the water flow to the fixtures may be noticeably lower when you're done. If you're working on a house that has less than 45 lbs. of pressure or a flow rate of less than 4 gallons per minute, make sure you install home runs, and consider going up in size to 3/4-in. pipe. A simple way to test water pressure is to hook up a hose bib pressure gauge (sold at home centers) to your spigot. To check your flow rate, just see how many gallons of water flow into a 5-gallon bucket in one minute.

KINK

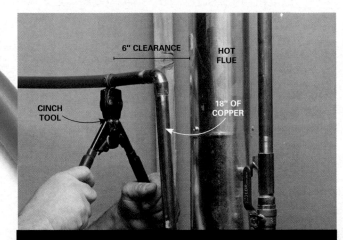

6" CLEARANCE

HOT
FLUE

CINCH
TOOL

18" OF
COPPER

Repair or replace kinks

Kinks happen. You can repair kinks with a heat gun, but PEX tends to rekink in the previously kinked spot, especially if the pipe needs to make a bend at the kinked location. It's best to cut kinks out and use the shorter sections of pipe elsewhere. If you get a minor kink in the middle of a long, straight run and you don't want to cut it out, heat the pipe with a heat gun and then cover the damaged area with a hanger or abrasion clip. That will help the pipe keep its shape.

Keep PEX away from hot stuff

PEX is plastic, and plastic melts. So keep your PEX pipes away from hot stuff. Codes commonly require PEX to be at least 18 in. away from the water heater and 6 in. away from single-wall flues on gas water heaters. And stay well clear of furnace flues, wood-burning stove pipes and any other item that gets hot.

COFFEE THERMOS

Warm up cold pipes

Most PEX manufacturers recommend you work with pipe at temperatures above freezing. The whole length of the pipe doesn't need to be warm, just wherever you make a connection. You can heat those cold pipes and fittings with a heat gun or hair dryer, leave them in a warm vehicle for a while or keep fittings in your pocket. Heck, you can even warm a pipe in a thermos of hot water.

Use the same stuff

There are several different manufacturers of PEX. It is *very* important that you know which brand of pipes you're working with and install only that manufacturer's connectors and fittings. If you mix and match materials, you will void your warranty and may fail your inspection. Worst-case scenario: You'll end up with leaky pipes and water damage. Not all products have recognizable markings on them, so leave a few of the packaging labels on-site to appease the inspector and for future reference.

WATTS   ZURN   UPONOR   VIEGA

Cinch clamps are easy

There are many different ways to connect PEX to fittings, but cinch clamps are one of the most DIY-friendly. They're readily available and relatively inexpensive, and you know when they're installed properly because the tab of the clamp will be visibly pinched.

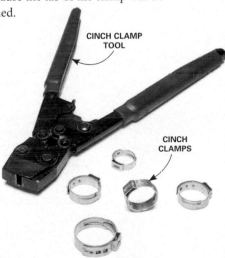

CINCH CLAMP TOOL

CINCH CLAMPS

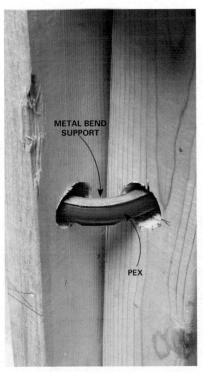

METAL BEND SUPPORT

PEX

Avoid kinks

PEX's flexibility makes it easy to work with. It can be bent around pretty sharp corners without the need for an elbow fitting. But if you try to bend it too much, you'll end up kinking it. Installing a bend support will prevent this, and it will also protect the pipe from abrasion.

PLASTIC BEND SUPPORT

Heating and cooling

Twist the fins to silence a whistling grille

If you have a grille or register that hums or howls, all you have to do is twist the fins and open them a little. A pliers alone will scratch and kink the delicate fins, so apply electrical tape to a hinge that's about the same length as the fins. Then grab each fin between the hinge leaves and twist slightly.

"Better" filters can damage HVAC systems

Expensive high-efficiency "allergy" type filters have a minimum efficiency reporting value (MERV) of 11 or higher. But these filters are so dense that they can cause equipment damage, high utility usage, poor airflow (particularly to rooms farthest from the furnace) and long run cycles. If your HVAC system uses a standard 1-in. filter, a cheaper MERV 7 or 8 furnace filter is better for most homes.

Furnace filter reminder

Whenever you buy a new box of furnace filters, write the months of the year on the individual filters. That way, you'll always know when you last changed the filter.

Cool down with a whole-house fan

Whole-house fans may seem old fashioned, but they're enjoying renewed popularity. The idea behind them is simple. A powerful fan draws cooler early morning and evening air through open doors and windows and forces it up through the attic and out the roof vents. This sends hot air up and out, cooling your house and your attic. These fans are commonly mounted in an upstairs stairwell or hallway ceiling where there's at least 3 ft. of clearance above the fan.

Main advantages

- Energy savings. They use 90 percent less energy than an air conditioner, and in dry climates with cool mornings and evenings, they can actually replace your AC system.
- Easy installation. With a helper and basic tools, you can install a whole-house fan in a weekend.

Main disadvantages

- They can't cool inside temps any lower than outside temps and they can't dehumidify.
- They can make allergies worse. Whole-house fans draw in outdoor pollen and dust.
- Larger fans move air quickly, but they cost more to purchase and install. They also require significant attic ventilation and make more noise than smaller attic fans.

For the best results, match the fan size to your floor plan, cooling needs and available attic ventilation. Call your local utility and check online to see which models qualify for local rebates and any possible federal tax credits. Fans cost $200 to $1,200.

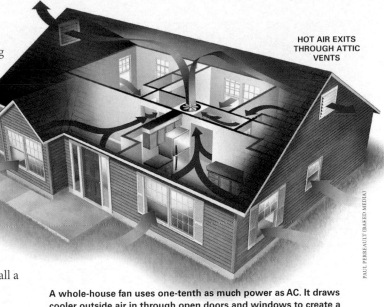

HOT AIR EXITS THROUGH ATTIC VENTS

PAUL PERREAULT (BAKED MEDIA)

A whole-house fan uses one-tenth as much power as AC. It draws cooler outside air in through open doors and windows to create a pleasant breeze that pushes hot air out through attic vents.

Newer attic fans have insulated doors that close in 30 seconds when the fan's not operating.

R-38–INSULATED SEALED DOORS

REMOTE CONTROL KIT

TAMTECH

Fix rotting A/C insulation

The black foam on one of my outside A/C lines is rotting and falling off. I suspect it's costing me money because the cold tubing is always covered with condensation. Is this something to worry about?

You're right—that condensation is reducing the efficiency of your A/C and raising your energy costs. You should remove all the old foam insulation and install the correct foam. Unfortunately, you won't find it at any home center. Measure the outside diameter on the larger of the two tubes (the skinny tube doesn't need insulation). Then contact a refrigeration supply house or online supplier for new foam and insulating tape.

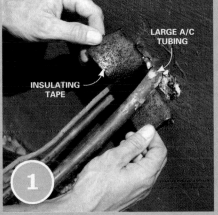

LARGE A/C TUBING

INSULATING TAPE

1

Seal the ends. Wipe off the condensation and wrap a few winds of the sticky poly tape on the tubing where it exits the house. Then dry and wrap the service valve on the condenser end of the tubing. Squeeze it in tight around the tubing.

ADHESIVE SEAL

2

Install new foam. Slip the new foam over the tubing and on top of the cork tape. Remove the adhesive liner, align the edges and press the seam together as you go. Be careful. Once the glued ends touch, you can't get them apart again.

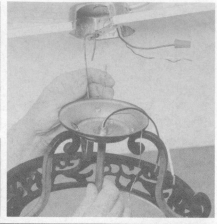

Chapter Six

ELECTRICAL AND LIGHTING

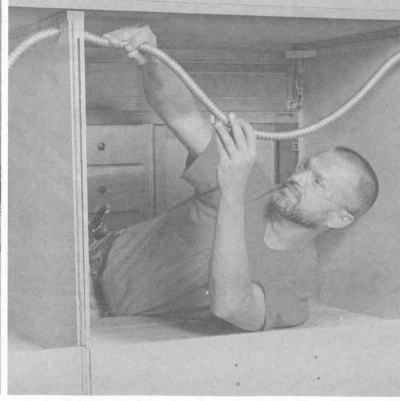

Switches and outlets

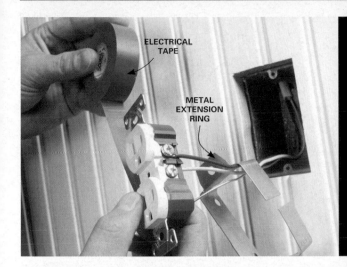

ELECTRICAL TAPE

METAL EXTENSION RING

When to wrap a receptacle

Wrapping an electrical receptacle with tape before you screw it to the box is not required. There's nothing about it in the National Electrical Code. It falls into that "prudent practice" category. We recommend that you use two to three wraps of electrical tape to cover the terminal screws of receptacles and switches when you're installing them inside a metal extension ring (shown) or onto a metal plaster ring. Both of these narrow the box opening and increase the likelihood that the terminal screws could inadvertently contact the metal sides, cause arcing and start a fire. Most often this occurs when you push in a plug and the receptacle slides slightly to one side. The wraps of electrical tape sufficiently insulate the terminal screws to avoid this incidental contact.

Sizing an electrical box

The National Electrical Code requires electrical boxes to have sufficient volume to hold all the wires, switches, clamps and other components that you intend to put inside them. You have to calculate the minimum size required for each box.

The basic rules are:

- Add 1 for each hot or neutral
- Add 1 for all ground wires combined
- Add 1 for all internal cable clamps combined
- Add 2 for each switch, or receptacle
- Multiply by 2 cu. in. for size 14 wire or 2.25 cu. in. for size 12 wire

Remodeling boxes have the volume or the number of wires that it can contain stamped onto the inside back of the box. To determine the volume of a metal box, measure and multiply the inside height by the width and the depth.

Which way is up?

When you show three-prong electrical outlets, the ground plug hole is always down. I was taught to install them with the ground plug up. What's the correct way?

Electricians endlessly debate which way to place outlets and vigorously exalt the virtues of installing it one way or the other, but we'll tell it to you straight—it just doesn't matter. Both ways are correct. The electrical code doesn't specify which direction the ground plug hole needs to face. One way isn't safer than the other—as long as the outlet is wired correctly.

It all comes down to aesthetics, so install them whatever way looks best to you. Incidentally, the ground plug is typically down in the United States, the opposite of how it's generally installed in Canada.

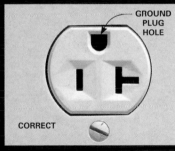

GROUND PLUG HOLE

CORRECT

STILL CORRECT

The electrical code allows outlets to be installed with the ground plug hole facing up, down or sideways. It's up to you.

Glow-in-the-dark switch

A dab of glow-in-the-dark paint means no more groping for the light switch at night. The paint dries clear and glows for about eight hours after exposure to light. Get it at a paint or craft store.

Multiple switches, one hot wire

A box with three switches is crowded enough without adding extra wire connectors and pigtails. Here's a wiring method that eliminates extra connections and creates a neater installation. Instead of running a separate pigtail from the hot wire to each switch, just leave the hot wire extra long. To connect the switches, simply score the wire with your wire stripper and push the insulation to expose about 3/4 in. of bare wire (Photo 1). Wrap this bare section at least three-quarters of the way around the screw terminal of the first switch. Repeat the process for the remaining intermediate switches (Photo 2). Connect the last switch in the usual manner, looping the wire around the screw in a clockwise direction.

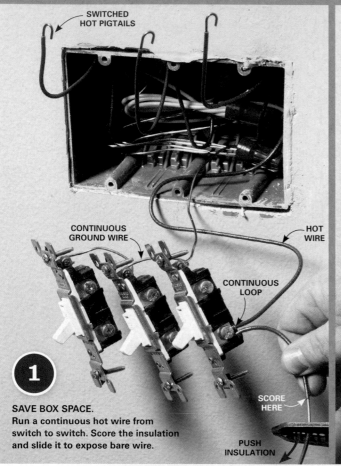

SWITCHED HOT PIGTAILS

CONTINUOUS GROUND WIRE

HOT WIRE

CONTINUOUS LOOP

1

SAVE BOX SPACE.
Run a continuous hot wire from switch to switch. Score the insulation and slide it to expose bare wire.

SCORE HERE

PUSH INSULATION

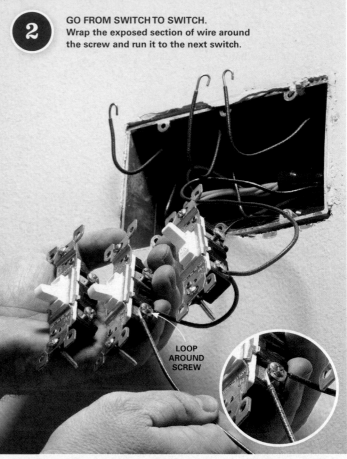

2 **GO FROM SWITCH TO SWITCH.**
Wrap the exposed section of wire around the screw and run it to the next switch.

LOOP AROUND SCREW

Circuit breaker ID

When you need to turn off the power to a circuit, there's no need to flip circuit breakers on and off until you find the right one. To end the guesswork, just write the corresponding circuit breaker number on the backs of the outlet covers and switch plates.

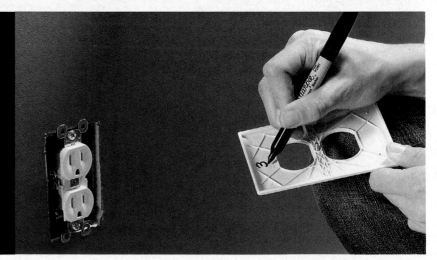

Wiring tips

Uncoil without kinks

Pulling plastic-sheathed cable through holes in the framing is a lot easier if you straighten it out first. If you simply pull the cable from the center of the coil, it'll kink as you pull it through the studs. The trick is to lift a handful of coils from the center of the roll (Photo 1) and toss them across the floor as if you're throwing a coiled rope. Next, walk along the length of cable, straightening it as you go (Photo 2). The electricians we talked to prefer this method because they can keep the cable contained in the plastic wrapper for easier handling and neater storage.

STRAIGHTENED CABLE

AVOID KINKS. Don't just pull cable from the roll. Instead, lift a few loops from the center of the roll. Four loops will reach about 12 ft.

STRAIGHTEN BEFORE PULLING. Toss the coil across the floor. Then straighten it by hand before pulling it through the framing.

Temporary extension cord protection

If you're having a graduation party or some other occasional event out in the yard, you may require extra electricity. Here's a great way to keep extension cord plugs dry. Cut notches in the opposite sides of a reusable plastic container and snap on the lid. Your plugs will stay dry if it happens to rain or the ground is moist.

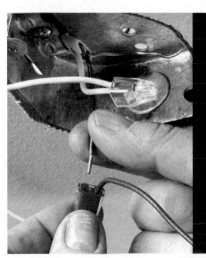

Short wires? No problem

When the wires in the box are too short, making connections is aggravating. You'll want to hunt down whoever installed them and throttle that person. But instead, just go to a home center and pick up a few stab-in connectors. In tight spaces, they're much easier to use than twist-on nuts. Push a "pigtail" (a new piece of wire) into the connector, then push the connector onto the old wire. Presto! You've got plenty of length to connect to the fixture's wires. Make sure the wire you use for the pigtail is the same gauge as the existing wire.

Avoid tight turns or kinked coaxial cables

The wire at the center of coaxial cable is molded inside a foam jacket to keep it away from the shielding and to block interference. If you kink the cable or bend it around a sharp corner, you crush the foam. At that point, the damage is done and there's no way to undo it. Never bend cable around a radius smaller than 3 in.

Pack boxes neatly

If you've done much wiring, you've probably had times when you could barely push the switch or outlet into the box because there were so many wires. The solution is to arrange the wires neatly and then fold them carefully into the box. Here's how to keep wires neat and compact: First, gather all the bare ground wires along with a long pigtail and connect them. Fold them into the back of the box, leaving the pigtail extended. Next, do the same for the neutral wires. If you're connecting switches as we show here, you don't need a neutral pigtail. Leave the hot wire extra long and fold it back and forth across the bottom of the box. (See "Multiple switches, one hot wire" on p. 110 for how to connect switches to this wire.) Put a wire connector cap on the hot wire to identify it. The neatly packed box makes it easy to identify the wires and leaves you plenty of room for the switches.

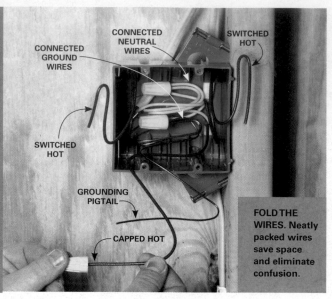

CONNECTED GROUND WIRES

CONNECTED NEUTRAL WIRES

SWITCHED HOT

SWITCHED HOT

GROUNDING PIGTAIL

CAPPED HOT

FOLD THE WIRES. Neatly packed wires save space and eliminate confusion.

How to plan a new branch circuit

DIYers often ask how many receptacles and lights they can install on a branch circuit and what size circuits they should install. We can give you some general guidelines, but electrical codes vary by state and local authority. Since your local codes always trump our advice, contact a local inspector before you start running cable.

1. You can usually mix lighting and receptacles on the same circuit. But it's not a good idea to place lighting and receptacles in the same room on a single circuit. If the breaker trips, you'll lose all the light fixtures and receptacles at the same time.
2. If you're wiring living areas, you can install 10 to 13 lights and receptacles on a single 15-amp circuit. Locate the receptacles so you're never more than 6 ft. away from one on each wall.
3. Run a separate 15- or 20-amp circuit for each of these watt-sucking appliances: garbage disposer, dishwasher, microwave, vent hood, trash compactor and space heater.
4. Run a separate 20-amp circuit to each bathroom and laundry room. Install a minimum of two 20-amp circuits for the kitchen. Protect the receptacles with a ground-fault circuit interrupter (GFCI) breaker or GFCI-style receptacles.
5. Use 12-gauge cable for 20-amp circuits and 14-gauge for 15-amp. Many cable manufacturers color-code the outer jacket of their cable, but the color schemes are not universal. So always double-check the wire itself to be sure.
6. New branch circuits to all "living areas" (bedroom, living room, family room, den, dining room, library, sunroom, closet, hallway and similar locations) must be connected to an arc-fault circuit interrupter (AFCI). AFCI breakers are pricey, so you may be tempted to buy an ordinary breaker. Don't. The electrical inspector will just make you change it out.

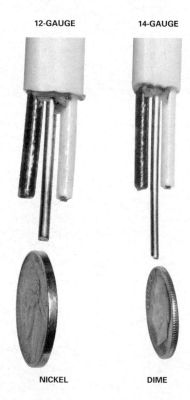

CHECK WIRE GAUGE WITH YOUR LOOSE CHANGE. Fourteen-gauge wire is the thickness of a dime; 12-gauge is the thickness of a nickel.

12-GAUGE

14-GAUGE

NICKEL

DIME

Lighting and ceiling fans

Stay-put solar lights

Solar lights along a driveway are great, but most of them come with flimsy plastic stakes that are impossible to pound into gravel or clay-packed areas. Replace the stakes with sections of 3/4-in. copper tubing. By coincidence, the diameter matches the bottom of most light heads. The tubes are much easier to pound into hard-packed soil, and they're less likely to be kicked over in high-traffic areas.

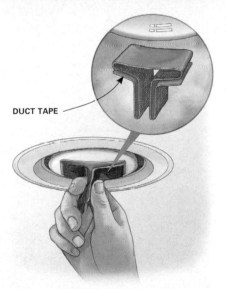

DUCT TAPE

Lightbulb handle

Removing a tight, burned-out lightbulb from a recessed fixture can be next to impossible because there just isn't enough room for your fingers. Make a lightbulb "handle" from a 15-in. strip of duct tape. Center the tape on the bulb; fold the two ends back to the middle, then fold each end over again on itself to form the handle.

Solar deck-light mounts

Want to put lights on your deck but hate the idea of running wire? Here's an easy way to mount solar lights and let the sun do the rest of the work. Remove the bottom plug from the lights and cut a short length of wooden dowel that fits inside the light tube. Run a screw up through the bottom of the railing (drill a pilot hole first) and then up through the dowel. Then just slip the light over the dowel and it becomes a permanent fixture.

Landing lights

If your night vision isn't what it used to be, try this nifty visual cue to help you back the car out of the garage at night. String a 6-ft. rope light along the edge of the garage door opening. To make it light up automatically when the garage door opens screw a socket connector into the bulb socket of the opener; that way when the opener light goes on, the rope light does too!

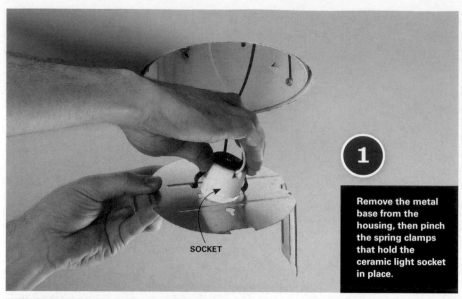

1

Remove the metal base from the housing, then pinch the spring clamps that hold the ceramic light socket in place.

SOCKET

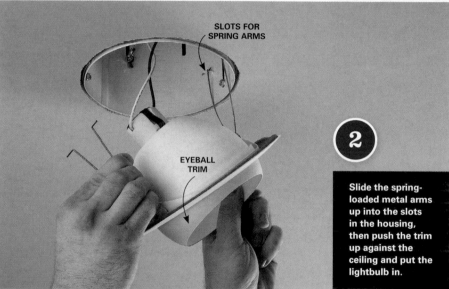

SLOTS FOR SPRING ARMS

EYEBALL TRIM

2

Slide the spring-loaded metal arms up into the slots in the housing, then push the trim up against the ceiling and put the lightbulb in.

Upgrade your recessed lights

Dissatisfied with the look of the recessed lights in your kitchen? You can change them in a few minutes just by changing the trim.

Remove the existing trim and bulb and look up inside the metal housing for a sticker with the brand name, the model number and compatible trim styles. If you can't find the information, or the brand isn't available, take the old trim to a lighting store and look for matches. Most manufacturers have several different types and sizes of housing that will accept a variety of trim styles.

Changing old, yellowed trim for new trim is simple—just pull out the old trim and attach the new trim in the same hooks. You can also replace standard trim with an eyeball-style trim that can be aimed in different directions, but it takes an extra step.

First, turn off the switch and circuit breaker and remove the bulb. Unscrew the wing nut that holds the base of the light in place and remove the socket (Photo 1). Then snap the socket into the top of the eyeball shroud and push the eyeball trim up into the can (Photo 2). Be sure to use the type of bulb recommended on the label in the housing.

Sizing a ceiling fan

A quick rule of thumb matches the diameter of the ceiling fan with the largest dimension of a room. For 12 ft. or less, use a 36-in. fan. For 12 to 16 ft., use a 48-in. fan. For 16 to 18 ft., use a 52-in. fan. And for dimensions larger than 18 ft., install two fans.

Placement of a ceiling fan for adequate air circulation is 7 ft. above the floor with the blades 8 to 10 in. from the ceiling. And to move more air at low speed, a fan with five blades is best.

Regarding energy savings, research has proven that ceiling fans can save energy during the cooling season by creating a gentle breeze. You get your savings then by raising your thermostat by a minimum of 2 degrees. This decreases air conditioning energy used by 10 to 15 percent, or 5 to 8 percent per degree.

RUBBER BAND

LIGHT SHADE

No-rattle ceiling fan

If the screws that hold the light globe to your ceiling fan tend to work loose and then hum or rattle, slip a wide rubber band around the neck of the globe where the screws grip it. The rubber band prevents the screws from loosening, dampens any noise and protects the globe from overzealous screw tighteners.

Don't change fluorescent bulbs until you have to

Some people think fluorescent tubes have to be changed when the ends of the tubes turn black. Not true. Continued use doesn't harm the starting ballast or significantly affect light output. Leave them alone until the bulb starts flickering or takes a long time to fire up. Then stick in a new bulb, because at that point the old one will damage the ballast.

Third hand for hanging light fixtures

Connecting a fixture takes three hands: one to hold the fixture and two to make the connections. If you don't have a third hand, hang the fixture from a scrap of wire or a coat hanger while you make the connections.

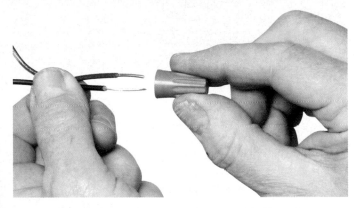

Make a strong connection

Light fixtures almost always require a connection between solid wire and stranded. That's frustrating because the connector twists and pushes the stranded wire but doesn't grab it. Here's the solution: First, cut off the old exposed solid wire and then strip off 1/2 in. of the insulation. On the stranded wire, strip off 5/8 in. Hold the wires together so the stranded wire extends about 1/8 in. beyond the solid wire and twist on the connector. The end of the stranded wire will bunch up inside the tip of the connector, locked in place for a secure connection.

Electrical repairs

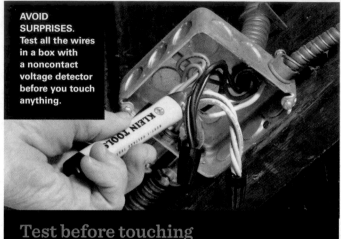

AVOID SURPRISES. Test all the wires in a box with a noncontact voltage detector before you touch anything.

Test before touching

When you've done a lot of wiring, it's easy to get complacent about whether the power is off. But don't. Use a noncontact voltage detector to check every wire in the box or area you're working. Always check the tester on a wire or cord you know is live to make sure it's working before you rely on it. Noncontact voltage detectors are available at home centers, hardware stores and online and range in price from $5 to $25. The tool shown here has a green light that indicates it's turned on and working—a nice feature that's well worth the extra money.

Repair stripped electrical box threads

If you have an older home with metal electrical boxes, you're bound to encounter a stripped hole sooner or later. Don't think you can get away with ramming a drywall screw into the stripped hole. That doesn't meet code, and it'll loosen up over time. If you have a tap-and-die set, use a No. 6-32 tap and try to reform the existing threads. If that works, you're good to go. If not, consider buying an electrician's tapping tool (sold at home centers). The shaft has tapping threads for the three most common thread sizes you'll find in electrical boxes. Turn off the power and insert the tapping tool as shown.

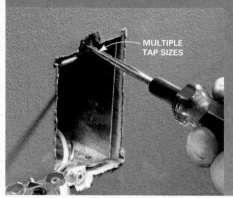

MULTIPLE TAP SIZES

REFORM STRIPPED THREADS—OR TAP NEW ONES. Twist the tapping tool into the stripped threads to reform them. If they're stripped beyond repair, push the tool in farther and twist to tap the cut and tap the next largest size.

Replace a problem plug

Plugs on lamp cords often have a weak point where the cord enters the plug. Pulling and flexing can break the wires at this point, leaving you with a lamp that flickers when you jiggle the cord. The cure is to replace the plug. To do this safely, choose a polarized plug. A polarized plug has one blade that's wider than the other so it fits into an outlet only one way. Before you buy a plug, take a close look at the cord. Along with other labeling, you should find "SPT-1" or "SPT-2." This refers to the thickness of the cord's sheathing, and the plug you buy must have the same listing

so it will fit over the sheathing. If you can't find the SPT listing, replace the entire cord.

The plug you buy may not look exactly like the one shown here, but installing it will be similar. Be sure to read the manufacturer's instructions. When you split the two halves of the cord (Photo 1), be careful not to expose any wire. If you do, cut back the cord and start over. Strip the wire ends and make connections (Photo 2). The neutral wire must connect to the wider blade. If you're not able to identify it, replace the entire cord.

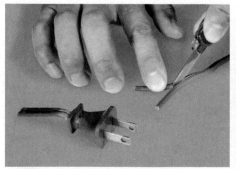

1 Cut the cord a couple of inches from the plug. Then split about an inch of cord with a pocketknife and strip off 3/4 in. of insulation.

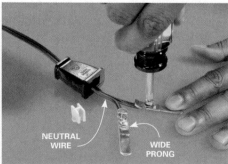

NEUTRAL WIRE

WIDE PRONG

2 Wrap the wires clockwise around the terminal screws of the new plug and tighten. The neutral wire must connect to the wider prong.

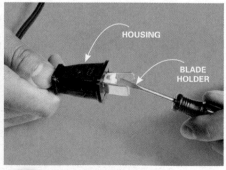

HOUSING

BLADE HOLDER

3 Slip the blades into the housing and push the blade holder into place.

Silence a humming dimmer switch

You might think that a dimmer turns down the lights by turning down the power flow. But it actually works like a super-fast strobe, switching the power on and off dozens of times per second. This electrical pulsation causes the filaments in lightbulbs to vibrate and that creates the humming sound you hear. An easy solution—which usually works—is to try different brands of bulbs. Some bulbs have beefier filaments, which vibrate less. You can even try "rough-use" bulbs meant for garage door openers or trouble lights. These bulbs have heavy filaments but are pricey ($2 to $5 each). If bulb switching doesn't stop the hum, upgrade your dimmer switch. Dimmers that cost about $20 usually dampen the electrical pulse better than models in the $10 range. Swapping out a dimmer switch is usually a simple matter of disconnecting and reconnecting three wires. Just be sure to work safely. Turn off the power to the circuit—and make sure it's off using a noncontact voltage detector.

CHANGING BULBS USUALLY STOPS THE HUM

High-quality dimmer switches are less likely to cause humming.

HIGH-QUALITY DIMMER

Stuck-bulb solutions

When a lightbulb is stuck in its socket, the culprit is usually corrosion between the socket and the bulb's metal base. This is most common outdoors and in damp places like basements and bathrooms. If you have a bulb that won't budge, put on heavy gloves and eye protection. Make sure the light switch is off. Then go ahead and twist as hard as you like. Don't worry about breaking the bulb. In fact, if the bulb just won't turn, your next step is to break it intentionally. Hold a screwdriver tip against the bulb and give the handle a firm whack with a hammer. This leaves the bulb's metal base in the socket.

Often, you can unscrew the base by inserting a pliers and holding the jaws open as you turn. A potato might work too: Round the end of the potato with a knife, jam it into the socket and turn. But if your bulb base is really stubborn, use hot glue and a 1/2 x 1/2-in. stick of wood (Photo 1). If you don't have a scrap of wood, buy a 5/8-in. dowel at a home center or hardware store. Save yourself all this hassle in the future by applying a special bulb lubricant to the new bulb.

STUCK-BULB BASE

HOT GLUE

BULB LUBRICANT

1 Apply a heavy blob of hot glue to a stick and press it into the broken bulb's base. If the glue doesn't fill the base, inject glue into any voids. Let the glue cool for five minutes and turn the stick to screw out the base.

2 Coat the threads of the new bulb with a special lubricant designed for lightbulbs. The coating inhibits corrosion and makes future removal much easier.

Extend the box

If the junction box is recessed more than 1/4 in. from the surface of the wall or ceiling, you've got a code violation. This is common when a layer of drywall or wood was installed over the original ceiling. To correct it, add a box extender. If you don't find one for round or octagonal boxes at home centers, search online.

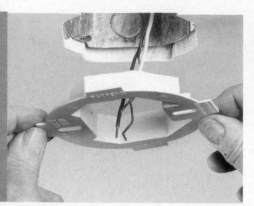

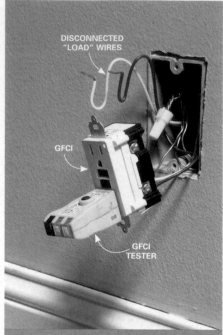

Clean contact points to let battery power flow

If new batteries don't revive your radio, flashlight or other battery-powered gizmo, don't toss it into the trash just yet. Corrosion on the battery contact points could be stopping the power flow. Rub the points with a pencil eraser. If the points are caked with heavy corrosion, you may need something more abrasive, such as an emery board or fine sandpaper.

CONTACT

Trouble-shooting GFCIs

We asked our electrical pros what problems they run into with GFCIs and how to solve them. For starters, we found that most complaints occur when several outlets are protected by one GFCI. There are several possible causes, ranging from a light or appliance with a ground fault that's plugged into a downstream outlet, to a defective GFCI or even a circuit with too much cable.

To determine whether the problem is with the GFCI itself, or downstream, turn off the power to the GFCI and disconnect the wires from the "load" terminals. Push the reset button (if it doesn't click, you'll have to reset it after the power is back on) and plug a GFCI tester into the GFCI outlet before you turn the power back on. If the GFCI trips after you turn the power on, replace it. If it holds, then the problem is with one of the downstream outlets. To avoid the time-consuming process of trouble-shooting the "load" outlets, the easiest and best solution is to replace each of them with a new, tamper-resistant GFCI.

TAB

Simple solution for a troublesome light fixture

Do you have bulbs that burn out quickly, lights that flicker, or a light fixture that simply doesn't work even though there's power to it? Try this 60-second fix before you call an electrician.

Turn off the power to the fixture and use a noncontact voltage tester to make sure the power is off. Then reach into the bulb socket with a flat-blade screwdriver and gently pry up on the tab that's centered at the bottom to restore good contact with the bulb.

Fishing wire

The tools you need

Flex bits and glow rods are the go-to tools for fishing wires. Flex bits are great for drilling holes in hard-to-reach spaces (see "Invest in a Bumper Ball," p. 121). The two most common lengths are 5 ft. and 6 ft., but extensions are also available. A 3/4-in. x 54-in. flex bit costs about $50 at home centers. Buy a bit that has a hole on the end of it so you can use the bit itself to pull wires.

Once your hole is drilled, you can shove a glow rod through the hole, attach your wire to the eyelet at the end and pull it back through. Glow rods can also be used to hook wires to pull them out. As their name suggests, glow rods glow in the dark. This makes them easier to spot when you're working in dark areas (which is most of the time).

Glow rods come in various lengths and thicknesses, and you can combine as many sections as the job requires. Thinner rods flex more and work better when you have to make sharp turns. A thicker rod can span longer distances and is better for hooking wires that are more than a few feet away. Glow rod kits are sold at home centers.

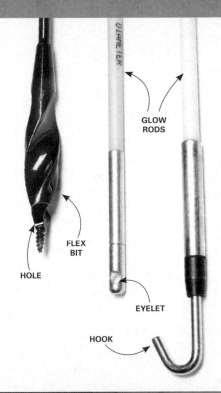

GLOW RODS
FLEX BIT
HOLE
EYELET
HOOK

Don't spin apart the glow rods

Sometimes you need to twist and spin glow rods in order to snake them past ductwork, pipes and other obstructions. A great way to lose a rod or attachment in a wall or joist space is to twist it so many times in the same direction that it unthreads and comes apart. Some pros wrap a little electrical tape around the connections to keep them secure.

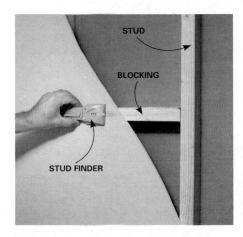

STUD
BLOCKING
STUD FINDER

Check the whole wall cavity with a stud finder

A decent stud finder is a must-have for every wire-fishing job, but don't throw it back in your pouch after you've located the studs. Use your stud finder to check the whole wall cavity for obstacles like blocking and abandoned headers. You don't want to find out the hard way that you should have fished your wire one stud cavity to the left or right.

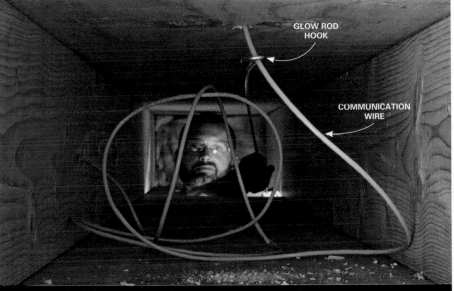

GLOW ROD HOOK
COMMUNICATION WIRE

Push through more than you need

When hooking a wire to pull it toward you, make sure there's more than enough wire to hook on to. Sometimes it's a real challenge to grab hold of a wire, and once you have it hooked, you don't want to lose it. Always makes sure that you have at least 5 or 6 ft. of extra wire to keep up the tension on the hook the whole time you're pulling on it.

FLEX BIT

ELECTRICAL CABLE

ELECTRICAL TAPE

Hook on to a flex bit

Sometimes you don't need to use glow rods at all. Most flex bits have holes in the ends of them. If you have access to where the flex bit pops out, attach your wire directly to the bit and fish the wire through that way. Twist the wire and tape it up to make sure it doesn't come off when you're pulling it back through (see "Hold On Tight," p. 121). Remove your bit from your drill before pulling so you don't accidentally spin the bit and twist up your wire.

Fish wires through the holes for recessed lights

When you're installing new recessed can lighting, fishing wires from one light to another is easy because you have a great big hole to pull the wires through. But even if you're not installing new lighting, you can use the existing openings. Many cans can be easily popped out of the opening by removing a few screws.

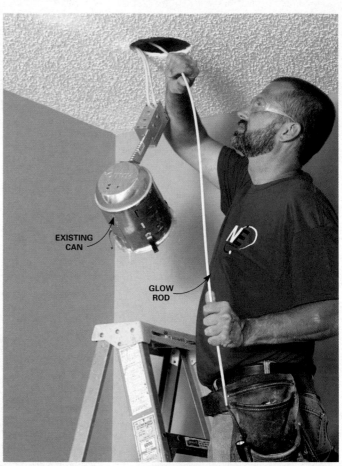

EXISTING CAN

GLOW ROD

Protect drywall with a mud ring

Mud rings, also called drywall brackets or low-voltage "old-work" brackets, are great for protecting the drywall when you're drilling with a flex bit or cranking on a glow rod. They're easy to install (just tighten two screws) and cost only a few bucks at home centers. Once the wires are connected, you can screw the wall plate to the mud ring.

Mud rings are approved only for low-voltage wires like communication and coaxial cables. If you need to install a regular gang box for an electrical receptacle or wall switch, install the mud ring temporarily to protect the drywall while you fish the wire, then remove it.

MUD RING

Seal the holes

If you're drilling holes through top and bottom plates or running wires through a fire wall in the garage, you must seal those holes with a fire-resistant caulk or foam sealant to comply with fire and energy codes. Most building officials won't make you bust out large holes in ceilings and walls in order to access hard-to-reach holes, but check with your local official before you begin your project. A can of fire-blocking insulated foam sealant costs about $10 at home centers and hardware stores.

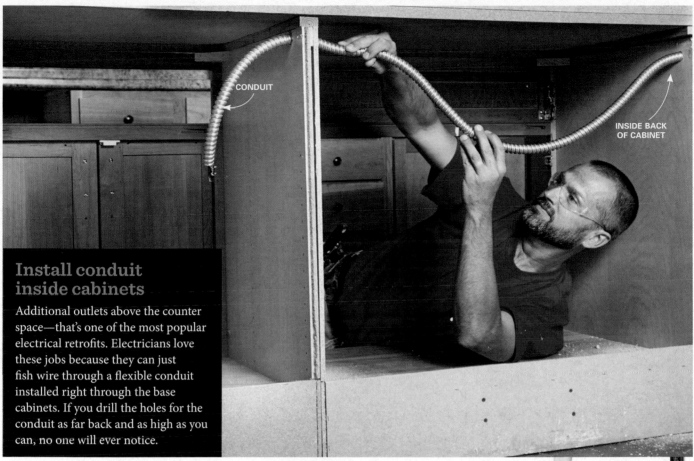

CONDUIT

INSIDE BACK OF CABINET

Install conduit inside cabinets

Additional outlets above the counter space—that's one of the most popular electrical retrofits. Electricians love these jobs because they can just fish wire through a flexible conduit installed right through the base cabinets. If you drill the holes for the conduit as far back and as high as you can, no one will ever notice.

Invest in a Bumper Ball

Wires aren't supposed to be installed any closer than 1-1/4 in. from a penetrable surface (the outside of the drywall). That means you shouldn't be drilling holes right next to the drywall. But it's not always easy to control where a flex bit goes. A Bumper Ball flexible drill bit guide installed on the end of your flex bit will help maintain the proper space between the bit and the outside of the wall cavity. You can buy a set of two at electrical suppliers or online.

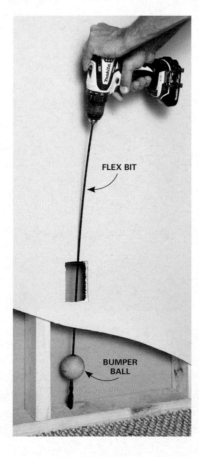

FLEX BIT

BUMPER BALL

Hold on tight

When you hook cable to the eyelet of a glow rod, strip the plastic sheathing back about 6 in., then cut off the hot and neutral wires. Then wrap the remaining ground wire through the rod's eyelet and wrap it back around the wire's sheathing several times. Finally, wrap the whole area with electrical tape.

When hooking coaxial cable, just tape the whole wire to the glow rod.

Use the same technique when working with communication cable like phone wire. If you try to hook one of the small communication wires, you could stretch and damage that individual wire several feet down inside the sheathing.

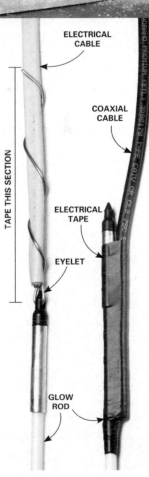

ELECTRICAL CABLE

COAXIAL CABLE

TAPE THIS SECTION

ELECTRICAL TAPE

EYELET

GLOW ROD

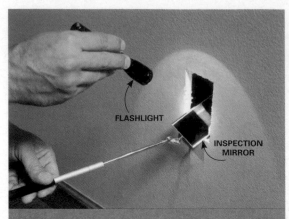

FLASHLIGHT

INSPECTION MIRROR

Get a better view with an inspection mirror

You know your wire is in there somewhere, but you just can't seem to find it. It's probably hung up on another wire or pipe, but guessing isn't going to solve the problem. Instead, shine a flashlight onto an inspection mirror to find out exactly what's going on. This is a simple, inexpensive tip that can save you a lot of time and frustration. Pick up an inspection mirror at an auto parts store for less than $10. Or bump it up a notch and pay a few more bucks for a mirror with small built-in lights, so you can see exactly what's going on.

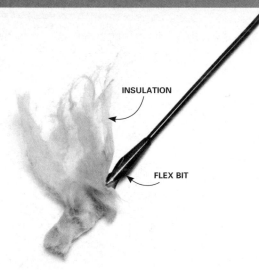

INSULATION

FLEX BIT

Don't spin the bit in insulation

The best advice for fishing wires through insulation is "Avoid it if you can." The potential is always there to damage the vapor barrier or bunch up insulation, leaving cold spots in the wall. If you must fish wires through exterior walls, the best tip is to avoid spinning the flex bit until you make solid contact with the wood you plan to drill through. If you drill too early, you'll end up creating a large insulation cotton candy cone, which will make retrieving your bit difficult, if not impossible.

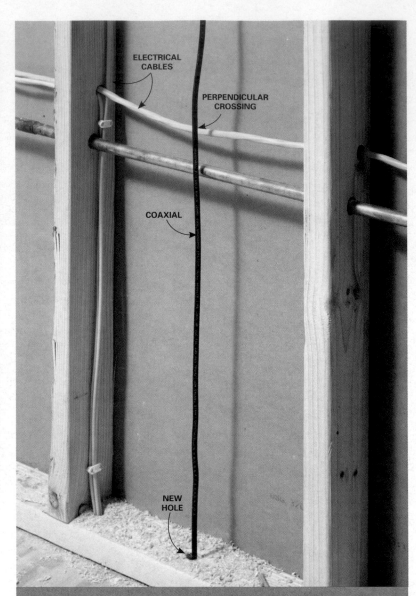

ELECTRICAL CABLES

PERPENDICULAR CROSSING

COAXIAL

NEW HOLE

Keep low-voltage wires away from electrical cables

It's really tempting to fish low-voltage wires (like coax and Cat-5e) through existing holes occupied by electrical cables, but don't do it! Even though cables are insulated, the high-voltage current can interfere with the signal in the low-voltage wires. This could result in bad TV reception or unreliable phone and Internet service. Drill a new hole, and keep the new low-voltage wire several inches away from electrical cables. It's OK to run low-voltage wires perpendicular to cables, and it's also OK to run low-voltage wires next to electrical wires that are encased in conduit or metal sheathing.

Buy extra wire

Have plenty of extra wire or cable on hand, because it's not likely that you'll be able to fish a wire in a straight line from Point A to Point B. There's also the possibility that your wire might get hung up on something, and you'd have to abandon it and start over.

Vacuum-assisted wire pulling

When you're pulling wire through conduit, start with a small wad of paper towel tied to a string. Suck the wad through the conduit with a vacuum. Then use the string to pull the wire through.

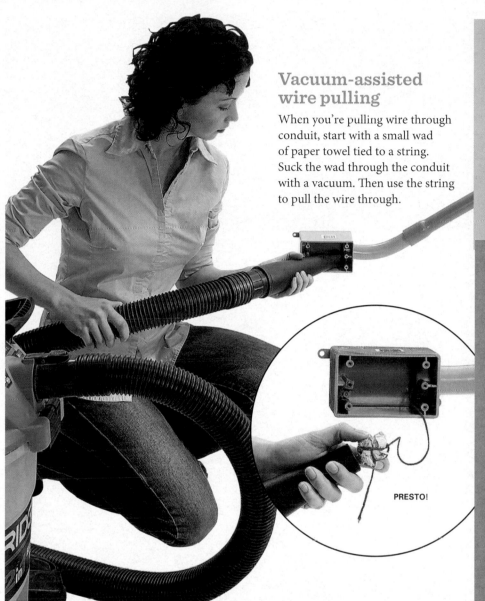

PRESTO!

A better way to fish wire

Trying to run a fish tape through an insulated stud bay is a nightmare. The fish tape curls up and snags the insulation, making it impossible to reach the hole you've cut out for your new junction box. Instead, try using a 10-ft. stick of 1/2-in. PEX as your fish "tape."

The PEX is rigid enough that you can slide it between the insulation and the drywall. Once the PEX reaches the hole, tape your Romex to it and pull the PEX back to the starting point of the operation. This also works great when you're fishing wire above a ceiling and below a batt of insulation between joist bays (to install a ceiling fan or light fixture, for example).

Run wires under a sidewalk

If you want to get power to a pond or just want an outlet in the back 40, you may have to run wires under a sidewalk. Here's how to do it. The idea is to drive a length of 1/2-in. rigid electrical conduit under the walk. You'll need to cap off both ends of the conduit: one end to keep the dirt out, the other so you can pound on it without damage. We recommend a 1/2-in. coupling and plug on both ends. Lift the conduit up off the bottom of your trench with some blocks, and bang away.

Chapter Seven

BUILDING, REMODELING AND REPAIRS

Planning and design

Plan for future upgrades if you can't afford them now

You don't have to wait until you can build your dream addition all at once. You can get started now and gradually add as your finances allow. But work from a master plan so you don't have to go back and tear out or upgrade what you've already done.

For example, consider:

- an electrical service with capacity for the future addition, workshop or hot tub
- in-the-wall wiring for electronics in every room or a future home theater
- rough plumbing for a future half bath or hot tub
- wiring for future lighting fixtures
- rough framing for future doors or windows
- French doors that open to a future deck.

Compare the price of remodeling with the cost of buying new

Your house is your most important investment as well as the place you call home. Although you may love your house and neighborhood, check how much your addition would add to the value of your home. Creating a luxury home in a modest neighborhood may not make financial sense. A real estate agent or home appraiser can make a close estimate. If you can't recoup at least 75 percent of the cost when you sell, at least consider the advantages of buying another house with the space or features you need. It may well be a better investment to move rather than to add on.

Shop for materials yourself

You won't save much by trying to stockpile lumber, drywall, electrical wiring or other basic building materials. But when it comes to the finish materials—carpeting, appliances, faucets, countertops, light fixtures—your own footwork will pay off. Not only do you get exactly what you want, but you also can find bargains, especially if you start collecting these items well in advance. You can even plan to reuse a stylish old stove, distressed hardwood flooring or other items that add a creative touch to a room. But clear your decisions with your contractor; installation costs might be higher for unusual requests.

Avoid moving the plumbing or changing the foundation

You can't always avoid it, but any alteration to these two systems typically adds thousands of dollars to a remodeling project. Neither is simple. New plumbing often requires breaking into walls and floors; resizing lines to meet newer plumbing codes; and replacing old, out-of-date pipes. New foundations usually require excavation, concrete and other heavy, expensive work. The price jumps whenever you add these two items, so ask yourself if you really need to move the kitchen sink during a kitchen remodel, or if you really need the extra space in a bathroom bump-out.

CORK FLOOR

LUXURY VINYL PLANKS

Two great basement floor coverings

Choosing material for a basement floor is tricky. Carpet is warm and soft but susceptible to moisture damage. Tile is good for areas that might get wet, but it's hard and cold underfoot. Still, there are a few choices that strike a good compromise.

Interlocking cork flooring is easy to install, sustainably harvested and warm underfoot. Make sure to buy top-quality cork flooring that has a durable, water-resistant core to prevent moisture damage. In basements, we recommend installing a floating cork floor over a padded underlayment that includes a vapor barrier. This can go directly on dry concrete or over a dimple mat.

The second flooring choice we recommend is luxury vinyl tile or planks. Luxury vinyl is waterproof and virtually indestructible. It's also easy to install and looks great. It's available in a plank form that looks like wood, and squares that look like tile. Floating luxury vinyl floors connect with self-adhesive tabs or interlocking edges. You'll find luxury vinyl at flooring stores, home centers and online.

Add a gas fireplace

You can't go wrong adding a gas fireplace to your basement remodeling plans. Matt Cook, our basement expert, estimates that more than 80 percent of the basement remodeling jobs done by his company include a gas fireplace. In addition to the obvious benefit—everybody loves fireplaces—a fireplace can be a great source of extra heat to warm up a room fast on cold winter days.

One advantage of gas fireplaces is that you may not need to run a chimney through the roof. In some situations, you can run the flue directly through the side wall. A DIY gas fireplace kit starts at about $2,000.

FINISHED BASEMENT COMPANY

Baseboards:
5-1/4 in.

Chair rail:
2-1/4 in. plus 5/8 in.
(2-7/8 in.)

Crown molding:
2-1/4 in.

Right-sized trim

To accentuate—rather than dominate—colorful walls, choose chair rail that's about two-thirds of the baseboard width and crown about one-third the baseboard width. For a more traditional look, choose crown that's about two-thirds of the baseboard width.

Demolition

ANGLE-CUT JAMB

Cut the jamb and pull

You can knock a jamb sideways out of its opening, but the nails or screws holding it in place put up strong resistance to the shear force you apply.

An easier way is to cut one of the sides in half with a reciprocating saw and then pull the rest straight away from the framing. You can easily pull away any nails or screws holding the doorjambs in place simply by using the leverage of the jamb itself. Make your cut at an angle so the two cut sections don't wedge against each other, preventing you from pulling them apart. This same technique works for pulling out windows.

Cut around the window with a recip saw

Spray foam insulation does an excellent job of insulating around a window— and a surprisingly good job of keeping the window or door in place. Even if you remove all the fasteners holding in a window, you won't be able to pull the window out until you deal with the spray foam.

So don't bother pulling the nails or screws out of an old window. Just run a recip saw between the window and the framing and cut the fasteners and the foam at the same time. You may want a buddy on the other side of the window to keep it from falling out when you're done cutting around it. With a long enough blade, you can even slice through the nailing flange at the same time. That's important if you're trying to save the siding around the opening.

Blow the dust outside

Set a box fan in a window and blow the dust out of your work area. Wedge the fan into place with scrap pieces of foam and a few rags. For the best results, open windows beyond the dusty area or on the opposite side of the room to help keep the air moving in the right direction.

RECIPROCATING SAW

BOTTOM PLATE

Cut off the nails on the plates

After you've bashed the studs out of place, use a reciprocating saw to slice off the nails that held them down. Even if you're not planning to reuse the plates, it's a good way to avoid stepping on a nail. Make sure you use a saw blade for nail-embedded wood; it'll slice right through the nails.

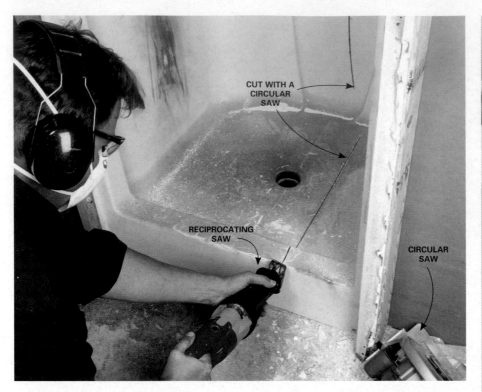

CUT WITH A
CIRCULAR
SAW

RECIPROCATING
SAW

CIRCULAR
SAW

Bust up cast iron tubs (and other stuff)

Cast iron tubs are ridiculously heavy. So unless it's a priceless collector's item, you don't want to have any part of moving one. Your best bet is to bust it up in place. It can be tough to get the cracking started, so begin hitting the tub at the edge. Once it does start breaking, pound your way along the smashed edges.

Throw a tarp or thick sheet of plastic over the top to cut down on flying shards of iron. And wear your safety gear, especially hearing protection—busting up a cast iron tub is like having a front row seat at a church bell convention. This tip works on just about anything brittle: old toilets, radiators, concrete laundry tubs, etc.

Cut fiberglass surround into pieces

Some bathrooms are built around a shower or tub surround. This means that even if you manage to remove all the fasteners holding it in place, the odds are you're not getting that surround out the door in one piece. You're going to have to slice it up. Make the long cuts with a circular saw, and finish the curved areas with a recip saw. Wear eye protection because fiberglass throws a bunch of chips when it's cut. And a dust mask is a must—fiberglass dust is not something you want to breathe in. Most important, thoroughly investigate the areas where you'll be making your cuts, to avoid severing any electrical wires or plumbing pipes.

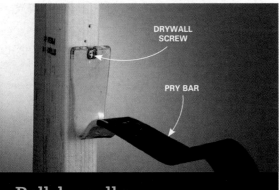

DRYWALL
SCREW

PRY BAR

Pull drywall screws

When you pull drywall from a wall, the screws usually stay in the studs. Unscrewing them with a drill is not the most efficient way to remove them because the screw heads are usually deteriorated or full of drywall mud. Use a pry bar or your hammer claw to pull them out just like you would with nails. Drywall screws are brittle, so if some joker used 3-in. screws to install the drywall, snap them off with your hammer.

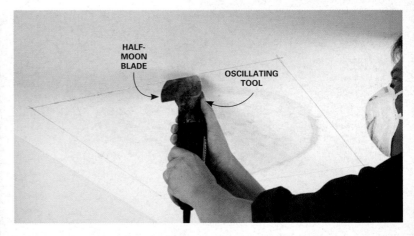

HALF-
MOON
BLADE

OSCILLATING
TOOL

Slice up drywall with a multitool

There seems to be no end of odd jobs that can be done with an oscillating tool, and here's another one: If you have to remove a section of damaged drywall, cut it out with a multitool equipped with a half-moon blade. The tool will cut almost as fast as you can pull it. And because the oscillations on the blade are so short and the teeth are so fine, the tool creates half the dust of a reciprocating or keyhole saw. Plus, the recess you cut will be much straighter and cleaner, making the patching work much easier.

Be a smart packer

Renting a trash bin isn't cheap, so take advantage of every square inch of it by strategically placing the debris in the container instead of tossing it in willy-nilly. Long boards should always run the length of the container. Set in large, hollow items like bathtubs or sinks open side up so you can fill them in instead of creating a void.

Use small pieces to fill in and around large ones. Think of the debris as puzzle pieces, each with its own proper spot. If your trash bin has a door, don't park the bin so close to the house that you can't open it. Walking in heavy items is a lot easier than lifting them over the side. Also, make sure you order the proper size. If you explain your project to the sanitation company, the staff should be able to suggest a bin size that's right for your project.

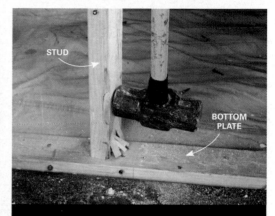

STUD

BOTTOM PLATE

Knock out studs sideways

A sledgehammer works great for busting up studs, but don't take a whack at the middle of the studs—they'll just wobble back and forth and probably bounce the head of the sledge right back in your direction. Hit the studs as close to the bottom plate as you can, but not so hard that you pull out the nails on the top plate—that's a good way to catch a falling stud in the noggin. Hit the bottom of each stud just far enough to dislodge it from the nails that were holding it. Then grab hold of it and pull it off the top plate.

Cut it up with a circular saw

Sledgehammers, pry bars and reciprocating saws aren't the only demo heroes on the job site—your circular saw can be used for a heck of a lot more than cutting studs and sheets of plywood. Fitted with the right blade, your circular saw can cut up roofing, tin, concrete, rebar, steel doors and fiber cement. With a demo blade, you can cut up nail-embedded debris all day long.

Suck out insulation

VACUUM HOSE

Tearing down a drywall ceiling is not a super-pleasant experience, but tearing down a ceiling that has 14 in. of blown-in insulation on top of it is a complete nightmare. Avoid that gigantic mess by sucking out all the insulation in the attic before pulling down any drywall.

The huge vacuum required for the job costs about $220 a day to rent, but if your local rental center doesn't carry them, call an insulation contractor in your area. Many blow-in insulation installers also have the equipment to suck out the insulation. But this service isn't cheap: Expect to pay about $1 to $1.50 per sq. ft. You might be able to get a deal if you use the same company to blow in the new insulation. Make sure your insulation is fiberglass or cellulose. If you even suspect there's vermiculite insulation in the attic, get an expert opinion before touching the stuff—it could contain asbestos.

Wall framing tips

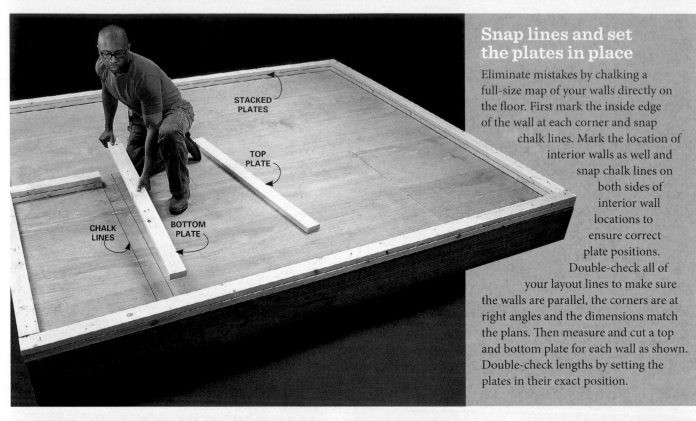

Snap lines and set the plates in place

Eliminate mistakes by chalking a full-size map of your walls directly on the floor. First mark the inside edge of the wall at each corner and snap chalk lines. Mark the location of interior walls as well and snap chalk lines on both sides of interior wall locations to ensure correct plate positions. Double-check all of your layout lines to make sure the walls are parallel, the corners are at right angles and the dimensions match the plans. Then measure and cut a top and bottom plate for each wall as shown. Double-check lengths by setting the plates in their exact position.

STACKED PLATES

TOP PLATE

CHALK LINES

BOTTOM PLATE

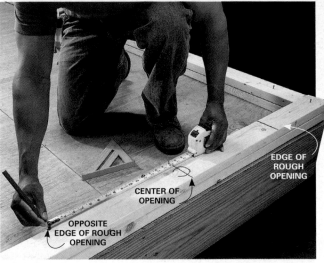

OPPOSITE EDGE OF ROUGH OPENING

CENTER OF OPENING

EDGE OF ROUGH OPENING

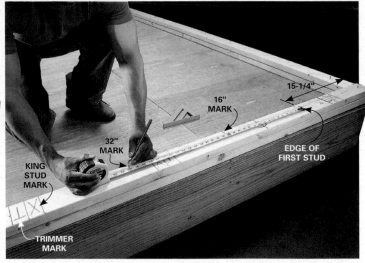

15-1/4"

16" MARK

32" MARK

KING STUD MARK

EDGE OF FIRST STUD

TRIMMER MARK

Mark windows and doors first, then lay out the studs

Find the center of each window and door opening. Then divide the "rough opening" (given on your plan or in the window literature) by two and measure out to the left and right of the center mark. Write a "T" to the outside of both marks to indicate trimmer locations. Measure over 1-1/2 in. and draw another line. Mark an "X" outside these marks for the full-height king studs.

With the openings marked, lay out the stud locations (right photo). The goal is to position the studs every 16 or 24 in. so that the edges of 4 x 8-ft. sheets of plywood align with the centers of studs. Subtract 3/4 in. from the first layout mark. Then hook your tape on a partially driven nail at this mark, and mark at each 16- or 24-in. multiple. Make an "X" on the same side of each layout mark to indicate the stud position. Mark studs that land between window or door trimmers with a "C" to indicate cripples rather than full-height studs.

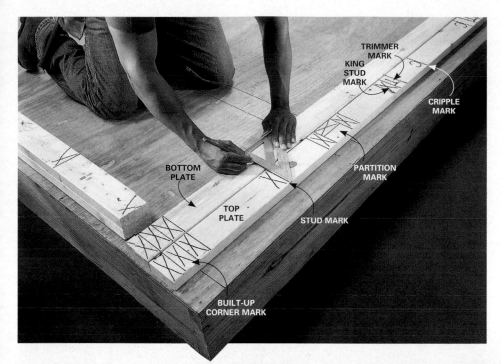

Transfer the layout marks to the bottom plate

Set the plates side by side and transfer the marks from the top plate to the bottom plate using a square. Some carpenters mark only the edge of the plates. We show marking the wide face, which will help you align twisted studs. Tack the pairs of plates together with 8d nails after marking them so they don't get separated and mixed with other plates. Then set them aside until you're ready to build that wall.

Nail full-height headers to the top plate

Calculate header lengths by adding 3 in. to the rough opening width. Add 6 in. to headers that require two trimmers on each side. Cut header parts and nail them together. Label the headers.

In many plans, headers are positioned against the top plate. If yours are, begin wall assembly by positioning and nailing these "full-height" headers to the top plate with 16d nails (top right photo). Then lay full-length studs between the plates and nail king studs to the headers and to the top and bottom plates (bottom right photo). Nail in all the full-height studs as well as corner assemblies. Note: Sight down each stud before you nail it in and orient any bow (crown) upward. Next install the trimmers (bottom right).

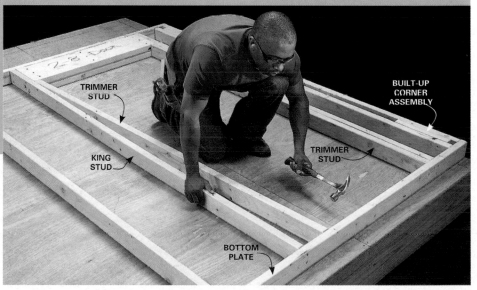

CRIPPLE
LOCATION

2-0 WINDOW

HEADER

KING
STUD

TRIMMER
STUD

Add cripples above headers and under sills

In wall plans that have openings with cripples above the header, cut and nail together the king studs and trimmers first. Then position and nail them to the plates. Set the header on the trimmers and nail through the king studs to hold it in place. Then measure, and nail the cripples into place (top photo). You have to toenail the bottom of the cripples to the header.

Window openings are just like doors but with the addition of a rough sill. Mark the top of the sill by measuring down from the header. Use the rough opening height for this dimension. Cut the lower cripples and place one under each end of the sill as a temporary support while you toenail the sill to the trimmers with a pair of 8d nails at each end. Align the cripples with the layout marks and nail through the sill and bottom plate to hold them in place. Use pairs of 16d nails. Some carpenters like to double the rough sill, especially on openings wider than about 3 ft. If you do this, remember to allow for the thickness of a double sill when you cut your cripples.

PARTITION
ASSEMBLY

2-0 WINDOW

ROUGH
SILL

CRIPPLE

Easy framing formula

You don't need a math degree to estimate framing materials for walls. Here's a formula that works every time, no matter how many doors, windows or corners your walls have:

- One stud per linear foot of wall.
- Five linear feet of plate material (bottoms, tops and ties) per linear foot of wall.

It'll look like too much lumber when it arrives, but you'll need the extra stuff for corners, window and door frames, blocking and braces. Set aside the crooked stuff for short pieces.

Frame soffits with wood I-joists

To create a soffit around a long run of basement pipe that has a perfectly straight bottom edge, use 14-in. I-joists. Hold them up to the floor joists and screw through the flange to hold them in place. Install two long I-joists on each side of the pipes to create the sides of the soffit. Then frame the bottom with 2x2s and cover it with drywall. The soffit will look great— straight as an arrow.

Build walls plumb with a plumb bob

One of the quickest and easiest ways to plumb up or down from any given point is with a plumb bob. We're using the plumb bob to transfer wall layout marks from the floor to the ceiling. Suspend the plumb bob about 1/2 in. above the floor and center the point exactly over the intersecting lines. Then mark the location on the ceiling. The key to accuracy is to wait for the bob to stop swinging. To speed things up, ask a helper to steady the plumb bob while you adjust the position of the string. Plumb bobs have one major drawback: They don't work in windy conditions.

MARK CEILING

2x10 BLOCKING

Drop the plumb bob from the ceiling and suspend it about 1/2 in. above your floor.

WALL LAYOUT MARKS

PLUMB BOB

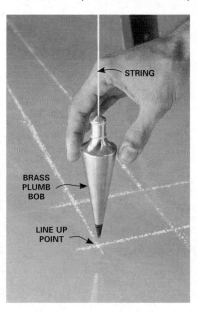

Ask a helper to steady the plumb bob and tell you which way to move the string to center it over the point on the floor.

STRING

BRASS PLUMB BOB

LINE UP POINT

Roofing

Minor leaks can cause major damage

Have a roof leak? Well, you'd better fix it, even if it doesn't bother you much or you're getting a new roof next year. Over time, even small leaks can lead to big problems, such as mold, rotted framing and sheathing, destroyed insulation and damaged ceilings. The flashing leak that caused this $1,000 repair bill was obvious from the ceiling stains for over two years. If the homeowner had dealt with it right away, the damage and subsequent repairs would have been minimal.

MOLD

ROTTING WOOD

DAMAGED SHINGLE

Roof gripper

An old foam cushion from a sofa or chair not only saves your knees but also grips asphalt shingles and keeps you from sliding down a steep pitch. It won't prevent falls, though, so it's no substitute for safety equipment like a harness and roof jacks.

Shingle cooler

If you're replacing damaged shingles on a hot summer day and struggling to break through the sealant strip, try this cool trick to ease the job. Rest an ice bag on the shingle for a couple of minutes before trying to break the sealant strip. The hot, sticky adhesive will cool down and pop up with ease.

Small holes

Tiny holes in shingles are sneaky because they can cause rot and other damage for years before you notice the obvious signs of a leak. You might find holes left over from satellite dish or antenna mounting brackets or just about anything. And exposed, misplaced roofing nails should be pulled and the holes patched. Small holes are simple to fix, but the fix isn't to inject caulk in the hole. You'll fix this one with flashing.

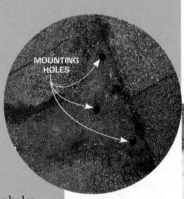

MOUNTING HOLES

PROBLEM: Leftover mounting holes can let in vast amounts of water.

SOLUTION: Seal nail holes forever. Slip flashing under the shingle and add a bead of caulk under and over the flashing to hold it in place.

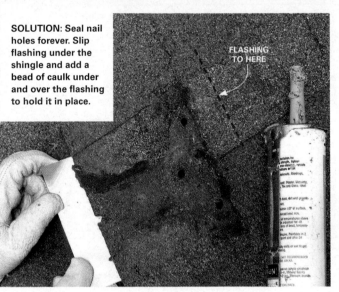

FLASHING TO HERE

TYPICAL NAIL LOCATIONS

1 Gently tap a flat bar under the shingles to break the seal-down strips free. Don't force it—shingles rip easily.

NAIL REMOVAL ZONE

NAIL

2 Wedge the notch of the pry bar under the shingle at the nail head, then pry up both shingle and nail.

3 Nail down the new shingle, propping the tabs above as you nail to avoid breaking them.

EDGE OF NEW SHINGLE

Replace a shingle

A broken shingle is both ugly and a leak waiting to happen. But as long as you can find matching shingles (and you're not afraid of heights), the repair is straightforward.

Pick a day when the weather is moderate to do the repair—too cold and the shingles can crack; too warm and the shingle sealants are tough to break.

Loosen the tabs under the broken shingle and the next two courses above it (Photo 1). Shingles are fastened with eight nails each—four at the center just above the tab slots and four through the shingle above it—and you have to lift up all the shingles that cover those nails to remove them.

After all the tabs are loose, push the flat bar up under the damaged shingle to each nail, centering the nail in the flat bar notch (Photo 2). To avoid ripping shingles, gently work the pry bar under both tabs as you push it up.

Pop out the nails by prying underneath the shingle instead of trying to dig the nail head out from the top of the shingle; that will wreck the shingle. Then push the shingle down from the nail head and pull out the nail. After removing the center row of nails on the damaged shingle, lift the undamaged shingles above it and remove the next row of nails. Then pull out the damaged shingle.

Slide the new shingle up into place. Nail the center row first, then the center row of the course above it, nailing 1/2 in. over from the old holes (Photo 3). Nail at the top of the slots between the tabs, just above the sealant strip.

No-slip tools

When you're working on the roof, wrap rubber bands around tools to help them stay put. The rubber will grip on roofs with up to a 6/12 slope.

RUBBER BAND

Jobsite tips

Folding-horse roundup

There are dozens of styles at home centers and online. Most carpenters prefer the folding metal type, but some prefer other breeds. So here's a roundup:

Metal horses

Folding metal horses are solid, easy to stow and inexpensive. However, some of the cheap, super-flimsy ones—the ones that often look like they're made of aluminum roof flashing—aren't stable. There are also a few impostors out there that use a strand of cable, instead of metal hinges, as cross braces: If you see them, run. If you use your horses inside and want to protect a finished floor, you can buy protective plastic feet for a few bucks and install them in minutes. And watch those fingers when you fold up metal horses; the sharp edges can inflict a painful pinch.

Metal bar horses

These are often made of square metal tubing. These draft horses of the sawhorse world are rock-solid and have the weight and price tag to prove it. Like the plastic ones, some aren't designed to accommodate a wood top slat—and you definitely don't want to saw into one of these.

Plastic collapsible horses

Most of these have legs that swing out to create an A-frame shape. They're light, easy to set up and easy to store. Some have height-adjustable legs, which are handy outdoors. Heavy-duty versions are tough enough for any job, some are only for light duty: We've seen legs actually buckle when slamming a sheet of 3/4-in. plywood onto them. Another drawback to many: No way to attach a wood top. If you cut too deep, you cut into the horse itself.

Metal brackets

These are simple brackets that use 2x4s—usually ones you supply—for the legs and crosspiece. Some have teeth that bite into the 2x4s; others use fasteners. They're height- and length-adjustable depending on the length of 2x4 used. They're inexpensive, but they can also fall apart or "rack" while in use or when you move them.

Tangle prevention

If you store a lot of gear under the backseat of your truck, it can get pretty cluttered under there. Stretch wrap can help to restore order. It's perfect for bundling items that would otherwise turn into one big frustrating tangled mess. You can also wrap your tow strap, tie-downs, jumper cables, raincoat, extension cord, bungees and extra pairs of gloves.

Windshield notes

It's a good idea to keep a dry-erase marker in your truck. If you're out in the yard or at a job site and think of things you need to pick up, make a list on the windshield. When you get a minute to hunt down your phone or a paper and pencil, you can transfer the list without worrying that you've forgotten something. Make sure to erase the list before you drive so it doesn't obstruct your view.

CARPET SCRAPS

No-mar horses

Meticulous carpenters say you've just got to have a set of sawhorses with carpeted tops for sanding or working with fine pieces of finished wood. Just trim carpeting scraps to size and hot-glue them to the wood tops of your horses. Now you can sand without getting scuff marks on the bottom of the workpiece and assemble prefinished work without leaving marks or scratches.

Load support

Next time you head to the home center to pick up long, floppy materials like trim, plastic pipe or vinyl siding, take your extension ladder. It provides a stiff support for your flimsy load. Include some heavy weights to hold down the end of your cargo and plenty of elastic cords to strap your load to the ladder. Also tie down the ladder so it doesn't slide from side to side.

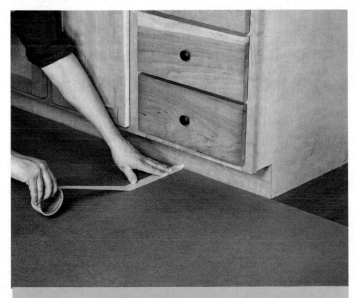

Protect finished flooring with hardboard

Rosin paper, cardboard and dropcloths are all legit ways to protect a floor—that is, until you knock your trim gun off the top of a 6-ft. ladder. If you really want to ensure that a floor stays dent- and scratch-free, cover it with 1/8-in. hardboard. It's pretty cheap, and as the name suggests, it's pretty hard. Cut the sheets with a circular saw or jigsaw, and to prevent scratches, make sure both the floor and the hardboard are perfectly clean before you lay the hardboard down. Tape the seams with masking tape to keep the dirt and debris from slipping through the cracks. When the job is done, pull up the sheets and save them for the next job.

Protect your tools

Tarps do a decent job of protecting tools from the elements, but it's hard to keep them in place, especially when you're traveling down the road. The wind always seems to catch underneath, which can send them sailing.

The next time you have to take your tools on a road trip, try wrapping them in a grill cover. The size and shape of a grill cover make it much easier to secure with a strap or bungee. The cover also protects your tools from rain or morning dew if you plan to leave them out overnight in your backyard. Home centers and discount stores carry grill covers in various sizes.

GRILL COVER

Hauling lumber

In most states it's illegal to haul lumber or other long items that protrude a set distance from the back of your vehicle, unless you attach a warning flag. Keep a spring clip handy and use that to clamp your warning flag to the end of your long load. It beats messing around with staples, nails or string.

TOOL SAFETY: DON'T BE A DUMMY

Don't crosscut against the table saw fence

Nigel the dummy is demonstrating one of the most dangerous table saw practices: cutting a board to length using the fence as a guide. There's a good chance the board will get pinched between the blade and the fence and get thrown back into his body with lots of force. That nasty incident is called "kickback." Broken thumbs, cracked ribs, ruptured spleens and punctured eyes are only a few of the resultant injuries you can suffer. About 35,000 people end up in the emergency room every year with table saw injuries, with 10 percent of them hospitalized. Industry experts estimate that about half of table saw injuries are caused either directly or indirectly by kickback.

In addition to avoiding the dangerous technique Nigel is using to crosscut a board, here are a few other ways to prevent kickback injuries:

- Don't cut anything that's longer than it is wide with the shorter side against the fence. If you want to crosscut with a table saw, use the miter gauge or a crosscutting sled.
- Avoid ripping wet, bowed or twisted lumber.
- Position your body to the right or left of the miter saw slots, not directly behind the blade.
- Don't let anyone walk behind you when you're operating the saw.

CAUTION: Don't use the fence as a guide for crosscutting. Instead, use the miter gauge or build a crosscutting sled.

NIGEL

DANGEROUS CROSSCUT

BLADE IS TOO HIGH

NOTE: No crash test dummies were harmed in the making of this story.

RED ALERT: Even a dummy should have enough common sense to avoid this technique. Nigel's finger is so close to the blade that a split second of inattention or a kickback could send him to the crash-test dummy hospital.

NO PUSH STICK

NO BLADE GUARD

Don't remove that blade guard!

Every table saw sold includes a blade guard, which has a splitter attached. The guard covers the blade, preventing you from accidentally touching it, and the splitter keeps wood from pinching on the blade and kicking back. Don't take them off! Sure, the guard may be a nuisance at times, but it's better to be inconvenienced than to lose one or more fingers. Of the 35,000 emergency room visits we talked about earlier, 83 percent involve contact with the blade.

If you're buying a table saw, consider spending extra for the SawStop brand. It's the only saw on the market that stops the blade when skin touches it. If your blade guard is missing, contact the manufacturer for a replacement. An add-on guard is a good option if your original guard is missing or doesn't work well. They're expensive, but your finger is worth it.

Even with a blade guard installed, you should keep your fingers away from the blade. Always use a push stick for rips less than 4 in. wide. If you're using your thumb to push the piece and the piece kicks back, you risk torn ligaments, tendons and broken bones. Push the cut piece past the blade, turn off the saw and wait for the blade to stop before retrieving the ripped piece. Don't reach near a spinning blade to remove a cutoff.

Don't put your hand directly behind a circular saw

There are an estimated 14,000 visits to the emergency room every year as a result of circular saw injuries. Many of these injuries result in lost or severely damaged fingers. When you're using a circular saw, remember that if the blade binds, the saw can shoot backward a lot faster than you can move your hand out of the way. Anything in the blade's path, including fingers, hands, legs or feet, is in danger of getting cut. Avoid the risk by clamping your work and keeping both hands on the saw whenever possible. Also keep your body to the side of the saw rather than directly behind it.

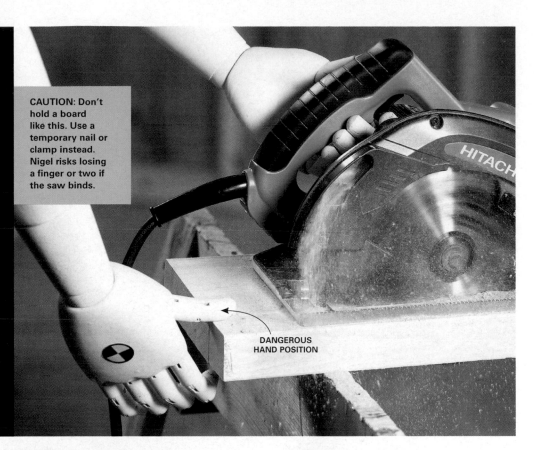

CAUTION: Don't hold a board like this. Use a temporary nail or clamp instead. Nigel risks losing a finger or two if the saw binds.

DANGEROUS HAND POSITION

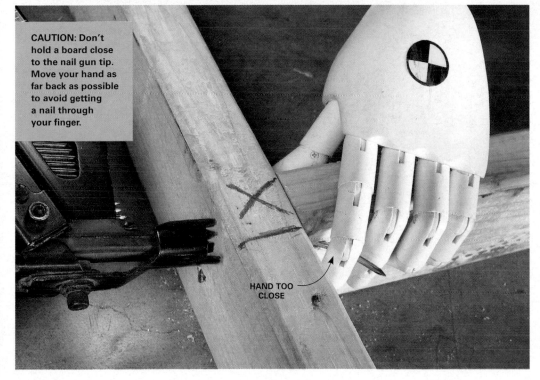

CAUTION: Don't hold a board close to the nail gun tip. Move your hand as far back as possible to avoid getting a nail through your finger.

HAND TOO CLOSE

Don't put your hands near a nail gun

Even if you're a nail gun expert, your nails won't always go straight. Wood grain or knots can deflect the nail and cause it to shoot out the side of the board. If you're driving the nail at an angle to toenail a board, there's a good chance the nail can glance off and go shooting into space. If you must hold a board with your free hand, keep it well away from the nail gun muzzle. If you're reaching over a board to hold it down, move your hand out of the nail's path. Also avoid shooting into large knots that can deflect the nail. And, of course, always wear eye protection when you're using a nail gun.

Don't get careless with a knife

Power tools are one thing, but did you know that utility knives are one of the most dangerous tools, accounting for a whopping 60,000 estimated emergency room visits a year? One slip is all it takes to put a deep cut in any body part that's in the way. And while most cuts are superficial and may only require a few stitches, permanent tendon and nerve damage is common.

The best way to avoid an injury is to clamp materials whenever possible to avoid having to hand-hold them. If you do have to hold something while you're cutting, imagine a line at right angles to the cutting line and keep your hand behind it (on the dull side of the blade).

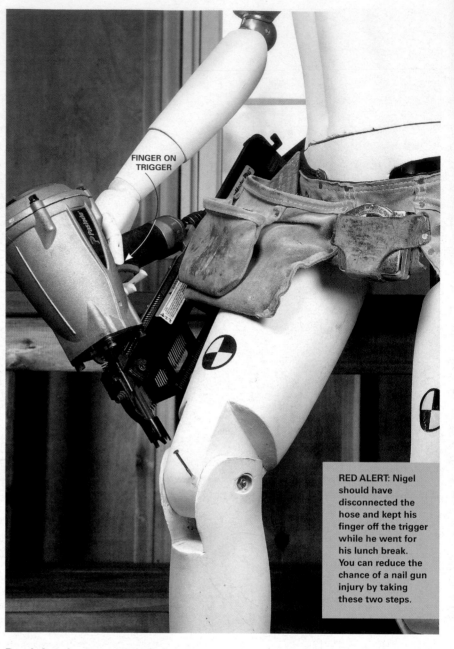

FINGER ON TRIGGER

RED ALERT: Nigel should have disconnected the hose and kept his finger off the trigger while he went for his lunch break. You can reduce the chance of a nail gun injury by taking these two steps.

RED ALERT: Nigel's finger is in the danger zone. If the knife slips, he'll end up with a nasty cut or worse. Keep your hands out of the blade's path.

Don't be sloppy with nail guns

You've all seen the news stories. X-rays of big nails embedded in someone's head, lodged in a spine or stuck in a foot. Ask any carpenter and you're sure to hear a story about a nail that went through a finger or hand. A tool that's powerful enough to shoot a 3-in.-long nail into wood can easily penetrate skin and bone. Depending on the type, some nail guns can be set to "bump-trip." In this mode, the operator can simply hold down the trigger and bump the nail gun nose against the surface to shoot a nail. This is great for speeding up jobs like nailing down plywood sheathing, but it creates a risk if you hold the trigger while carrying the nail gun. Bump your leg and you'll be heading to the emergency room. In incidents where accidental contact caused an injury, more than 80 percent of the time the operator had a finger on the trigger.

There are two ways to avoid this. First, get out your owner's manual and see if you can set your nail gun to sequential mode. This requires you to push down the muzzle and then pull the trigger for each nail. Second, keep your hand off the trigger when you're carrying a nail gun, or better yet, unplug the hose. Then there's no chance of accidental firing.

Windows

Replace broken glass in a jalousie window

Putting in a new piece of jalousie window glass is an easy, straightforward fix. However, because the glass is thicker than standard glass and has polished edges, it usually has to be special-ordered from glass companies or hardware stores. Bring exact glass dimensions and a chunk of the broken glass to get the right thickness.

Remove the setscrews in the metal housing at each end of the glass, then take out the metal wedges that hold the glass (Photo 1). Hold on to the setscrews—they're tiny and disappear instantly if dropped. Carefully pull the broken glass out when the wedges are out.

Clean any dirt and corrosion out of the metal housing at the ends, then slide in the new glass (Photo 2).

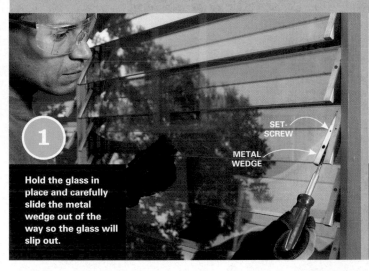

1 SET-SCREW
METAL WEDGE
Hold the glass in place and carefully slide the metal wedge out of the way so the glass will slip out.

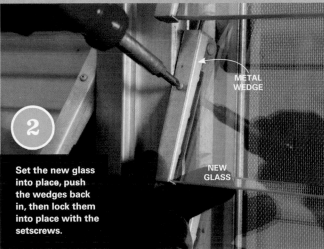

2 METAL WEDGE
NEW GLASS
Set the new glass into place, push the wedges back in, then lock them into place with the setscrews.

Remove old, dry glazing compound

First soften the putty with heat. A heat gun works best. Set it on low and direct the heat back and forth along the putty, slowly warming it. Be careful. If you hold the heat in one place on or near the glass, the glass will crack and you'll have an even bigger job on your hands! As the glazing compound softens, scrape it out with a stiff putty knife.

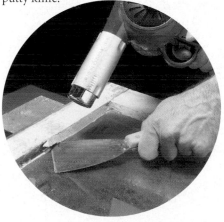

Lube a sticking vinyl window or door

When vinyl windows and doors don't operate smoothly, it's usually because gunk has built up in the channels. But sometimes even clean windows and doors can bind. Try spraying dry PTFE-type lubricant on the contact points and wiping it off with a rag. Don't use oil lubricants; they can attract dirt, and some can damage the vinyl. PTFE lubricants contain Teflon and are sold at home centers.

DRY LUBRICANT

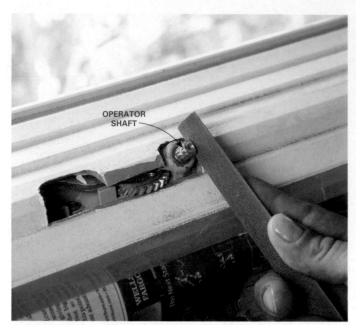

File a flat spot on the operator shaft, then insert a longer setscrew into the handle. The flat side lets the setscrew lock onto the shaft.

Fix a stripped crank handle

If you turn your window handle and nothing happens, the gears on your handle, crank operator shaft or both are probably stripped. Take off the handle and look for signs of wear. If the teeth are worn, replace the handle. If the shaft is worn, you can replace the whole operator. But here's a home remedy to try first.

Start by backing out the setscrew to remove the handle (some newer handles don't have setscrews and simply pull off—and this fix won't work). If you have a folding handle, mark where the setscrew is on the operator shaft when the window is closed and the handle is folded up. Remove the handle and file the shaft so the setscrew can lock onto the shaft (photo above). The metal is tough; it'll take about 15 minutes to get a flat side. Or use a rotary tool with a grinder bit to speed up the job. Vacuum the shavings out of the operator so they won't harm the moving parts.

Reattach the handle with a longer setscrew (available at hardware stores). If you open and close the window a lot, this fix may not hold up in the long run and you'll need to replace the whole assembly.

SETSCREW

Seal a drafty window

Weather stripping often becomes loose, worn or distorted when the sash drags or when the strip gets sticky and attaches itself to the frame, then pulls loose when the sash is opened. Windows have weather strip on the sash, frame or both. Regardless of its location, the steps for removing and replacing it are the same. Weather stripping is available from your window manufacturer. The window brand and glass manufacturer date are etched in the corner of the glass or in the aluminum spacer between the glass panes. You'll also need the height and width of your sash (take these measurements yourself).

If the weather strip is in good shape and loose in only a few places, like the corners, apply a dab of polyurethane sealant to the groove and press the weather strip into place. Otherwise, replace the entire weather strip. First remove the sash and set it on a work surface so you can access all four sides. If the weather strip is one continuous piece, cut it apart at the corners with a utility knife.

Starting at a corner, pull the weather strip loose from the sash. If the spline tears off and remains stuck in the groove, make a hook from stiff wire to dig it out.

Work the new weather strip into the groove, starting at a corner. You'll hear it click as the strip slides into the groove.

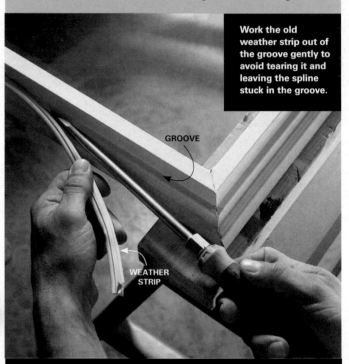

Work the old weather strip out of the groove gently to avoid tearing it and leaving the spline stuck in the groove.

GROOVE

WEATHER STRIP

Pro tip: If the window is stuck shut, it's likely that the weather strip is sticking. After you muscle it open, spray silicone lubricant on a rag and wipe it on the weather stripping. Don't use oily lubricants; they attract dust.

Doors

SHIM

Level the floor

The most critical step of any door installation is making sure the bottom of each doorjamb is at the proper height. If you're installing a door on a finished floor and the floor isn't level, you'll have to cut a little off the bottom of one of the jambs.

Use a level to check the floor. Rest a level across the opening and level it with one or more shims. Mark the shim at the thickest point, and measure the thickness of the shim at the mark. That's exactly how much you'll need to cut off the jamb at the opposite side of the opening.

Trim shims in a jiffy

When you install a door, the usual way to trim the shims is to score them with a utility knife and then snap them off. It's a slow way to go, and half the time you push the shims out of place. Other times, they don't break off cleanly. However, an oscillating tool does the job perfectly. Quick, clean, no hassles.

Easier door work

Before removing a door that will be reinstalled, snug a wooden wedge underneath it at the hinge side and duct tape the wedge to the floor. This makes reinstalling the door much easier because you'll get the height right on the first try.

Door stand

Keeping doors upright and stable when you're planing or sanding them just got a whole lot easier with this classic tip. This simple door stand made from shop scraps actually has upright arms to pinch the door and hold it rock-solid while you tune up your door. The secret to the pinching action is the 3/8-in. plywood base that bends from the weight of the door, forcing the tops of the 2x4s together. Here are the key measurements you'll need to make your own:

- 1-1/2-in. x 3-1/2-in. x 24-in. upright arms
- 3/8-in. x 3-1/2-in. x 24-in. plywood base
- 1-1/2-in. x 1-1/2-in. x 4-in. feet
- 1-1/2-in. x 3-1/2-in. x 12-in. 45-degree diagonal braces
- Two strips of carpeting hot-glued to the inside of the uprights

Cut these pieces and assemble them with screws. Be sure to position the uprights 3 in. apart excluding the carpet (a bit closer for thin carpet).

CARPET STRIPS

3"

3/8" PLYWOOD BASE

Align a patio screen door

There you are, balancing a tray full of burgers fresh from the grill, struggling to open the sticking patio screen door. Badly aligned rollers cause the screen door to bind and stick when it's opened or closed. Eventually this stresses the corner joints of the door, and if they open or loosen up, the door is shot. But you can adjust the door to run smoothly in minutes with just a screwdriver.

You'll find two adjustment screws at the bottom of the door, one at each end, that lift and lower separate rollers. Inspect the rollers for damage. First lower the door to the track (Photo 1), then raise it evenly (Photo 2).

Still runs rough? Clean the track. Chances are, leaves, grit or other debris is clogging it.

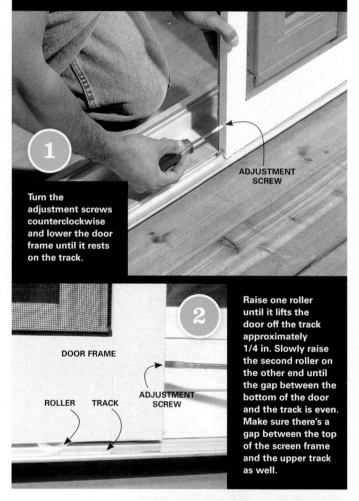

1 ADJUSTMENT SCREW

Turn the adjustment screws counterclockwise and lower the door frame until it rests on the track.

2 DOOR FRAME

ADJUSTMENT SCREW

ROLLER TRACK

Raise one roller until it lifts the door off the track approximately 1/4 in. Slowly raise the second roller on the other end until the gap between the bottom of the door and the track is even. Make sure there's a gap between the top of the screen frame and the upper track as well.

Install a door with corner cleats

To install an interior prehung door, a slick trick is to screw cleats across the two upper corners, and a 1x4 cleat across the opening a foot above the floor. Pushing the doorjamb against those cleats will ensure that it's parallel to the wall. If you shim out the cleats with a few sheets of heavy paper, the jamb will stay slightly proud to the drywall, so that the door casing fits nice and snug.

GOUGED-OUT HOLE

FENDER WASHER

Bifold doorknob fix

You're supposed to mount hollow-core bifold doorknobs along the edge closest to the hinge because that area is reinforced with solid wood. But that's also a "pinch zone," so many people mount the knobs in the middle of the hollow section. Eventually the screw head pulls through the thin veneer and the knob dangles out the front side. The fix is easy. Just buy a 3/16-in. x 1-in. fender washer at any hardware store. Remove the screw. Slide the washer down to the screw head and reinstall.

Tighten a rattling door

A loose, rattling door can be nerve-racking. Most strike plates have an adjustment tab to solve that problem. Unscrew the strike plate from the door. Bend the small tab toward the latch bolt opening. If the door continues to rattle, you might have to remove the plate and bend the tab several times to get it just right. If the door latch doesn't catch when you close the door, bend it back until the door latches tightly.

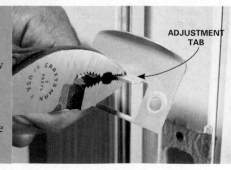

ADJUSTMENT TAB

Floors

7 tips for floor prep

When you're about to lay a new floor, you have the perfect opportunity to upgrade your subfloor to make it solid and squeak-free. While the specifics might vary a bit depending on your new flooring material, consider these issues:

- **Deflection/stiffness.** If you find soft spots in your floor or areas that "give" as you walk across them, stiffen them by adding framing from below or more underlayment on top. Ceramic tile floors require extra stiffness to keep grout lines from cracking.
- **Squeaks.** Drive screws through the subfloor into joists to eliminate the wood movement that causes squeaks. Use adhesive as well as screws to fasten new underlayment.

- **Bounce.** If the dinner plates rattle every time you walk across your kitchen floor, you're getting too much vibration or bounce. Corrections must be made from below.
- **Flatness.** Now's the time to level off high spots and fill low areas so your new floor runs true.
- **Surface flaws.** Some flooring, like vinyl, linoleum and carpeting, requires perfectly smooth subfloors or underlayments. Otherwise, every flaw will show through in the surface.
- **Moisture in concrete.** Always check the moisture level in concrete before laying flooring over it. Trapped moisture will ruin the floor and encourage mold.
- **Asbestos.** Asbestos, a proven carcinogen, was used in many types of flooring and adhesives. While old flooring isn't hazardous if left undisturbed, don't rip it out unless you know it's asbestos-free. Call your local health department for instructions about how to collect a sample and have it tested for asbestos.

5 tips for adding new floors

The next time you're thinking about adding a new floor, consider these potential problems:

- Will all the appliances fit? Pay careful attention to the refrigerator if it has a cabinet directly over it with minimum clearance.
- What about the transition from one room to another? A difference of 1/2 in. to 3/4 in. is usually acceptable, but steeper transitions can look awkward and pose a tripping hazard.
- If the floor adjoins a staircase, are the stair risers still consistent? Too much buildup on the floor can make the lower or upper step height dangerously different from the rest. Most building codes mandate that no step on a staircase

vary in height by more than 3/8 in. from the rest.
- Door heights can be affected as well. Interior doors can be cut fairly easily, but you usually can't cut off an exterior door at all, much less raise a threshold. And there may be no room for a "mud" rug under the door as it swings into the room.
- Consider the toe-kick space under the cabinets. It should be greater than 3 in. or you could get your work boots caught between the floor and the cabinet.

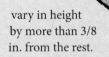

TRIM SCREW

Patch a chip in laminate flooring

Drop a knife or other sharp-edged item and you'll get an instant chip in your laminate floor. But you don't need to call in a pro, because this repair is strictly DIY. If you have the chip or an extra plank, take it to a home center and match it up with a tube of laminate floor patching material. You may have to buy the two closest colors and mix them to match. While you're there, buy a matching brand of cleaning solvent.

Clean the flooring with the solvent and let it dry. Next, squeeze a dollop of filler onto a scrap piece of flooring or a mixing board and mix it (Photo 1). Then press a shallow layer into the chip. Don't try to fill the entire chip in one application. Clean off any excess with solvent. Let the first coat set for one hour before applying the next.

After the filler hardens, use a knife and markers to add grain pattern (Photo 2).

1

WORK THE FILLER UNTIL IT STIFFENS, THEN APPLY: Blend two colors together or knead a single color with a putty knife until it begins to stiffen.

2

ADD GRAIN TEXTURE: Duplicate the grain pattern by making small cuts with a knife. Darken the cuts with furniture touch-up markers.

Silence a squeaky floor

To fix a squeaky floor under carpet, locate the floor joists with a stud finder, then drive in a trim head screw through the carpet, pad and subfloor, and right into the floor joist.

Be sure the top inch of the screw doesn't have threads or the subfloor won't suck down tight to the joist. We like trim screws because screws with larger heads pull down and pucker the carpet. If that happens, back out the screw and drive it back down. Keep adding screws until the squeak stops.

Rent a walk-behind floor scraper

Some old vinyl sheet or tile floors are super easy to pull up. Others are so thoroughly glued down that you're lucky to remove quarter-size chunks with every whack of your handheld floor scraper. If a shovel and hand scraper are just not getting the job done, rent a walk-behind scraper. You can save yourself a bunch of time and prevent a whole lot of wear and tear on your back and wrists. Many floor scrapers have an attachment for busting up ceramic tiles as well.

Walls and ceilings

Vacuum while you cut

If you're cutting or drilling drywall, you'll have to drag out the vacuum sooner or later anyway. So do it now and suck up the dust before it spreads. If your plans include lots of drywall dust, consider buying a HEPA filter, which will catch even the smallest particles. Standard paper filters trap only the larger particles while your vacuum blasts the rest throughout your house.

ADJUSTABLE SUPPORT ARM

Quick fix for drywall holes

Before self-adhesive drywall patches were invented, fixing holes in drywall and plaster involved sliding a wood backer behind the hole, attaching it with screws, and then cutting a patch to fit. With drywall repair patches, it's as easy as sticking on a Band-Aid.

Just stick the self-adhesive patch over the hole and cover it with joint compound. The perforations in the patch allow the joint compound to ooze through, creating a stronger patch and better bond. The patches are available in 4-, 6- and 8-in. squares.

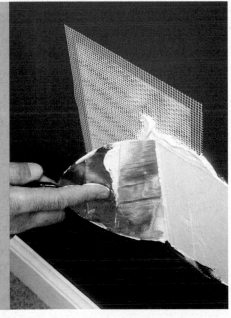

Lifts work for walls, too

A lift works on upper wall sheets just as well as it does on ceilings. After loading the drywall, push the lift to the wall, position the sheet, tip the top edge against the wall and crank it snugly against the ceiling.

Measure tight but cut loose

Putting drywall up and then taking it down to shave an edge that won't fit is a waste of energy, especially if you're alone. Instead, subtract 1/4 in. from your measurements to make up for rough cuts and wavy walls. It's easier to fill slight gaps with joint compound than to struggle with a tight fit.

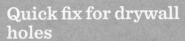

Capture dust at the source

Painting a room almost always involves some wall patching and sanding. And you know what a mess that dust can be! For less than $20, you can practically eliminate the problem with a dustless drywall sanding attachment for your shop vacuum. They're available with a 6-ft. hose and adapters to simplify the connection to your vacuum cleaner.

Tips for a quieter ceiling

How much time and effort you spend on soundproofing depends on what your goal is. Preventing the deep bass of a home theater from rocking the whole house is complicated and expensive. But if you're just looking to quiet footsteps from the floor above or reduce the impact of your teenager's video game, then there are a few simple steps you can take. If you do nothing else, consider adding fiberglass batts to the joist spaces. Anything will help. You can add a 3-1/2-in. layer, or better yet, fill the joist spaces with fiberglass.

For even more noise reduction, isolate the ceiling drywall from the joists with resilient channels as shown here. Screw the channels to the joists, spacing them 12 or 16 in. apart (ask your building inspector what's required). Then screw the drywall to the channels, being careful not to drive screws into the joists. This creates a "floating ceiling" that reduces sound transmission. You may have to visit a drywall supplier to find resilient channels.

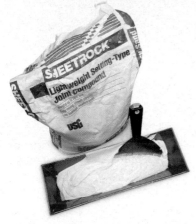

Quick-setting mud for speedy repairs

It's a good idea to keep a bag of this 20-minute setting-type joint compound around for patching and repairs. It's great for small jobs because it sets up fast enough for you to apply two or three coats in a few hours.

Unlike regular joint compound, which has to dry to harden, this stuff hardens by a chemical reaction that starts when you add the water. And within 15 or 20 minutes, it's hard enough to shape with a rasp or coarse sandpaper, and recoat. It's also handy for filling holes that are too deep to fill with regular joint compound. You'll find 20-minute joint compound at home centers and drywall suppliers.

STAIN

PLASTIC

BLEACH AND WATER MIXTURE

Bleach away a water stain

Do you have a water stain on your ceiling? Before you start painting or respraying, try this fix: spray it with bleach and water solution (10 percent bleach), and wait a day or two. If it's an old stain, try a mold and mildew remover. You'd be surprised how often this takes care of the problem. It works on both flat and textured ceilings.

Wear safety goggles, and make sure you protect the walls and floors with plastic.

Hide a hole with a smoke detector

From the quick and dirty department: A small hole in a ceiling can take a lot of time to fix, since anything bigger than a nail hole will need a few coats of compound, sanding, priming and painting. And you may even have to paint the whole ceiling to make it blend in. If you don't have the time right now, just cover it with a smoke detector. You may need one anyway.

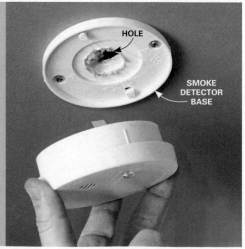

HOLE

SMOKE DETECTOR BASE

How to avoid 7 ugly drywall mistakes

HERE ARE THE MISTAKES TO AVOID

6. Joining pieces at the corner of a door

5. Creating extra joints by using small pieces

4. Cutting for a "too-tight" fit

3. Forcing drywall over outlet boxes (three occurrences in photo)

1. Leaving out backers at inside corners

2. Forgetting to mark framing before installing the drywall

7. Installing tapered edges along corners

① Framing at inside corners is often inadequate or lacking altogether, making it impossible to fasten the edge of the drywall.

The solution is to inspect the framing before you start hanging drywall. Make sure there's at least 1 in. of exposed framing at corners. If not, add another 2x4 alongside the existing framing (photo right). Especially check along the top of walls that run parallel to the ceiling framing. Normally blocking is nailed to the top plate of the wall during the framing phase, but it's often missing. If you have to add blocking and don't have room to swing a hammer, drive screws into the blocking at an angle from below.

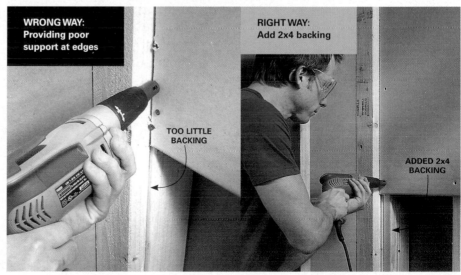

WRONG WAY: Providing poor support at edges

TOO LITTLE BACKING

RIGHT WAY: Add 2x4 backing

ADDED 2x4 BACKING

WRONG WAY:
Guessing at framing locations

NO FRAMING MARKS

SCREWS MISS

RIGHT WAY:
Mark the framing

LIGHT PENCIL MARK

JOIST CENTER MARK

2 If you forget to mark the location of framing members before you cover them with drywall, you'll have a hard time placing the screws accurately (top left). For foolproof screw placement, make these marks and use them as a guide to draw a light pencil line across the sheet (top right). Then you'll be able to place screws quickly and accurately. And you won't have to waste time removing screws that miss the framing.

Mark the location of ceiling joists on the top plate of the wall framing. Then mark the center of each stud on the floor. Make note of unusual framing so you'll know where to place screws after it's covered with drywall. After the ceiling drywall is hung, mark the stud locations on the ceiling with a pencil before you start to hang drywall on the walls.

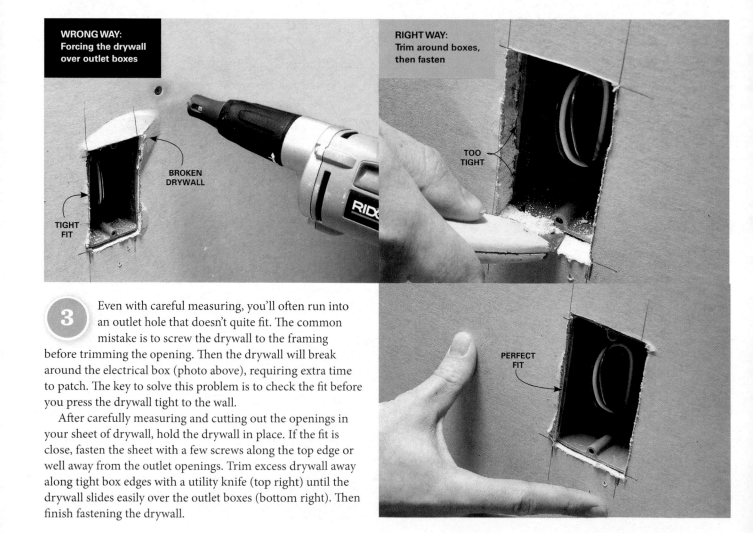

WRONG WAY:
Forcing the drywall over outlet boxes

BROKEN DRYWALL

TIGHT FIT

RIGHT WAY:
Trim around boxes, then fasten

TOO TIGHT

PERFECT FIT

3 Even with careful measuring, you'll often run into an outlet hole that doesn't quite fit. The common mistake is to screw the drywall to the framing before trimming the opening. Then the drywall will break around the electrical box (photo above), requiring extra time to patch. The key to solve this problem is to check the fit before you press the drywall tight to the wall.

After carefully measuring and cutting out the openings in your sheet of drywall, hold the drywall in place. If the fit is close, fasten the sheet with a few screws along the top edge or well away from the outlet openings. Trim excess drywall away along tight box edges with a utility knife (top right) until the drywall slides easily over the outlet boxes (bottom right). Then finish fastening the drywall.

4 There's no reason to measure and cut drywall for an exact fit. It'll usually just cause trouble. Jamming in a piece that's too tight will crumble the edge or break out a corner (first photo at right). And removing a piece to shave a too-tight edge is messy and time consuming. A loose fit avoids this problem. Cut it to leave about a 1/8-in. gap at edges. In fact, when you're hanging the ceiling, keep in mind that 1/2 in. along the perimeter will be covered by drywall on the walls. And the same is true of inside wall corners. So you can safely cut these pieces 1/4 in. less than the actual measurement and leave a gap in the corner if necessary. Even a piece whose edges aren't covered should be cut a little short. It's easier to fill a 1/8-in. gap with setting-type compound than to cut and repair a broken edge or corner.

WRONG WAY: Cutting for a tight fit

TOO TIGHT

RIGHT WAY: Leave 1/8-in. gaps at edges

1/8" GAP

1/8" GAP

WRONG WAY: Creating unnecessary joints

8' SHEET OF DRYWALL

BUTT JOINT

8' SHEET OF DRYWALL

BUTT JOINT

RIGHT WAY: Use the longest sheet possible

12' SHEET OF DRYWALL

12' SHEET OF DRYWALL

5 Taping drywall is time consuming and tedious enough without adding extra joints, especially those hard-to-tape butt joints (photo left). So plan your job to use the longest and largest sheets possible. And don't scrimp on materials. Drywall is cheap.

If the walls you're planning to drywall are between 8 ft. 1 in. and 9 ft. 1 in. tall, consider ordering special 54-in.-wide sheets of drywall to avoid an extra horizontal joint. You'll find 54-in.-wide drywall at drywall suppliers, or you can special-order it from most home centers and lumberyards. You'll also speed up

your job by using 12-ft.-long sheets of drywall rather than standard 8-footers (photo right). However, hauling 12-ft. sheets is difficult and getting them into the house can be challenging. For large jobs, have the drywall delivered. Many drywall suppliers will even stack the drywall in the house for an extra fee.

BAD
JOINT
LOCATION

NO
JOINT

NOTCH
AROUND
DOOR

6 Avoid lining up a sheet of drywall with the edge of a door or window opening (photo left). Your home tends to shift and settle slightly, and that movement shows up at the corners of windows and doors. A joint at this location, even if it's well taped, is weaker than solid

drywall. Chances are it'll crack in the future.

It's better to notch drywall around openings rather than to make a joint. For interior walls, simply continue over the opening with a full sheet and cut out the opening after you fasten the sheet (photo right). Windows on exterior walls

are a little trickier. Measure and notch the sheet before hanging it. Get help when hanging notched sheets because the skinny section above the opening is often fragile. It's OK to join sheets over an opening (and often easier if you're working alone) as long as the joint isn't in line with either side.

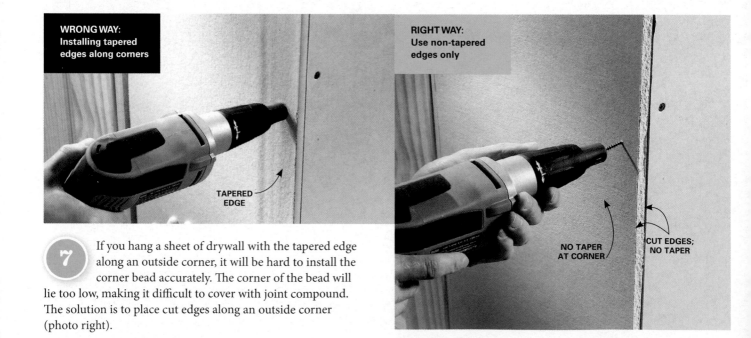

TAPERED
EDGE

NO TAPER
AT CORNER

CUT EDGES;
NO TAPER

7 If you hang a sheet of drywall with the tapered edge along an outside corner, it will be hard to install the corner bead accurately. The corner of the bead will lie too low, making it difficult to cover with joint compound. The solution is to place cut edges along an outside corner (photo right).

Pro tips for better trim

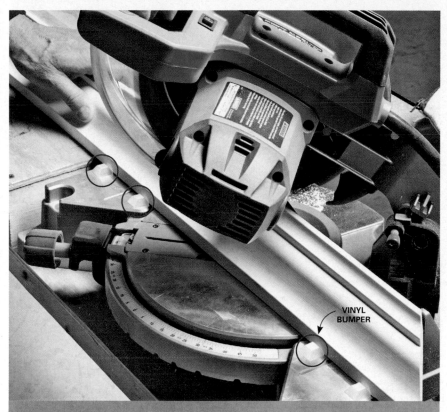

VINYL
BUMPER

Clever crown molding cutting guides

Installing crown molding? Here's an easy way to lock it into position on your miter saw using self-stick vinyl bumpers. Position the molding and stick bumpers to each side of the table and you're ready to go! The bumpers will last all weekend with amazing sticking power. When the project is finished, pull off the bumpers and the saw is ready for your next handyman task.

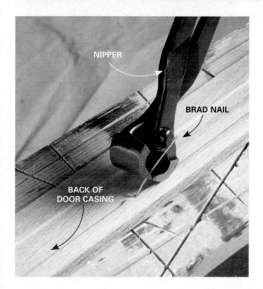

NIPPER

BRAD NAIL

BACK OF
DOOR CASING

Pull nails with a nipper

If you're replacing windows, doors or flooring and you want to salvage the trim, end-nipper pliers are a handy tool to pull out brads and finish nails. The rounded end provides plenty of leverage, and if the nail breaks, you can always cut it down flush. Don't squeeze too hard when gripping the nail, or you may nip it off prematurely.

No framing— no problem

Once in a while, you may need to attach moldings where there's no framing behind the drywall to nail into. For example, if you're making frames on your wall out of moldings, it's likely that one of the vertical moldings won't have a stud behind it. The solution is to apply a thin bead of panel adhesive or construction adhesive and then tack the molding to the wall with a nail gun. For a better grip, shoot a pair of nails next to each other and at opposite angles so they form a wedge. If nails alone won't hold the molding, press it tight with 1x2s wedged against the opposite wall or the ceiling to hold it until the adhesive dries.

Nail, finish, fill, finish

For natural trim and woodwork, it's best to wait until the first coats of stain and varnish are on the wood before you fill nail holes. That way the wood is close to its finish shade and color, and it's sealed so putty stays only in the hole. Get several shades of putty and mix them until they match the wood.

Cope moldings with a drum sander

Use a drum sander in a hand drill to quickly create perfectly coped inside corners on molding. First, nail one molding piece in the corner so the end meets flush with the wall. Next, cut a 45-degree miter (if the corner is 90 degrees) on the corner end of the second molding piece, then clamp it to a steady work surface. With a coarse-grit sanding sleeve in an electric drill, sand away the mitered end. Be careful to sand only to the line, running the drum back and forth along the joint line to ensure a smooth contour. If your molding has intricate curves, use a rotary tool with a small drum sander to finish these areas. Test-fit, resand as necessary and nail on the second piece.

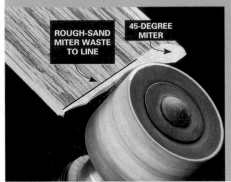

ROUGH-SAND MITER WASTE TO LINE

45-DEGREE MITER

FINISH-SAND TO LINE WHILE BEVELING UNDERCUT SLIGHTLY

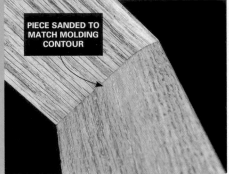

PIECE SANDED TO MATCH MOLDING CONTOUR

Shim with a screw

If there's a gap, sometimes a drywall screw is the perfect adjustable shim. For example, when you're applying baseboard, the drywall at floor level often tapers back, making it hard to get the baseboard corners to line up well. A couple of screws driven into the bottom of the wall will quickly solve the problem, and do it a lot faster than filling the area with joint compound.

Glue baseboard to follow a hollow

Walls sometimes have gentle hollows that are not apparent to the eye, making it hard to attach trim without leaving a gap. If the trim is at all flexible, you can apply construction adhesive to the top and bottom edges and then figure out a way to apply pressure to it. A 2x4 against the floor works for crown, and for baseboard you can cut a couple of scraps and nail them to the floor at an angle.

Burnish an outside miter to close it

Sometimes just the act of nailing a miter joint causes it to open slightly. If the gap isn't too big, you can close it by rubbing a smooth metal tool hard against the corner. This crushes the wood fibers inward. Just about any tool will work, like the utility knife shown, or the round shank of a screwdriver.

SCRIBING TIPS

Wainscoting: Fit a board to a corner that's not plumb. Use a level to hold the board plumb. Set the compass for the widest gap and scribe the line. Saw or plane away the wood to the outside of the line.

Shelving: Fit a shelf to a corner that's not square. Slide the shelf into the corner, keeping the long back edge tight to the wall. If the shelf fits between two walls, cut it about 1/2 in. too long and set it in at an angle. Run a pencil along the wall to scribe the line. Saw along the line. Repeat the process on the opposite end of the shelf.

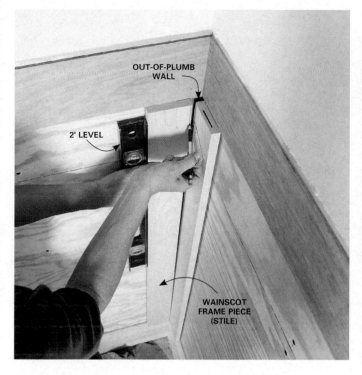

OUT-OF-PLUMB WALL

2' LEVEL

WAINSCOT FRAME PIECE (STILE)

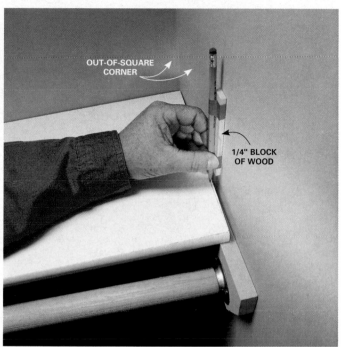

OUT-OF-SQUARE CORNER

1/4" BLOCK OF WOOD

Window stools: Notch your window stool and set it in place. Measure the gap between the back edge of the stool and the window and set your compass for 1/16 in. less than this measurement. Run your compass along the wall behind each end of the stool. Saw or file away the material to the lines.

Irregular edges: Scribing helps you fit a cabinet side, paneling or molding to irregular surfaces like brick. First support the paneling or molding so its edge is plumb. Then set the compass a little wider than the widest gap and scribe the line. Be careful to hold the compass perpendicular to the surface being scribed.

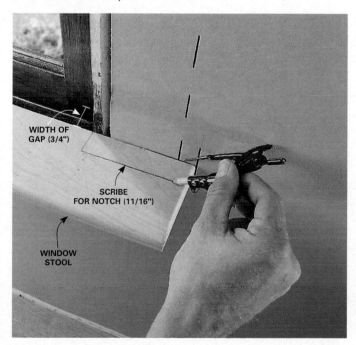

WIDTH OF GAP (3/4")

SCRIBE FOR NOTCH (11/16")

WINDOW STOOL

HOLD COMPASS SQUARE

Chapter Eight

SAFER HOME AND FAMILY

Generators and emergency equipment

Buy a standby generator if you can afford it

Portable generators are great in a pinch, but they're often noisy and they require frequent refueling. They also have to be stored when not in use, and connected and started when the power goes out.

A standby generator is permanently connected to your home's electrical system and goes on automatically when the power goes out, providing seamless power. Standby generators can run on propane or natural gas, eliminating the need to monitor the fuel. And they're quieter.

You can buy one large enough to power everything in your house, or you can buy a smaller unit and choose the most critical circuits to power. Standby generators start at about $1,800, plus installation. (And they do need to be installed by a pro.)

The difference in cost between a portable generator and a standby unit may not be as great as you think. Remember, a portable unit requires either expensive extension cords or a transfer switch. Standby units can run on less expensive natural gas, which will save you money in the long run.

Buy a generator you can get serviced locally

You may find a great deal on a generator by shopping online. But what will you do if you can't get it serviced locally? Sometimes it's worth spending a little extra to buy from a local dealer. Parts will be available, and the dealer will be familiar with maintenance and repair procedures for your model. So before you buy a generator, make sure there's someone nearby who can provide parts and service.

Propane is easier than gas

When it comes to portable generators and ease of use, liquid propane (LP) sure beats gasoline. Gasoline is a handy fuel, but it's not without problems. Storing enough gasoline to get you through a several-day power outage requires constant vigilance. First you have to buy several 5-gallon gas containers and find a safe place to store them. Then you have to add stabilizer and ideally replace the gas after several months to make sure it's still fresh when you need it.

Propane-powered portable generators solve these problems and more. You can store and use liquid propane (LP) indefinitely (it doesn't go bad). Refueling is simple and safe; just replace the propane tank with a full one. And you don't have to worry about the carburetor on your generator getting gummed up with old gasoline. Search online for "propane generators" to see what's available.

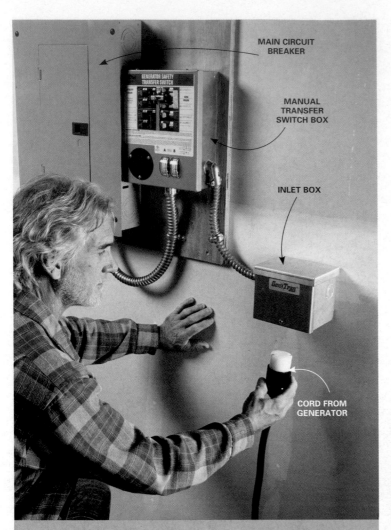

MAIN CIRCUIT BREAKER

MANUAL TRANSFER SWITCH BOX

INLET BOX

CORD FROM GENERATOR

Furnaces, well pumps and electric water heaters require a transfer switch

You can use extension cords from your portable generator to power any device with a plug, but anything that's directly connected to your home's wiring, including essentials like your well pump, furnace and electric water heater, requires a transfer switch.

A manual transfer switch is essentially a small circuit breaker box that you mount next to your main electrical panel. You match the capacity of the transfer switch to the wattage of your generator. Then you choose which circuits to connect to the transfer switch. The manual transfer switch shown here came prewired for six circuits and included the inlet box (generator connection) and the cord to connect the generator.

A transfer switch is the only safe way to connect your generator to house wiring because it requires you to disconnect the house wiring from the incoming power lines at the same time you switch to generator power. This prevents the possibility of "backfeeding" generated power into the power lines, which creates a potentially lethal hazard for power line workers.

Connecting a manual transfer switch is an advanced electrical project. An electrician should be able to complete an installation similar to the one shown here in about three hours.

Add up your watts—then add extra for motor start-up

If you're the adventurous type, you can just go with our recommendation of a 5,500-watt generator (see p. 159) and make the best of it. But if you really want to know what size generator you need to power everything you want, then the only way is to add up the wattage of all the lights, appliances and motors that you intend to run simultaneously.

Generator manufacturers and resellers have charts you can refer to that list the average wattage used for various appliances and motors. Or you can check the nameplates on the appliances you want to power. If wattage isn't listed, you can derive it by multiplying volts by amps. For example, if the plate lists 2.5 amps at 120 volts, multiply the two to get 300 watts.

There's one caveat, though. Motors require an extra surge of electricity to get started, and you have to factor this into the equation. Add up the wattage of everything you want to run. Then determine the largest motor you need to run (the furnace, for example), multiply the wattage requirement by 2 to get the approximate start-up wattage required, and add this number to the total.

Buy gas cans when you buy the generator

A 5,500-watt generator will run about eight hours on 5 gallons of gasoline, so gas management is critical if you want to be prepared for an extended power outage. That may mean running your generator for shorter periods and coasting on things like refrigeration.

Having several filled 5-gallon gas cans available is prudent, but you'll need to add stabilizer to extend the shelf life. Even then, after six months or so you should pour it into your car's gas tank and refill the cans with fresh fuel. The generator itself should be run dry for storage or filled with stabilized fuel. That fuel should be replaced every six months as well.

A good size for emergency backup is 5,500 watts

If you're shopping for a portable generator—that is, one on wheels that's not permanently connected to your home's electrical system—a generator that supplies 5,500 watts is about the right size. This is enough to power a few critical appliances like a refrigerator, furnace, microwave, TV and some lights.

Of course, you can't run a whole-house air conditioner and an electric water heater at the same time with 5,500 watts, but a generator this size will get you by until the power comes back on. You can buy a good-quality 5,500-watt generator for about $700.

HONDA

Don't wreck your TV with a cheap generator

Computers, TVs and many modern appliances contain sensitive electronics that can be damaged by the "dirty" power produced by less expensive generators. Inverter-type generators provide the cleanest power but are very expensive, especially in sizes large enough to power a house. But for a little extra money, you can buy generators with power conditioning that provides cleaner power. Total Harmonic Distortion (THD) is a way to measure the quality of electricity from a generator. Look for a generator with a THD of less than 5 percent to safely operate most electronics.

You can buy a quiet generator— but it'll cost more

One problem with portable generators is the noise that you—and your neighbors—have to put up with. You can compare decibel ratings to find quieter models, but keep in mind that there's no industry standard, so you may be comparing apples and oranges. Standby generators are quieter, and for a stiff premium you can buy a really quiet portable generator like the 6,500-watt model shown here. It costs around $4,500.

You'll need heavy-duty extension cords

Remember, if you decide not to install a manual transfer switch, you'll need a lot of expensive, heavy-duty extension cords. Using undersize cords presents a fire hazard and can damage motors as well as stress your generator. To run a refrigerator, depending on how energy efficient it is and how far from the generator, you'll need at least a 12-gauge cord. A 50-ft. 12-gauge cord will set you back about $50. Multiply that by five or six and you can see that a transfer switch starts to sound like a better deal.

Coping with natural disasters

Don't get shocked in a flooded basement

The water in a flooded basement probably isn't electrified by your home's electrical lines. But it could be. So instead of finding out the hard way, just consider it an energized pool of instant death until you call your utility company to disconnect your power. Then you can dive in. And after the water is gone, remember that anything electrical in the basement may still be wet, damaged and dangerous. So it's best to leave the basement power off until your utility company or an electrician gives you the OK.

Flooded basement? Turn off the gas

Floodwater and floating junk can lead to damaged gas lines and malfunctioning gas controls. Leaked gas then bubbles up through the water, giving your basement an explosive atmosphere on top of the flood. And the smell of gas may be masked by other floodwater odors. So call the utility company to shut off your gas even if you don't smell it. If you do smell gas, get out of the house before you make the call.

More than half of flood-related drownings involve a vehicle.

Keep your wheels on dry land

Driving through a few inches of water seems safe enough, but it kills people every year. Floodwater hides washouts and the road itself, and you can suddenly find yourself in deep water. In just 6 in. of water, some cars partially float and become hard to control. And any passenger vehicle, even a monster SUV, will become a rudderless barge in 2 ft. of rushing water. When you find a flooded road, better to turn around than risk drowning.

Keep your generator away from the house

A generator is the best thing to have in a blackout. But it can make you black out (or die). Like any internal combustion engine, a generator engine exhausts carbon monoxide gas, which can give you a headache, knock you out or even kill you. This is easy to avoid, though: Don't run a generator in your garage or porch, and keep it at least 10 ft. away from your house.

Hurricane Katrina led to more than 50 cases of carbon monoxide poisoning.

Stay dry in a flooded basement

Furniture isn't the only stuff floating in your basement. Chances are, the water contains chemicals stored downstairs and a dose of sewage that backed up through basement drains. That's not just disgusting, but also a toxic soup that can make you sick. Before you go down there, gear up with rubber boots and gloves to prevent skin contact. Also wear gloves when cleaning up the polluted sludge left by the flood.

Lightning: Don't get struck indoors

Your home is probably the safest place to be in an electrical storm. But lightning can still get to you through the conductive paths in your house; that means your wiring, your plumbing and water. Talking on a corded phone, taking a shower or bath, working on your desktop computer or handling power tools during an electrical storm isn't much safer than standing outside. It's best to stay away from all water and appliances until the storm passes.

Stay out of gushing floodwater

Six inches of floodwater doesn't look dangerous. But if it's moving fast enough, it's enough to sweep you off your feet and carry you into the hereafter. Rushing water also erodes roads and walkways, creating drop-offs that you can't see under the torrent. A long pole, stick or pipe lets you probe for drop-offs and might help you stay on your feet. Still, the smartest move is to stay out of flowing water.

Flooding is the No. 1 cause of weather-related deaths in the United States.

Don't burn down your house

When the power goes out, lots of people light lots of candles. And lots of people burn down their home. There's no good reason for this: Today's LED flashlights and lanterns burn brighter and last longer than candles, without the fire risk.

Candles cause about 15,000 house fires in the United States every year.

A 1-in. hole in your roof can let in a gallon of rainwater every minute. And a few gallons can do thousands of dollars of damage.

First aid for roof damage

Minor roof damage can lead to major water damage inside your home. But if you keep a few simple materials on hand, you can seal most roof injuries in just a few minutes.

A section of flashing is the perfect patch for smaller holes—often caused by blown-down tree branches (photo above). Don't forget to caulk around the hole. Special roof sealant is best, but any type of caulk is better than nothing.

For larger areas, a tarp is the best bandage. But before you spread a tarp, screw plywood over large holes in the roof. Left unsupported, a tarp will sag into a hole, fill with rainwater and possibly leak. If shingles have blown off but there

are no holes in the roof, you can lay the tarp directly over the roof sheathing. Stretch the tarp so it lies smoothly over the roof and batten down the entire perimeter (except the ridge). Just a few inches of loose tarp will allow strong winds to drive in rain or rip the tarp to shreds. Use screws and any type of lumber you have on hand to secure the tarp. Whenever possible, extend the tarp over the roof ridge (Photo 2) so water won't flow down and under it. If there's no way to run the tarp over the ridge, slip sections of flashing under shingles and over the upper edge of the tarp. Then drive nails through both the flashing and the tarp.

FIRST AID KIT FOR YOUR ROOF
A 9 x 12-ft. tarp is big enough to cover a large area but small enough for one person to manage. If you have a large roof, keep two or three of them on hand. Also buy a 14-in. x 10-ft. roll of aluminum flashing.

ROOFS ARE DANGEROUS!
Emergency roof repairs often mean walking on a wet roof and wrestling with tarps, which can catch the wind like a sail. We strongly recommend you wear a roof harness.

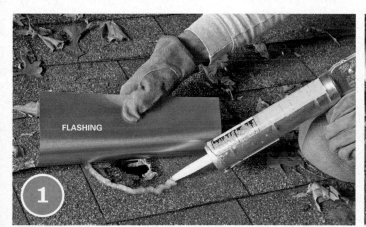

PATCH A SMALL HOLE: Cover a small hole with metal flashing. Slide the flashing under the shingles above the hole, run a heavy bead of caulk around the hole and nail down the exposed corners of the flashing.

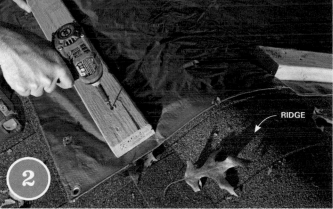

TARP LARGE AREAS: Even if the damage is near the lower end of the roof, extend the tarp over the ridge so water won't run under the tarp. Screw down boards to secure the tarp.

Home security

Don't keep the garage door remote in your car

A thief who breaks into your car can grab the remote for easy access to your garage. This isn't just a problem when your car is parked in the driveway; the registration card in your glove box gives a crook your address.

So get rid of the remote on your visor and buy a keychain remote ($25 and up). You can easily take it with you every time you leave the car. Home centers stock only a small selection of remotes, but you'll find more online. Start your search by typing in the brand of your opener, followed by "remote."

VINYL FENCE PICKET

RON DIPPEL

Sliding door security

Securing a patio door by putting a wooden stick in the track isn't very attractive because it doesn't match the white vinyl. Instead, try a vinyl fence picket. The color is a good match, and you can easily cut it to fit a smaller door.

Automatic door closer

This device allows the door to stay open for a set amount of time, then closes it. You set the timer and can override it on those summer days when you're working in the garage.

New-style lock and shackle laugh at bolt cutters

These days even the dumbest crooks carry bolt cutters. In less than five seconds, they're into your shed and carting off your expensive tools.

Thwart the bums (or at least make them break a sweat) with a high-security hasp and hidden shackle lock. Attach the hasp to your doors with carriage bolts. Then slap on a bump-proof, case-hardened lock. It completely covers the hasp, protecting it from bolt cutters. And crooks can't pry the lock off because it's surrounded by a ring of high-strength steel. Both the lock and the hasp are available online or at home centers.

HASP

LOCK

Add an eye bolt to your concrete projects

When you're pouring new steps, a driveway, a patio or a footing for some other project, embed an eye bolt in the concrete. Place it so it won't interfere with daily foot or vehicle traffic, but also where it's accessible to serve as a secure anchor for hooking up your trailer, generator, motorcycle, grills, bikes and other items. You can find stainless steel and galvanized eye bolts at home centers and marine suppliers (used for dock building). If you don't want to sink a permanent concrete pier, you can buy screw-in ground anchoring products instead.

Know who's there

Install a wide-angle door viewer so you always know who's at your door. The one shown here is available at hardware stores and home centers. To install, just drill a hole from each side and screw it in.

WIDE-ANGLE DOOR VIEWER

Use the shortest chain possible

Don't use an overly long chain or cable to lock your bikes and other stuff. Slack in a chain makes it easy for a thief to pry off the chain or smash the lock.

Protecting home and family

Stop water vandalism

We heard a terrible story recently. A family went on vacation and while they were gone, vandals stuck the end of a garden hose through their mail slot, turned on the hose and flooded their house! If you're leaving your house empty for a long period of time, it's a good idea to turn off the water.

A slight turn of the dial makes water heaters safer

Plain old tapwater can be dangerous. Water heaters set too high send thousands (mostly children) to hospitals each year with burns. Most safety experts recommend a setting of 120 degrees F. But finding that setting on the dial isn't easy—most dials aren't labeled with numbers. If the stickers on the water heater don't tell you how to set the temperature and you can't find the owner's manual, use this method: Run hot water at the tap closest to the water heater for at least three minutes. Then fill a glass and check the temperature. If the water is above 120 degrees, adjust the dial, wait about three hours and check again. Repeat until you get 120-degree water. For a final test, check the temperature the following morning, before anyone uses hot water.

COOKING THERMOMETER

TEMPERATURE DIAL

Test your sump pump before the beginning of the rainy season

The most common time for a sump pump to fail is the first heavy rainfall after months of not being used. The submerged or partially submerged portions of cast iron pumps can rust and seize. And they'll burn out when they switch on. Don't get caught with your pump down and the water rising. After a long dry (unused) spell, pour a bucket or two of water into the sump to make sure the pump kicks on.

Chimney fires destroy homes

Creosote buildup may not look dangerous, but it ignites at a mere 451 degrees F, and once it starts burning, it expands like foam sealant. In less than a minute, it builds to more than 2,000 degrees F and can engulf your entire chimney and destroy your home.

Even if you clean your chimney regularly, you should still have it inspected by a qualified chimney sweep once a year. Certified chimney sweeps are trained to recognize chimney deterioration and venting problems and can assess your chimney's condition.

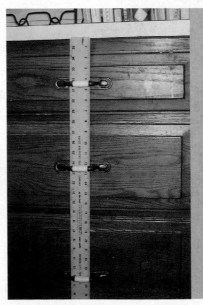

Safety in a second

If toddlers visit your home only occasionally, you don't have to mar your cabinetry with a safety latch to make it childproof. Keep a set of drawers from being opened by sliding a yardstick through the handles. Now the kids are safe and you didn't have to buy a special safety latch or get out your drill.

5 THINGS TO CHECK BEFORE A ROAD TRIP

It's time for the beloved family road trip and everybody's itching to get going. Better do a quick check of your car's health first. Some discoveries can prevent "towable" experiences; others are safety issues. It would be best to run through this five-minute checklist a week ahead of departure so you'll have time to get the car repaired if a mechanic is needed.

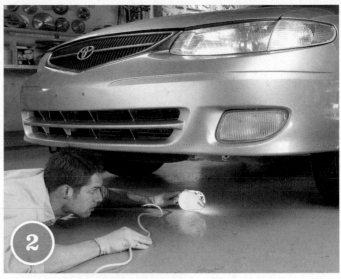

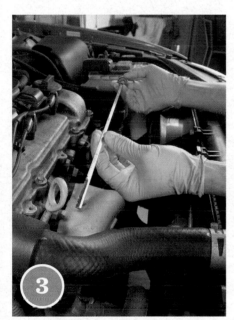

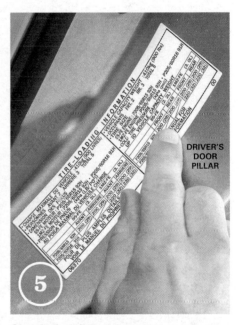

Check the condition of all belts. Broken belts are one of the most common reasons for roadside assistance calls. Replacement belts are easy to locate and replace near your home. But the belt for your car may be tough to find in rural areas. Twist the belt slightly to expose cracks or glazing. Replace any belt that is cracked, worn or delaminating.

Check for fluid leaks. Small leaks often turn into gushers once you leave town, and that can be costly. The most common sources are the radiator, engine oil pan, transmission oil pan and hoses, power steering hoses, steering rack, and heater and radiator hoses. Use a flashlight to check for leaks. Note the color of the fluid and trace the fluid trails back to their source.

Check and top off all fluids. With the engine off, check power steering fluid, brake fluid, coolant, windshield washer and engine oil. Most automatic transmissions must be checked with the engine hot and running and the gearshift in "park." Check your owner's manual to confirm. Look for the power steering fluid level to reach the COLD mark on the dipstick. If it's low, check your owner's manual and buy the right fluid for your vehicle.

Check all exterior lights. They're easy to check, and inexpensive to replace. Bulb numbers and replacement procedures are listed in your owner's manual. Turn the key to the "accessories" position (there's no need to start the engine). Operate the turn signals, brake lights and backup lights, and check for reflections in your rearview mirror. Perform the same checks on the front turn signal lights, headlights, high beams and running lights.

Check the tire pressure. Low tire air pressure causes engines to burn more gas and tires to wear faster and run hotter. Hot tires are more prone to blowout during extended highway drives. Check them all (including the spare) before you leave town. Look for the correct air pressure on the decal located on either the driver's door or the door pillar or check your owner's manual. Make sure the tires are cold when you check tire pressure.

TIPS FOR OUTSIDE THE HOUSE

1 **No place to hide.** Trimming back shrubs and other plantings near the house deprives prowlers of a place to hide. Strategically placed thorny plants—a hedge of rosebushes ringing the perimeter of the house, for example—can also be a deterrent. Consider putting gravel on pathways and under windows to prevent an intruder from approaching silently.

2 **Down and out.** Protect basement windows with metal grates or bars or specially designed plastic bubbles. However, check local building and fire codes before blocking the exit from any window.

6 **Get a good look.** Install a wide-angle peephole on the entry door.

7 **Install dead bolt locks** on all exterior doors, and on doors leading to the basement and the garage. If double-cylinder dead bolts are used, always keep a key within easy reach of the door to prevent being trapped in a fire.

8 **The strong, solid type.** Make sure all exterior doors are solid-core to provide strength against intruders.

3 **Window of opportunity?** Secure ground-level double-hung windows with keyed pin locks. Also install these locks on any upper-level double-hung windows that are accessible from garage roofs, shed roofs, etc.

4 **Bulk up the doors.** Secure bulkhead-type basement doors from the underside with sliding crossbars. Recess the hinge barrels in concrete to protect them.

5 **Show them the door.** Placing lights on both sides of the entrance door should provide ample nighttime illumination, even if one light fails. For added security, consider converting at least one light on the front of your house to an emergency light, which flashes on and off when you flip the light switch twice. When the switch is flipped once, it functions as a regular light. Easy-to-install emergency light kits are available at hardware stores.

9 **Moving targets.** Motion-detecting lights go on when someone approaches the house and enters the sensory field. Install them on your house's exterior so they illuminate areas that can't be seen from the street—back and side yards, for example, as well as areas that are screened by shrubs, trees, or other vegetation. Place the lights high enough so they can't be reached without a ladder.

10 **Open-and-shut case.** If you have an automatic garage door opener, consider replacing it with one that has a "rolling code." This defeats the "code grabbing" devices that thieves sometimes possess, and that allow them to access the electronic code that opens your door. To improve security and safety, you can also purchase remote-control devices that will open the garage doors and turn on interior and exterior lights—all without your having to get out of the car.

11 **Don't forget the garage.** Reinforce the panels on wooden garage doors. If there are windows in the doors, consider replacing them with shatterproof glass. When going away for long periods, padlock the garage door track, or if it is an electric door, turn off the power. Garage doors should reverse if they touch anything while closing.

12 **Grounding an intruder.** Use vinyl rather than metal drainpipes, since vinyl is less likely to support a climber. Also, cut back tree limbs that a burglar could use to climb onto the roof. Place trellises and picnic tables away from the house.

13 **Sliding home.** Secure sliding glass doors with keyed pin locks that are screwed into the inside frame. The fixed panel of the door should also be screwed into the frame so it can't be lifted out.

14 **A well-lit path.** Installing low-voltage ground lighting makes outdoor walkways safer at night. Place timers or light sensors on the lights so they go on automatically at dusk.

TIPS FOR INSIDE THE HOUSE

15 **If you smell gas, evacuate the house immediately.** Call the fire department from a neighbor's house with your cell phone—using the landline phone or any appliance can be dangerous when gas is in the air.

16 **Be savvy about smoke.** Install at least one smoke detector on each level of the home, including the basement and attic, and in the garage. If bedrooms are more than 40 ft. apart, place a smoke detector outside each bedroom. Smoke detectors are also needed at the top of stairwells and at the bottom of the basement stairs. Smoke detectors can be part of a whole-house security system that includes protection against break-ins.

17 **And about security.** An electronic security system is a good idea. The most secure are the monitored systems, but unmonitored systems also help protect against burglary. Put a sign in front of the house indicating the presence of an alarm system or a watchdog.

18 **Quick call.** Program the police and fire department numbers into your phone's autodial, and post the numbers on the wall.

19 **Put timers on lights** and possibly on appliances such as the air conditioner, television and radio so you can program them to go on and off while you are away.

20 **Store fire extinguishers** in various locations in the house, most importantly the kitchen, basement and any room where there is a fireplace.

21 **Store valuables in a fireproof, waterproof safe** to protect them from theft, flooding and fire.

22 **A well-planned escape.** Make sure there is a fire escape ladder in each bedroom and in any other frequently used room above the ground floor.

23 **Carbon monoxide alert.** Install a carbon monoxide detector on each level of the house, including the basement and attic, and in the garage. However, do not place a detector near a source of combustion, such as a furnace or gas stove.

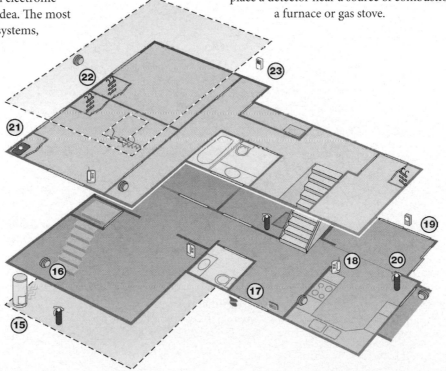

INSTANT FIXES

Silicone repair tape

This tape is unique. It has no adhesive; it's just pure silicone. When you wrap it around something, the silicone essentially welds to itself to form a single flexible unit. No gaps, no slipping and no end to come undone. Silicone tape is amazing stuff: It's an electrical insulator and it resists just about everything (oil, solvents, acids, salt water). It's heat proof to 500 degrees F and flexible at arctic temperatures. Use it to fix electrical cords, wrap cables on a trailer and make a heat-proof grip for a frying pan. There are stories of people using it to make gaskets, repair high-pressure hoses, even make an emergency fan belt by wrapping the tape around rope. In short, it's a miracle worker. It has only one drawback: It ain't cheap. A 12-ft. roll, 1 in. wide, is about 10 bucks. Expensive or not, it's a must-have addition to your toolbox.

Bend the hinge pin

Every time I leave the door to my bedroom slightly ajar, it swings wide open. It's annoying. Do I have to take the door down and adjust the frame?

You're certainly right that the door frame isn't plumb and causes the door to swing open. But before you go through the hassle of disassembling everything, try this trick. Grab a hammer, a few scraps of wood, a large nail and a shim. Take them into the room and close the door. Stick the shim loosely between the door and the jamb to hold the door in position when you drive out the upper hinge pin (Photo 1). Then bend the pin slightly with a firm whack. Reinsert the pin and check the results (Photo 2). If the door still won't stay where you want it, do the same with the lower hinge.

PIN

SHIM

NAIL

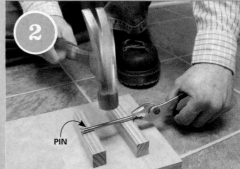

PIN

Bed leg boot

How many times have you stubbed your toe on your metal bed frame? Ouch! Here's a creative way to protect your piggies. Cover the bare metal leg and wheel with a foam beverage can holder. It'll save your toes and prevent carpet dents and hardwood floor scratches to boot!

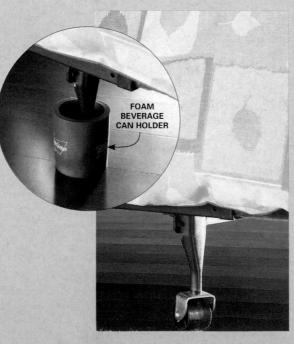

FOAM BEVERAGE CAN HOLDER

Patch holes in aluminum and vinyl siding

All houses gradually accumulate holes in their siding from fasteners and from phone and cable lines. The only way to repair these holes perfectly in vinyl or aluminum is to replace the entire piece—a repair that ranges from challenging in vinyl to almost impossible in old aluminum.

For an easier, nearly-as-good fix that keeps water out and is almost invisible from several feet away, fill the hole with a color-matched caulk. Home centers don't usually stock it, but siding wholesalers that sell to contractors carry caulks specifically blended for dozens of different shades of siding. If you know the manufacturer and color name of your siding, you can get the exact blend developed for that shade. Otherwise, bring a sample piece or take a photo and ask a salesperson to help you match it.

Before filling the hole, wipe the siding clean. Squirt enough caulk into the hole to fill the area behind the hole. Avoid smearing excess caulk all over the surrounding siding—the less you get on the siding, the less obvious the repair will be. Once the caulk is fully cured (which could be several days, depending on the type), trim it even with the siding with a razor blade.

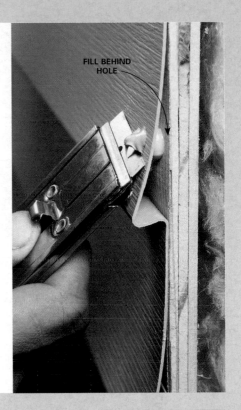

FILL BEHIND HOLE

COLOR-MATCHED CAULK

Trim the hardened caulk flush with the siding using a straightedge razor blade.

Oven won't heat? Check the clock

Blame it on the technology. It so happens that if you set the "time cook" function, the oven, much like a programmed VCR, won't turn on until the appointed time. You may have done this inadvertently, but if your digital display reads "hold," "delay" or "time cook," then the timer is engaged. You'll have to clear it first by pushing the "off" button. On ovens with dials, be sure the knob is turned to "manual."

Pro Tip: "I usually tell the callers right on the phone to check the timer setting. I really don't want to charge them $80 to come out and tell them exactly what's in their owner's manual."

Two turns of a wrench will correct a crooked fridge door

A sagging refrigerator or freezer door doesn't just look bad. It can cause the door gaskets to seal poorly, and that means your fridge will work harder to keep the milk cold. It can also lead to frost buildup in the freezer. To realign the door, just pry off the hinge cap and loosen the hinge screws. Then align the door with the top of the refrigerator. Adjust only the top hinge to straighten an upper door. To realign the lower door, adjust the middle hinge. Moving the middle hinge will affect the upper door, so you may have to adjust the top hinge afterward.

1

LOOSEN

LIFT

2

RETIGHTEN

HINGE

Chapter Nine

CLEANING

Bathroom

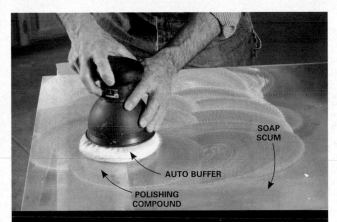

SOAP
SCUM

AUTO BUFFER

POLISHING
COMPOUND

Buff off heavy grime

If you have glass shower doors in your bathroom and don't keep on top of the cleaning, you can end up with soap scum so tough that it's nearly impossible to remove. That's when you bring out the heavy equipment.

Pick up some polishing compound at a home center or an auto parts store and use an auto buffer to polish off the offending scum. If you don't own a buffer, you can buy one for as little as $20 or borrow one from a gearhead friend. If possible, remove the doors and take them out to the garage to avoid messing up the bathroom.

Remove tough grime with less scrubbing

Whether it's built-up soap scum on the shower walls, ground-in dirt on the floor tile, or dried toothpaste on the vanity top, a Magic Eraser sponge will make short work of it. Just dampen it and rub it on the offending mess. In most cases, the mess will come right off. These sponges are especially useful for removing ground-in dirt from porous floor tile and getting those pesky nonslip strips in the bottom of your tub clean.

Magic Eraser sponges are available at grocery stores, hardware stores and wherever cleaning supplies are sold. Unlike regular sponges, they wear out pretty fast, so stock up.

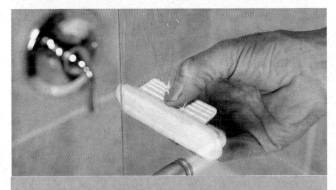

Protect your shower doors from mineral buildup

When the beads of water left on your glass shower door dry out, they leave minerals behind that are at best unsightly, and at worst can be tough as nails to remove if you let them build up (see previous tip). You can avoid beading water altogether by coating the glass with an auto-glass treatment.

We're using Aquapel, but Rain-X will also work. Follow the instructions on the package to apply the treatment to your shower door glass. You can buy autoglass treatments at any auto parts store or online.

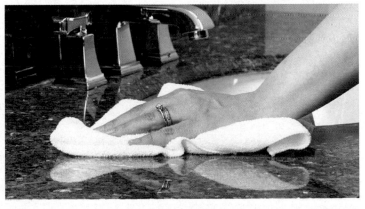

Polish with a microfiber cloth

Microfiber cloths excel at putting the finishing touches on mirrors, countertops, and even tile and fixtures. After cleaning surfaces with your favorite cleaning solution and drying them off with a terry cloth rag or a separate microfiber cloth, polish them to a mirror finish with a dry microfiber cloth.

Microfiber cloths are perfect for this because they pick up dust, wipe off smudges and don't shed any fibers. You'll find microfiber cloths wherever cleaning supplies are sold. You can even buy them in bulk at wholesale clubs and use them throughout your house for all kinds of other cleaning chores.

Best handy hint for simple cleaning

Remove stains from a sink, bathtub or other porcelain fixture by filling the basin with warm water and dropping in denture-cleaning tablets. Use two for a sink or toilet and five for a tub. When the water stops fizzing after about 15 minutes, drain the fixture and lightly scrub. The tablets will remove light grime and help soften heavier buildups for easier cleaning.

Install a detachable toilet seat

It seems like no matter how hard you try, you can never get the hinges on the toilet seat clean. There's always a bit of cleaning solution that seeps underneath and creeps out later. Installing a detachable toilet seat solves the problem. This type of seat is easy to remove by just twisting two hinge caps about a quarter of a turn. Then you have easy access to clean under the hinges. Detachable seats cost about $20. Installation is straightforward and only requires a wrench.

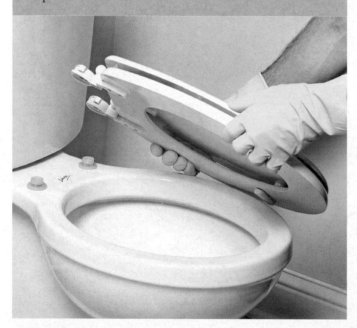

Vacuum first, then scrub

Do you ever find yourself chasing strands of wet hair or running into dust balls in the corners with your sponge or cleaning rag? You can eliminate this nuisance by vacuuming the bathroom before you get out your cleaning solutions.

For a really thorough cleaning, start at the top, vacuuming the dust from light fixtures and the top of window casings. Then work your way down. And finally, vacuum the floor methodically so you cover every inch. You don't want to leave any stray hair or dust bunnies to muck up your cleaning water. A soft-bristle upholstery brush works best for this type of vacuuming.

A scrub and a wax

Keep fixtures looking new. Every three months, use calcium, lime and rust remover and an old toothbrush to clean all the faucets and lavatories. Then apply an automotive car wax and buff after the wax hazes.

Stubborn stuff

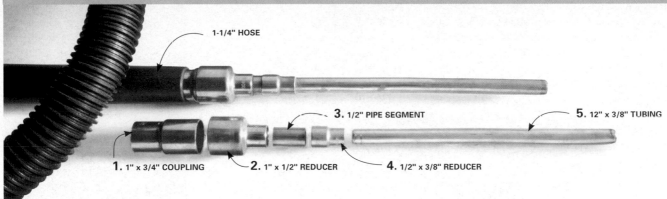

1-1/4" HOSE

3. 1/2" PIPE SEGMENT

5. 12" x 3/8" TUBING

1. 1" x 3/4" COUPLING

2. 1" x 1/2" REDUCER

4. 1/2" x 3/8" REDUCER

Crevice tool from copper fittings

You only need a few copper pipe fittings and short pieces of copper pipe to make this dual-purpose nozzle for your 1-1/4-in. shop vacuum. It'll blow dust like an air compressor nozzle or vacuum the tightest crevice. Just switch the vacuum hose from the exhaust port to the intake port on the vacuum. To make one, you need:

1. A 1-in. x 3/4-in. copper reducing coupling with stop
2. A 1-in. x 1/2-in. copper fitting reducer
3. A 1-in. piece of 1/2-in. inside-diameter copper pipe
4. A 1/2-in. x 3/8-in. copper fitting reducer
5. A 12-in. piece of 3/8-in. soft copper tubing

Glue the parts in the order shown with epoxy or cyanoacrylate glue. Now press-fit the 1-in. outside-diameter copper end into the 1-1/4 in. hose nozzle (the inside diameter is 1 in.) and put it to work. When using the vacuum as a blower, you can either grip the nozzle and hose so the nozzle won't blow out of the hose, or duct-tape the connection.

Remove metal scratches from porcelain

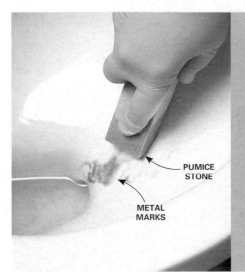

PUMICE STONE

METAL MARKS

You're supposed to use a closet auger to remove toilet clogs. But many DIYers don't have one and use a regular snake. Sure, it works, but it can also leave metal scratches on the bowl. If that happens to you, don't freak out. Just pick up a pumice stone from any home center. Wet the stone and keep it wet while you gently scrub the marks. Don't scrub too hard or you'll scratch the porcelain. And don't be surprised if the stone wears away quickly—that's normal.

Reach cobwebs at the ceiling

If you've got cobwebs, dust or bothersome bugs lurking in the upper reaches of a skylight or ceiling, simply duct tape a length of PVC pipe to the nozzle of your vacuum cleaner nozzle, then clean away.

Easier bottle cleaning

Clean those narrow-necked jars and vases with small gravel (aquarium gravel works the best). Fill one-third of the jar with water. Add a handful of gravel, and then stir and shake the jar. The gravel will scour the inside of the jar clean. Dump the gravel into a strainer, give it a quick rinse (so it doesn't stink!) and save it for next time.

AQUARIUM GRAVEL

Pet repellent for furniture

To train your pets to stay off furniture, place plastic carpet protectors—prickly side up—on their favorite perch. Available in office supply stores and the carpet/flooring department of home centers for a few dollars per ft., the protectors can be cut to the size you need with a scissors or a utility knife. The plastic teeth will train your pet to associate the couch with "uncomfortable." Soon they will seek cozier spots to relax on and leave the easy chair to you. Just remember to remove the protector before you sit down.

COOKING SPRAY

Simple sap remover

If you have a lot of trees on your property, you probably get sap on your hands occasionally. Here's an easy trick to get rid of it: Use cooking spray. Just a small squirt and a quick wipe with a paper towel are all it takes. Keep a can of cooking spray out in your garage. It removes most oil-base paints and primers too.

Cleaners that work

There are five basic types of cleaning chemicals: surfactants, alkalis, acids, solvents and disinfectants. Develop a basic understanding of these and you can pick the right cleaner for any job.

Surfactants, found in almost every cleaning product, help carry the ingredients into tiny cracks and pores. They also help loosen, emulsify (disperse in water) and suspend soils for removal.

Alkalis, which have a pH higher than 7, are best at removing (neutralizing) acidic soils, which have a pH less than 7. Alkalis chew up acidic fats and oils (from hamburger grease to body oil to plain old mud), breaking them into smaller particles that can be washed away. Alkaline cleaners range from mild liquid dishwashing detergent and glass cleaner to strong lye (sodium hydroxide) drain openers and degreasers.

Acids work best on neutralizing alkaline soils (tough water stains), such as lime scale, soap deposits, rust and more. Acids break stains into small particles to be washed away. Acidic cleaners range from mild (vinegar, lemon juice) to heavier cleaners such as phosphoric acid (found in toilet bowl and tub/tile cleaners) and hydrochloric or sulfuric acids (found in toilet bowl cleaners).

Solvents such as mineral spirits work by dissolving soils rather than neutralizing them like alkalis or acids. They're distilled from petroleum or plant products and are mostly used on oily and greasy soils.

Disinfectants, such as quaternary ammonium or pine oil, are added to cleaners that tout antibacterial power. They kill germs that smell, cause disease, stain clothes and spoil food.

Pro tip: Make sure you don't use a bleach-containing product on rust —it will set the stain.

Pro tip: If scrubbing doesn't remove hardened mineral deposits on a faucet aerator screen, unscrew the spout tip by turning it counterclockwise. Soak it overnight in vinegar, then scrub it with the toothbrush and flush with water before reinstalling.

Controlling sawdust

Make a plastic passage

Hanging sheets of plastic from the ceiling is a good way to isolate a room that's being remodeled. But instead of hanging one continuous sheet to keep the dust in, hang two and overlap them 4 ft. or so. That way you'll have a handy door to walk through, which beats having to duck under the plastic every time you come and go. Lay a scrap piece of lumber on the bottom of the plastic to keep it in place.

Cover the return air vents

A furnace is an extremely efficient tool to spread dust from a room under construction to all the other rooms in the house. Sure, an expensive furnace filter may catch most of the dust, but it'll also get clogged in hours, instead of weeks, and running a furnace with a clogged filter could result in costly furnace repairs.

Avoid these problems by covering the return air vents in, or near, the area where you're working. If you're kicking up a dust storm, shut the furnace down until that phase of the job is done, and replace the furnace filter once the whole job is done.

Before / After

No sawdust in the house!

To keep sawdust off your clothes and avoid tracking it in the house, pick up a pair of nylon athletic pants and a nylon rain jacket at a thrift store. Just slip them over your street clothes when you're kicking up dust in the shop—nothing sticks to them. Your clothes will last longer too!

Floors and carpeting

Floor-friendly feet for furniture

Most manufacturers put small metal buttons on furniture legs. Metal feet slide easily across factory and warehouse floors, but they can damage any type of hard flooring in your house (even ceramic tile). On carpet, a spilled drink can even lead to rust stains. So when you get a new piece of furniture, run to your local home center or hardware store, where you'll find a variety of inexpensive furniture feet.

Remove metal buttons on furniture legs. If a button is sunk deep into the wood and you can't pry it out, drill a 1/4-in. hole and lever it out with a small screwdriver.

Stick self-adhesive pads to the legs or drive in nail-type feet. On hardwood legs, drill a pilot hole slightly smaller than the nail shank.

PADS
Felt or cloth pads are gentle on floors, but they don't slide as easily as plastic feet.

GLIDES
Plastic glides slide smoothly across hard flooring, but don't use plastic or rubber on wood flooring—chemicals in plastics can stain wood finishes.

Clean your bagless vacuum filter, or else...

"Bagless vacuums are good for business," according to one vacuum repairman. The problem isn't design or manufacturing but user negligence. Vacuum owners empty the dirt canister but often don't clean the filters. Plugged filters lead to an overworked motor. And sooner or later, the motor burns out. Motor replacement costs at least $100.

People avoid cleaning filters because it's a messy job. The typical method is to tap the filter against the inside of a trash can until most of the dust falls off. But this raises a thick cloud of dust and doesn't get the filter completely clean. Here's a faster, neater, more thorough approach: Take the vacuum out to the garage and clean the pleated filter with a shop vacuum. Some pleated filters have a special coating that you can damage, so be gentle with the shop vacuum nozzle. Clean prefilter screens and post-filters the same way.

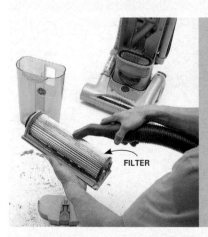

FILTER

Fluff up furniture dents in your carpet

To remove furniture footprints from carpet, dampen the carpet with a white rag (colored fabric can leave dye in the carpet). Then heat the area with a hair dryer as you rake the carpet yarn gently in all directions with a spoon. In most cases, the crater will completely disappear in five minutes or less. If not, let the carpet dry completely and repeat the process.

Remove carpet burns

Snip tips of burned carpet threads with sharp scissors. Feather out area around damage.

Repair carpet snags

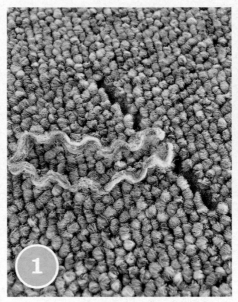

Cut away loose yarn and save it. Mask off repair area with tape. Squeeze a heavy bead of carpet seam sealer into the run.

Use a nail set to press each "scab" of the saved yarn's dried glue into the carpet's backing and seam sealer until a loop is reestablished.

Remove tough stains from vinyl flooring

Sheet vinyl "resilient" flooring is so easy to clean that it may never require anything beyond damp mopping with a cleaner intended for vinyl floors. But if your floor has marks or stains that still won't come off, you can use stronger stuff. Although the methods described here won't harm most vinyl floors, we strongly recommend that you test them in a closet or on a section of flooring that's hidden by furniture. Use white rags only; chemicals that dissolve stains can also make fabric colors bleed and stain your floor.

Isopropyl alcohol, sold as a disinfectant at drugstores, is a mild solvent. It's the best cleaner for heel marks and works on other tough stains too. You can also use lighter fluid or mineral spirits. Remember that all these products are flammable; turn off any nearby pilot lights and hang rags out to dry before throwing them away.

Bleach will often erase stains left by liquids like fruit juices, tomato sauce and wine. Mix one part household bleach with four parts water, soak a rag in it and lay the rag over the stain. Bleach works slowly; you may have to leave the rag in place for an hour or so.

Oxalic acid is the solution for stubborn rust stains. It's often labeled "wood bleach"—but not all wood bleach contains oxalic acid, so check the label. Most paint stores and some hardware stores carry oxalic acid. If the stain won't rub off, wet a rag with the acid solution and lay it over the stain for 10 minutes. If the stain remains, rewet the rag and repeat. When that's done, rinse the floor with clean water.

Dampen a white rag with isopropyl alcohol and rub away heel marks.

Mix oxalic acid powder with water and dab rust stains to remove them. Protect your hands with rubber gloves and open a window for ventilation.

Speed cleaning

Cut grease with a hot rag

Grease and dirt build up on kitchen cabinets over time. To clean your cabinets, heat a slightly damp sponge or cloth in the microwave for 20 to 30 seconds until it's hot. Put on a pair of rubber gloves, spray the cabinets with an all-purpose cleaner containing orange oil, then wipe off the cleaner with the hot sponge. For stubborn spots, let the cleaner sit for five minutes first. Wipe in the direction of the wood grain. Rinse and reheat the sponge as it becomes saturated. Then wipe the cabinets with a cool, damp cloth. The orange oil leaves a shiny coating. This works for any wood or metal surface.

Electric polisher

Here's a bright smile of a tip. Use a battery-powered toothbrush (the expensive type) to polish brass or silver project parts or scrub out stripper from carved areas of antique furniture. One section of bristles rotates and the other section oscillates, aggressively digging out polish and stripper from the narrowest recesses. Go on—give it a spin!

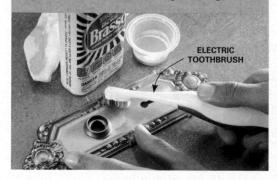

ELECTRIC
TOOTHBRUSH

Big-league stench stopper

Hockey equipment has a less than flowery reputation, so we asked Rick Bronwell, the assistant equipment manager for the Minnesota Wild hockey team, how he keeps the pros' stuff smelling good (or at least tolerable). "The most important thing is to air everything out," he said. "In addition to that, we've had success with a product called SportSense. It eliminates bacteria that cause odors, but just as important, it eliminates bacteria that can cause a skin infection."

Other brands are also available. Check sporting goods stores or search online for "sports spray odor eliminator."

Use a doormat

Eighty-five percent of the dirt that comes into the home is from shoes! So nag your family members to take them off. Place shoes on doormats to contain the dirt. Mats are sold at discount stores.

Up-high duster

Unless you're super-tall, dusting ceiling fans and other high, out-of-reach objects is a real chore. Wrap a dryer sheet around a clean painting roller and secure the ends with rubber bands. Attach an extension handle to the roller and dust away.

Remove pet hair with duct tape

That's right. There's another use for duct tape—cleaning. The stickiness of duct tape makes it perfect for a makeshift pet hair remover. Wrap duct tape around a paint roller cover, sticky side out. Roll the paint cover over furniture or carpet to pick up the pet hair. It also works on seats in vehicles. A sponge or cloth wrapped with duct tape works great for getting into corners. Add more tape as the surface gets full of hair. This method is faster than vacuuming.

Cleaning a vent hood grease filter

Running a vent hood grease filter through the dishwasher or scrubbing it with "grease cutting" household cleaners doesn't always work well. But you'll get great results when you use water-based degreaser from the auto parts store. Fill the sink with hot water and degreaser, drop in the filter and let the degreaser do all the work. The filter will come out sparkling clean in just a few minutes. Then just rinse it off.

Dealing with pests

Pro tip: Before you sweep up mouse droppings, always spray them with a disinfectant spray such as Lysol. Mice can pass disease to humans through their waste.

Don't feed the mice!

Store pet food in a lidded metal trashcan, as mice cannot climb the slick, vertical sides of the can. Sealed plastic containers are also a good option.

Soda-bottle bee trap

Cut the upper one-third off the top of a 2-liter plastic soda bottle with a utility knife. Pour a few ounces of soda pop into the bottom, then invert the top of the bottle and nest it inside the bottom part. Bees and wasps are attracted to the sweet smell and find their way through the bottleneck but can't find their way out. Eventually they get exhausted and drown.

5-gallon squirrel solution

A determined squirrel can usually figure out a way to have a banquet at your bird feeder even if it's a squirrel-proof model. But you can defeat them by cutting off the bottom of an empty 5-gal. plastic water bottle with a jigsaw. Drill a hole through the neck of the bottle, slide the bottle over the pole and hang it from the feeder with a short length of coat hanger. You're in business (and the squirrels are out of luck). They'll try to get around it, but they can't.

CRITTER-PROOF YOUR HOME

OPENING

1 Inspect the underside of your siding using a mirror. If you find a gap, mark the location with masking tape so you can seal it later.

WEATHERSTRIPPING

2 Seal doors, windows and basement sashes with adhesive-backed weatherstripping. Clean the surface first so the weatherstrip will adhere well.

DAMPER

3 Examine dryer vents to ensure the damper isn't stuck open or broken off completely. Also check that the seal between the vent and the wall is tight.

CAULK

4 Fill gaps between trim and siding with acrylic latex caulk. Keep a wet cloth handy to clean up any stray caulk. Smooth the bead with a wet finger.

EXPANDING FOAM

5 Pull nests from the soffit gaps and then fill these openings with expanding foam. After the foam hardens, cut off the excess with a utility knife.

COPPER MESH

6 Stuff in a generous amount of copper mesh with a screwdriver, leaving about half an inch of space for expanding foam sealant. Seal gaps with foam.

EXPANDING FOAM

7 Trim the foam flush using a utility knife after allowing the foam to harden overnight. To trim off a thicker section of foam, use an old steak knife.

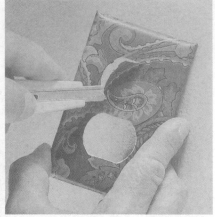

Chapter Ten

PAINTING AND DECORATING

Did you buy the right paint?

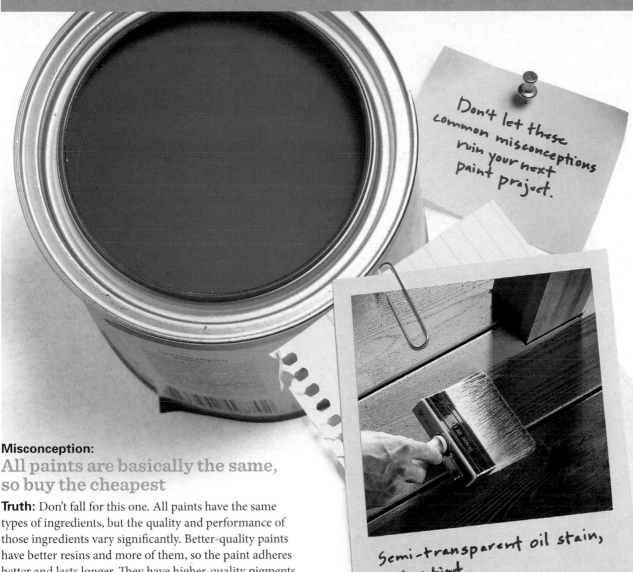

Don't let these common misconceptions ruin your next paint project.

Semi-transparent oil stain, cedar tint

Misconception:
All paints are basically the same, so buy the cheapest

Truth: Don't fall for this one. All paints have the same types of ingredients, but the quality and performance of those ingredients vary significantly. Better-quality paints have better resins and more of them, so the paint adheres better and lasts longer. They have higher-quality pigments that cover better and are less likely to fade. And they have additives that help you brush them out faster and smoother. All in all, the ingredients in higher-quality paints cost more, and you won't find them in the cheaper paints.

Misconception:
It's best to paint your deck with an opaque stain

Truth: Solid stains are a good choice for smooth outdoor surfaces like siding and deck rails, but they're not a good choice for decking. The wood won't absorb enough stain to withstand the abrasion of foot traffic and it'll soon show wear. Semi-transparent stains or tinted sealers are better choices because the wood will absorb more stain, giving it better protection. Still, you have to clean the wood and renew the stain every two to three years.

Misconception:
Oil primers are better than latex primers on bare wood

Truth: In general, both oil and latex primers work well on bare wood. But in some cases one works better than the other. An oil primer will work better than latex on new wood that has a "mill glaze," that is, a polished surface caused by the planer during the smoothing process. You can usually spot the shine if you examine the wood closely (see left). Or sprinkle a little water on the surface. If it beads up rather than sinks in, choose an oil primer, since the wood will usually absorb it better than it does latex. If you want to use latex, first sand to dull the shine.

A latex primer will work better than oil to "spot prime" knots and pitch pockets (dried). Choose a special "stain blocking" type for this purpose. Once the spot priming dries, prime the entire surface with an oil or latex primer.

BEADED WATER

SHINY MILL GLAZE

Misconception:
You don't have to reprime factory-primed building materials

Truth: Beware! Sometimes the manufacturers of siding and other materials prime their products only to protect them in transit and on the job site. The coating isn't always intended to be the base coat for paint. To determine if you have to reprime, read the manufacturer's finishing recommendations for the product you purchase.

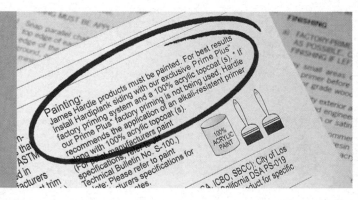

Misconception:
Outdoors, oil stains are better than latex stains because they last longer

Truth: It depends on the surface. Oil stains generally penetrate wood better than latex stains and perform best on rough surfaces like rough-sawn wood and cedar shingles, which will soak up a lot of stain. Semi-transparent oil stains excel here because you can apply several coats and achieve good wood protection without hiding the natural texture and grain. You can expect the stain to last from four to seven years. They're easier to renew, too. You can simply power wash to clean and recoat.

However, latex stains (especially solid ones) excel on smooth wood surfaces. They won't erode as quickly as oil stains. You can expect a solid latex stain on smooth, vertical wood to last four to six years. Keep in mind that no stain will last more than two to three years on horizontal surfaces that are exposed to the sun and rain.

ROUGH-SAWN BOARD

SEMI-TRANSPARENT OIL STAIN

Misconception:
You shouldn't put an oil primer over latex topcoats

Truth: Generally speaking, applying oil primer over latex isn't a problem. A clean, solid, well-prepared base for the new paint is the most critical issue. However, several situations specifically call for an oil primer.

1 If the old topcoat shows significant chalking, that is, the pigment comes off on your finger when you rub the topcoat, then scrub the surface well using a detergent and brush, rinse and apply an oil primer when the surface thoroughly dries.

2 If the topcoat shows extractive staining (water-soluble substances in cedar and redwood; photo below) bleeding through the surface, scrub, let dry and prime with a stain-blocking oil primer.

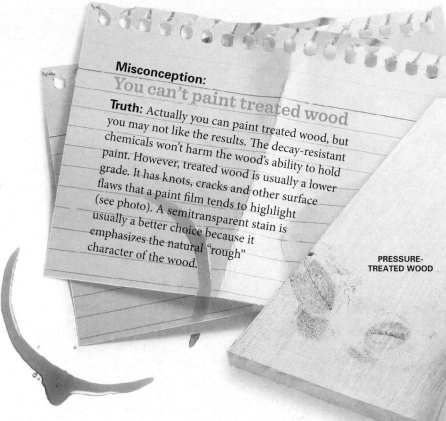

Misconception:
You can't paint treated wood

Truth: Actually you can paint treated wood, but you may not like the results. The decay-resistant chemicals won't harm the wood's ability to hold paint. However, treated wood is usually a lower grade. It has knots, cracks and other surface flaws that a paint film tends to highlight (see photo). A semitransparent stain is usually a better choice because it emphasizes the natural "rough" character of the wood.

PRESSURE-TREATED WOOD

Extractive bleed — use stain-blocking oil primer!

3 If you notice wax bleed on older types of hardboard siding, thoroughly scrub the surface and apply an oil primer. Heat from the sun sometimes causes the wax used as a water repellent to migrate to the surface and create a dark, blotchy appearance. Then apply 100 percent acrylic latex topcoats to yield the best long-term durability.

Misconception:
You can't paint wood once you've applied a water repellent

Truth: Using a water repellent on bare wood in areas vulnerable to moisture—such as windowsills, trim and siding near the ground, and board ends in exposed locations—is the best thing you can do to prevent peeling and extend the life of your paint job. Unfortunately, paintable water repellents can be difficult to find. Don't paint over a water repellent unless the label specifically says that you can. The label often specifies that you use an oil primer.

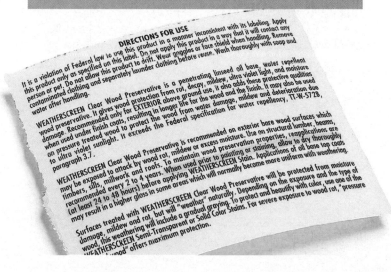

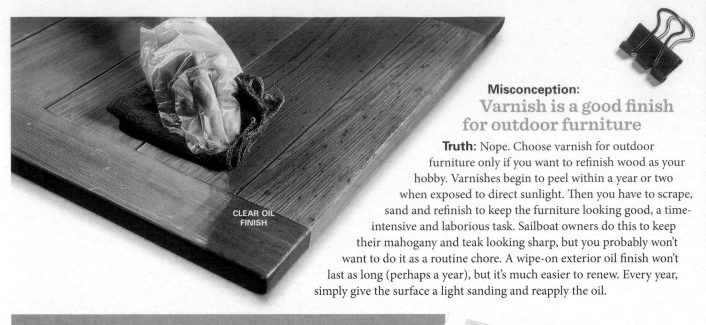

CLEAR OIL FINISH

Misconception:
Varnish is a good finish for outdoor furniture

Truth: Nope. Choose varnish for outdoor furniture only if you want to refinish wood as your hobby. Varnishes begin to peel within a year or two when exposed to direct sunlight. Then you have to scrape, sand and refinish to keep the furniture looking good, a time-intensive and laborious task. Sailboat owners do this to keep their mahogany and teak looking sharp, but you probably won't want to do it as a routine chore. A wipe-on exterior oil finish won't last as long (perhaps a year), but it's much easier to renew. Every year, simply give the surface a light sanding and reapply the oil.

Misconception:
You can't paint vinyl siding

Truth: Actually, it's no problem to paint vinyl siding. The old color won't peel because the pigments are mostly mixed into the material itself. But it can fade, or you may simply want a color change.

If it's new and you want to alter the color, wash it with a detergent, then rinse. If it's older and somewhat faded, you have to be a bit more aggressive. Scrub it with a brush and detergent and water to remove chalking and mildew as well as dirt. Then apply two coats of a 100-percent acrylic paint. You don't need a primer.

Misconception:
Enamel paints are the best choices for woodwork and trim

Truth: In general, it's true that enamel is the best choice for trim, but the word enamel can be confusing, and is no longer helpful when you're making paint decisions. Enamel once referred to resin-rich oil paint, that is, paint that contains a high proportion of oils to make it brush out more smoothly and dry to a glossy finish. Now it can also refer to resin-rich latex paints, which have similar qualities.

To avoid confusion, it's better to avoid the word enamel and choose your trim paint based on type (oil or latex) and sheen (gloss or semigloss).

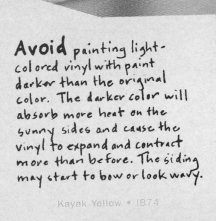

Avoid painting light-colored vinyl with paint darker than the original color. The darker color will absorb more heat on the sunny sides and cause the vinyl to expand and contract more than before. The siding may start to bow or look wavy.

Kayak Yellow • IB74

Too dark!

Bright Amethyst • IB103

Decorating

Add style with arches

If you want high style on a low budget, you can't beat a drywall archway. It takes a few hours to frame and finish an arch, but the materials cost is usually less than $20. And an arch looks like a million bucks. This isn't a complex job; if you've done some basic wall framing and drywall taping, you can handle it. To see how to frame an arch in a new or existing wall opening, go to familyhandyman.com and search for "drywall arch."

Perfect keyhole template

When you're installing a wall hanging that has keyhole slots on the back, create a template to help you position the wall screws. Lay a piece of paper over the slots and do a pencil rubbing a la Sherlock Holmes. Level and tape the guide to the wall. Mark the top of the keyholes with a nail and your screws will be in perfect position.

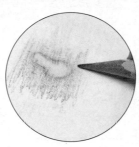

A sample box for future decorating and remodeling

Every homeowner ought to have a box filled with scraps and samples left over from decorating and remodeling projects. When shopping for a new sofa, you can pull out the carpet, wallpaper and drapery samples and take them along. For home improvements and repairs, you'll have molding scraps, paint chips and flooring samples to help you find matching materials. Keep spare hardware in the box too, in case you need replacements.

Tips for hanging artwork

■ **Hang artwork centered at eye level.** You view some pictures primarily while standing (such as in a hallway or kitchen), others primarily while sitting (dining room or family room). Hang artwork accordingly at "sitting" or "standing" eye level.

■ **Never hang artwork in direct sunlight.** Even with protective UV-blocking glass, prolonged exposure can fade images.

■ **Don't hang artwork above sources of heat.** Temperature swings can cause condensation to form inside a frame, damaging the image.

■ **Position artwork within 4 to 8 in. above the back of the sofa.** This distance can be even less when hanging pictures over desks, chests and sideboards.

■ **Space 'em right.** One rule of thumb says pictures should not be hung more than the width of a hand apart.

■ **Plan before you hang.** Make a newspaper or paper-bag template of your picture and tape it to the wall before you install hangers. If you have multiple pictures, try different arrangements on the floor before hanging them.

■ **Treat groupings like an individual picture.** Groupings should follow the same guidelines as individual pictures: the group should be centered over pieces of furniture and at eye level.

■ **Light it right.** Too much light creates glare and wash-out, so illuminate artwork at the lowest level possible for enjoyment. Incandescent and halogen light is less harmful to artwork than fluorescent light.

■ **Use the right hanger.** For pictures exceeding 8 x 10 in., use two hooks for stability. Dabs of mounting putty or self-sticking cabinet-door bumpers on the lower corners keep the piece hanging straight.

Tips for locating nails

Disappearing marks

When you're hanging a group of pictures or marking the stud locations on a wall, you usually have to go back and get rid of your marks. Make it easier to erase your tracks by using a disappearing-ink fabric marker. A damp cloth will remove the marks—sometimes they even disappear on their own.

Positioning pictures with thumbtacks

It's tough to position a nail in the right spot for hanging a picture. Next time, give this a try: Stick double-faced tape on the head of a thumbtack and stick it directly under the picture's mounting bracket. Hold the picture right where you want it and push on the top of the frame to make your mark with the thumbtack. Now you have a tiny mark to guide you for placing the hanging nail or hook.

Lick picture-hanging problems

Here's how to hang pictures quickly and easily. Lick your middle knuckle and grab the hanger on the back of the picture with the wet finger. Press your knuckle against the wall when the picture is exactly where you want it. The saliva will leave a light mark for placing a nail.

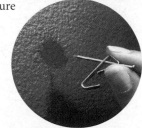

Wallpaper tips

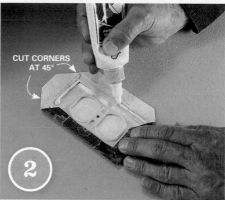

MATCH PATTERN

CUT CORNERS AT 45°

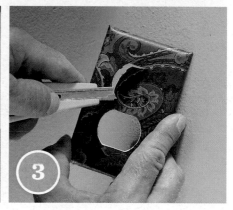

Perfect match outlet covers

To cover and create outlet or switch plate covers that match the pattern of the surrounding wall, follow these steps: Match the pattern on a scrap piece of wallpaper with that on the surrounding wall (Photo 1). Wet or apply paste to the paper, position it and gently remove the wallpaper and plastic cover

from the wall. Next, fold the edges back around the cover and secure them with wall covering seam repair (Photo 2). Cut the corners for crisper folds. Finally, cut out and remove the excess wallpaper using the openings in the plastic cover as a guide (Photo 3).

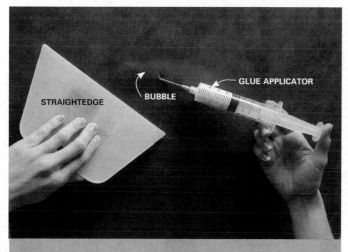

STRAIGHTEDGE

BUBBLE

GLUE APPLICATOR

Bubbling wallpaper

Fix bubbles in wallpaper by cutting them with a razor knife. A small slit is all that's needed. Then insert the end of a glue applicator in the slit and squeeze in a little adhesive.

Wipe away excessive adhesive with a damp sponge and press the wallpaper against the wall to force out the air, using a plastic straightedge.

The glue applicators and adhesive are available at paint stores and home centers.

Use vinyl paper in high-traffic rooms

Wallpaper made from paper absorbs moisture and can be hard to clean. Vinyl products are better suited for bathrooms and kitchen and hallways, but not all vinyl wallpapers are the same. Some are solid vinyl, others have a vinyl face with a paper backing, and some are mostly paper with a thin vinyl coating. Solid vinyl wallpaper is the most resistant to moisture and the most washable. To avoid confusion, many manufacturers have a "Best Uses" label on each roll.

Fix a wallpaper seam

If you have a seam that's coming apart, reactivate the paste around the gap with a rag soaked in warm water. Hold the rag over the area for a minute or two, and then carefully open the gap a little larger so you'll have more room for the sealer. Squeeze seam sealer (Elmer's Glue works in a pinch) into the gap, and press the paper to the wall with a roller. Clean off the excess sealer with a sponge.

SEAM SEALER

Better wallpaper scraper

Scraping off wallpaper is no picnic. Wallpaper scrapers are tiring because you can only use one hand. Putty knives have the same problem and can also damage the drywall surface. And neither gives you much of a reach. Here's a way to make the chore easier and faster. After wetting the wallpaper with a sponge, use a long-handled windshield ice scraper to remove it. The handle makes reaching high spots a breeze, and the scraper won't gouge the wall unless you get too aggressive.

WINDSHIELD ICE SCRAPER

Map out the room

A. Use a roll to lay out the wall
Use a full roll of paper as a guide to lay out the room. Butt a roll into the corner where you plan to start, and make a pencil mark on the wall at the edge of the roll. Slide the roll down to that mark, and make another pencil mark at the other edge of the roll. Keep doing this until you know where every seam is going to fall. You may have to cut down the first panel to avoid hanging small strips (3 in. or less) near doors and corners.

B. Work away from the door you enter
Wallpaper seams on straight walls are butted, not overlapped, but seams are less visible if you place them at the point farthest from where the first panel was installed. Minimize the visibility of seams by starting in the area opposite the most-used entrance to the room.

C. Start with a plumb line
Don't assume the corner you're starting in is plumb. Use a level and draw a straight plumb line about 1/4 in. past where you want the first panel of paper to end. Take into account that inside corner seams need to be overlapped at least 1/8 in.

D. Hide the last seam
If you're hanging paper that has a repeatable pattern, the pattern on the last seam is not going to line up, so try to hide it in a low-visibility area. The corner just above the entry is usually the best spot.

Tough removal tools for tough wallpaper

Chemical strippers: Some chemical strippers work as wetting agents that prevent the water from evaporating while you remove the paste. Others have enzymes (check the label) that actually break down the molecular structure of the paste, making it easier to remove. You can buy premixed liquid, powdered or gel chemical wallpaper removers at home centers and paint stores. Strippers can get pricey on big jobs. To save money, use hot water to remove most of the paper and glue and then apply a small amount of the gel at the end to remove the most stubborn paste and backing.

Scoring tools: A scoring tool punches hundreds of tiny holes in the wallpaper facing so the water can penetrate the backing. If you can pull off the facing, you probably don't need to use one. But if you have a waterproof facing like a glossy paper or vinyl, a scoring tool can really help. But use it carefully. Plaster walls are impervious to abuse, but scoring tools used aggressively can easily punch tiny holes in drywall. You can find scoring tools at home centers and wallpaper stores.

PAPER TIGER

Electric steamers: Steamers are the tool of last resort. They're messy, difficult to work with and time-consuming to use. But in truly stubborn cases, they'll get the job done … eventually. Steam removal is more dangerous than other methods because you can burn yourself, and you can also damage the paper drywall surface if you hold the steamer on the wall too long. But if nothing else is working, rent a steamer.

CLAY

WHEAT

STARCH

Choose the right paste for your paper

There are three basic types of paste: clay, wheat and starch. Each group has several subcategories. Most wallpaper instructions will indicate which paste to use. Avoid the "universal" paste unless the paper you're hanging specifically calls for it.

Prep and painting

ANKLE SECTION OF GYM SOCK

Buy special ceiling paint

While there are exceptions, in general you'll get the best results with paint that's formulated for a ceiling application. For a ceiling, you want paint that doesn't spatter, has a long open time (dries slowly), and is flat instead of glossy. Most ceiling paints are formulated with these qualities. And of course you can have ceiling paint tinted if you want a color other than "ceiling white."

Well-armed tape dispenser

Use your wrist as a masking tape dispenser during your next painting project. Cut a 4-in. piece from the ankle section of a gym sock, slip it on your wrist, then slide the tape over your hand. The sock protects your arm so the tape won't scratch it. The tape is always close at hand, leaving both hands free for your work.

Cut in before you roll

Cutting in just before you roll allows you to cover most of the brush marks with the roller. Carefully brush paint along the edge of the ceiling a section at a time. Cut in about 10 linear ft. and then roll that section. This method has a couple of advantages over cutting in the entire room at once. First, the cut-in section will remain wet until you roll, so it blends in better. It's also simply less boring to alternate between cutting in and rolling.

Preserve picture holes

A fresh coat of paint can fill in and hide small nail holes. So if you plan to hang pictures in their same locations when the job is done, stick toothpicks into the nail holes. Leave the toothpicks protruding about 1/8 in. so you can roll right over them. After painting, you can pull out the toothpicks and then put nails and pictures exactly where they were.

Tape off the carpet

When painting baseboard, some painters slip masking tape under the baseboard. But this is time-consuming and doesn't create a seep-proof seal between the baseboard and the carpet. Try this instead: Press the tape against the baseboard, covering about 1/4 in. of the bottom edge. Press down hard on the carpet while you apply the tape. That way, the tape will hold the carpet down while you paint. Later, when you remove the tape, the carpet will rise and cover the unpainted edge of the baseboard.

Use a high-quality tape for this job because it will grab and hold the baseboard better. Then add a strip of cheap tape to create a wider shield over the carpet. Finally, spread a drop cloth over the tape. This technique won't work if your carpet has a very low pile or if you have no padding under the carpet.

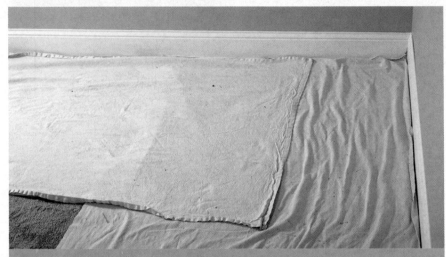

Narrow drop cloths are better

Large drop cloths work great if you're painting a ceiling, but they're overkill if you're only painting walls and trim. Drop cloth runners are usually 3 to 4 ft. wide and are much easier and safer to work with because you don't have to fold them several times. Folded drop cloths are easy to trip on, and nothing good results from tripping with an open paint can in your hand.

Runners no longer than 10 or 12 ft. work best. When they get dirty, wash them at a laundromat that has oversize washers and dryers.

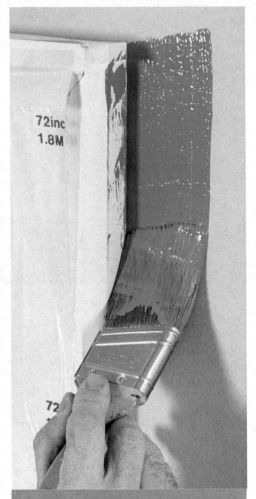

72inc
1.8M

72

Don't flood the masking tape

Masking tape is a precaution, not a guarantee. No matter how careful you are, there may still be a void or two between the tape and the trim. If you expose the tape to a bunch of paint, some is bound to get through. The trick is to pretend the tape isn't there. Don't force a lot of paint into the corner at an angle. Instead, lightly load the paintbrush and run it down parallel to the trim.

CLEANING
BRUSH

Clean up with old brushes

Even though you diligently clean your brushes, they will eventually wear out. Consider saving a couple of different sizes to repurpose as cleaning brushes. An old paintbrush is an excellent tool for dusting off window trim or whatever else needs a light touch.

Completely cover windows and doors

The masking tape you installed to protect the outside edge of the trim won't necessarily protect windows or doors. So it's important to cover them completely, especially if you're painting the ceiling. Here's one way to do it: Hang plastic with a Hand-Masker tool, which dispenses the tape and a folded piece of plastic in one pass. Before unfolding the plastic, tape off the perimeter of the trim. Then unfold the plastic so it completely covers the door or window and sticks it to the trim tape.

Set your tape

After you apply masking tape, run a putty knife, or a 5-in-1 tool, over it to "set" the tape to the trim. This bonds the tape to the surface and helps stop paint from seeping under the tape and up onto the trim.

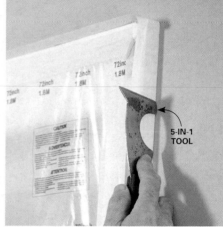

5-IN-1 TOOL

Cut the paint before pulling the tape off

When you remove masking tape that has been left on too long, the tape can pull chunks of paint off with it. It's best to pull off the masking tape while the paint is relatively wet. But when the tape stays on too long, gently cut the tape along the line where the paint meets the trim. This prevents the paint from sticking to the tape and coming off the wall.

Create a smooth path along the ceiling

It's hard to create a straight line when you're painting the wall along a textured ceiling. As you move your paintbrush along, the bristles get hung up on the texture, which creates noticeable paint globs. Use your 5-in-1 tool or a screwdriver to remove about 1/8 in. to 1/4 in. of texture, creating a clear path for the brush.

Slip-proof wood steps

Before winter hits, apply a coat of paint and traction grit on slippery wood steps. Sand and aluminum oxide grit are cheap, but both require constant stirring. And they show up as dark specks as soon as the paint starts to wear. Instead, try polymeric plastic grit, available at home centers and paint stores. Polymeric grit stays suspended in the paint as you apply it, and because it's clear plastic, it won't show up as dark specks as the paint wears.

If you want grit that's easier on bare feet, add rubber grit to the paint. Use the broadcast method shown to apply it.

SPRINKLE THE GRIT ON WET PAINT. Apply a fresh coat of paint to the steps. Then immediately sprinkle a generous coating of rubber grit to the surface. Allow it to dry. Then add a second coat to seal the grit.

Sand before you paint

Over time, and as the layers of paint build up, bumps and crud can get stuck to the ceiling. On untextured ceilings, start with a quick once-over sanding with 100-grit drywall sanding paper. This helps ensure a perfectly smooth paint job and increases paint bonding. The easiest way to do this is with a sanding pole. When you're done sanding, wipe the ceiling with a damp sponge to remove the dust.

Paint twice as fast with this extra-wide roller

An 18-in.-wide roller setup like this may not be for everybody. Painters use them for the obvious reason that they can paint twice as fast as they can with a standard 9-in. roller.

If you have a lot of large, unbroken walls and ceilings, the investment in a large paint pail, 18-in. roller cage and 18-in. cover makes sense for you, too. You'll definitely save a bunch of time. Plus, because the roller is supported on both edges instead of just one, it's easier to apply consistent pressure and avoid roller marks left by paint buildup at the edge of the roller.

You'll find 18-in. roller equipment at most home centers and paint stores.

Painting windows, door and trim

DRYING RACK

Create a paint station

A pair of sawhorses makes the perfect platform for painting or staining long stuff. But where do you lay 25 pieces of wet trim while they're drying? How about right in front of your nose. Make simple racks from scrap 3/4-in. plywood—custom cut the slots based on your needs. Screw them to the sides of your horse and then go to work.

A faster way to paint sashes

Most people slop paint onto the glass when painting windows, then scrape it off with a razor. But if you're good with a paintbrush, you can cut in along the glass. You won't have to scrape, and better yet, you'll leave the paint seal intact between the wood and the glass.

Load your brush and lay off the paint on the sash, staying about 1/2 in. from the glass. As soon as the brush is about half unloaded, go back and cut in closely. Let the brush bristles just barely touch the glass so the paint seals the tiny gap between the wood and the glass. If paint does drip on the window, scrape it off with a razor after it dries.

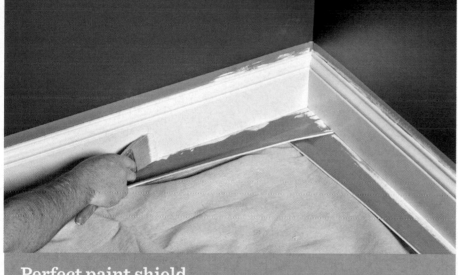

Perfect paint shield

Here's a great paint shield—aluminum roof flashing. It comes in 10-ft. lengths, and you can cut it to any length you want. It's rigid, so you can actually get it up under the baseboard and completely isolate the carpet from the baseboard. Plus, it's bendable, keeps its shape and is reusable. Tape the sharp edges for safety.

Use sanding sponges for trim

Sanding trim between coats of paint is the key to an ultra-smooth finish. But instead of reaching for sandpaper, use a sanding sponge. Sponges conform to the shape of the woodwork and get into the crevices where sandpaper can't go. They also apply even pressure to knock down rough spots over the entire surface.

Mask pet scratches with stain

Dogs and cats still haven't figured out how to open doors, but that's never stopped them from trying. Painted doors can be spackled and repainted to hide the damage, but natural wood doors can be more of a problem. However, if the scratches aren't too deep, you can usually mask the damage with stain and varnish.

Sand the damaged area lightly (Photo 1), feathering the sanding into the surrounding undamaged area. Wipe off all dust.

If you don't have the original stain or finish, find a matching stain at a paint store. Gel stains (available at home centers and paint stores) work best. Buy a small piece of matching wood and experiment with it first, or bring a photo of the door to the paint store for help. Start with a lighter stain—it can always be darkened. You can also buy a few different colors and blend them or streak them together.

Wipe the scratched area with a rag dipped in thinner to keep the stain from looking blotchy. Put a small amount of the gel stain on a rag, then dab a little on a dry brush. Wipe excess stain on the rag. Drag the brush lightly along one edge and quickly wipe it dry to see how the color looks. Leave the stain on longer, apply additional coats or blend in other colors to darken it (Photo 2).

If the stained area looks too dull after it dries, lightly spray the area with clear finish, feathering it into the surrounding area.

CLAW MARKS

FINE SANDING BLOCK

1 Lightly sand the scratches and the area around them.

2 Brush the stain over the sanded area with a dry brush, mixing colors to match the old finish.

Get a smooth finish on doors with a special mini roller

The best way to avoid brush marks is to avoid using brushes. High-density foam mini rollers spread paint smoothly and evenly, without brush marks and without the bumpy surface that standard-nap rollers leave. They also have rounded ends that almost eliminate lap marks and let you paint into corners without leaving scrapes or ridges.

Edge in around windows and panels with a brush first, then coat the rest of the door with the foam roller. Use the rollers for both primer and paint. They spread a thinner coat of paint than brushes or conventional rollers do, so you'll need at least two coats. Foam rollers are available at home centers and paint stores.

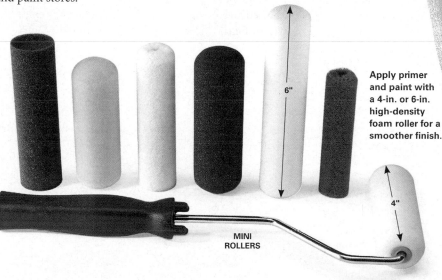

6" FOAM ROLLER

Apply primer and paint with a 4-in. or 6-in. high-density foam roller for a smoother finish.

6"

4"

MINI ROLLERS

Trim-painting shortcut

If you have lap siding to paint, you can save a lot of time by painting the edges of window and door casings the same color as the siding. Most pros do it this way, and the beauty is, nobody will ever notice this little shortcut. Caulk the joint between the casing and the siding as usual. Then when you paint the siding, just extend the paint onto the edge of the casing instead of meticulously cutting in. If you get paint on the face of the casing, wipe it off with a wet rag to create a neat edge.

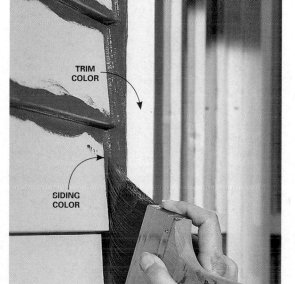

TRIM COLOR

SIDING COLOR

Choosing wood

A board with tight, straight grain holds paint well. Wide bands of darker "latewood" lead to peeling. Regardless of grain, look out for "mill glaze," a wood surface that looks glossy and paint won't stick to.

Good for paint

NARROW BANDS
OF LATEWOOD

Bad for paint

WIDE BANDS
OF LATEWOOD

GLAZED
SURFACE

Don't start a brushstroke on already-smoothed paint

Setting the paintbrush on an area that's already been smoothed out with laying-off strokes will leave an unsightly mark. Try to start laying-off strokes at the end of a trim piece or board, or in an unpainted area. Brush toward the finished area. Then sweep the brush up and off, like an airplane taking off from a runway, to avoid leaving a mark.

BRUSH MARK

Prevent peeling paint on exterior wood

How do you prevent peeling paint? This is the million-dollar question when you're painting your house, right? And the answer may be the best-kept secret in the painting world—use a water repellent preservative (WRP). WRP is perfect for moisture-prone spots like garage door trim and windowsills. But most painters—pros and DIYers alike—have never heard of it. Here's how it works:

Peeling often begins with a tiny crack in the paint. A little water sneaks in and the wood swells, stretching the paint and causing more cracks. As the surface warms and the water evaporates, it pushes against the paint from behind. Each time this cycle occurs, the crack grows and the paint bond weakens. Peeling soon begins.

WRP prevents this cycle. Applied to bare wood before primer and paint, it keeps wood from absorbing water after the paint cracks. WRP is very effective, but it needs to be applied with a light hand.

A small amount of WRP greatly reduces the amount of water entering the wood, but it also decreases paint adhesion. So there are two competing things going on. Ultimately, the slight decrease in adhesion is more than made up for by the absence of water trying to push the paint off when the surface is warmed.

WRP may be the best-kept secret in the painting world.

Finding a paintable WRP is a little tricky. Labels don't always make it clear whether the product is paintable or not. Here's a list of some widely available paintable WRPs:

- Blue Label Penofin
- Cuprinol Clear Deck & Wood Seal
- Olympic Clear Wood Preservative
- Weatherscreen Clear Wood Preservative
- Woodlife Classic
- Woodlife Coppercoat

It's also important to keep sunlight from hitting the bare wood during paint prep. Sunlight destroys lignin, the natural glue that holds wood fibers together. If you apply paint to a surface without lignin, it won't be long before that surface peels away from the rest of the wood.

Prep your wood for paint in small sections so the bare wood is exposed to the sun for minutes instead of hours or days. Scrape off the paint, sand the top layer of wood, apply a paintable WRP to moisture-prone areas and follow the manufacturer's instructions about how long to wait before priming and painting. Everywhere else, prime immediately after sanding.

Painting gear

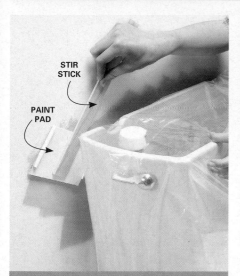

STIR STICK

PAINT PAD

Fresh tape

Sometimes, masking tape that's been sitting on a shelf for years won't pull off the roll without tearing. Freshen it by microwaving it for 10 seconds. Heat softens the adhesive for easy release.

Paint pad for tight spots

If you have a tight spot to paint, remove the pad from a paint edging tool. Hot-glue the pad to a stir stick, and you've got a painting tool that will fit behind toilet tanks and radiators.

Plastic-bag paint containers

A paint job with lots of colors requires cleaning brushes and containers whenever you switch colors. To make cleanup easier, put the paint in zipper lock bags. When it's time to change colors, just change the bag in the paint bucket. It's a great way to save time.

Cosmetic touch-up tool

Disposable cosmetics applicators are great for small touch-up jobs. They let you put a dab of paint or finish precisely where you want it. No mess, no brushes to clean up.

Stay-put roller sleeves

This is for anyone who's been frustrated by roller sleeves that slip off the end of the roller frame as you paint. Use the corner of a metal file to cut a bunch of shallow notches into the bars of the roller frame. The sleeve will stay put for hours of painting.

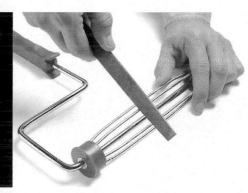

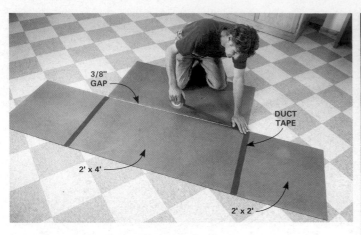

Stowable spray booth

You can make a great folding spray booth from three sheets of 1/4-in. hardboard, cutting one in half for the ends. Build your booth any size. Leave about a 3/8-in. gap between the panels when you make the duct-tape "hinges" or the tape will tear. You have to redo the hinges occasionally, but that's no biggie. As useful as this spray booth is, when you're done, just fold it into a 1/2-in.-thick sandwich and tuck it out of sight.

3/8"
GAP

DUCT
TAPE

2' x 4'

2' x 2'

Use a thick, premium roller cover

Here's a tip that applies to most paint jobs but is even more important for ceilings. You want to get as much paint on the ceiling as you can in the shortest amount of time possible while minimizing spatters. To do this, you need the best roller cover you can buy. Most pros prefer a 1/2-in.-nap lambswool cover. If you've never tried a lambswool roller cover, you owe it to yourself to experience the difference. And if you're worried about the cost, keep in mind that lambswool covers are easy to clean and can last a long time if you take good care of them.

LAMBSWOOL
ROLLER

INEXPENSIVE
ROLLER

You don't need an expensive pole

You can buy all kinds of fancy extendable paint poles, but a simple wooden broom handle is cheap and light and will do just as good a job.

Tablecloth drop cloth

Vinyl tablecloths—the kind usually used on picnic tables—make great drop cloths. They're tougher than plastic sheeting, and if you put the smooth side face down, they don't slip around on hard flooring the way canvas drop cloths do. On carpet, put the smooth side face up. These tablecloths are cheaper than drop cloths, too: you can find them for a few bucks at discount stores.

Cleanup and storage

Remove the fuzz

Some tools need cleaning even when they're brand new. Some new roller covers (usually the cheaper ones) have a layer of fuzz that detaches from the cover. The first time you load up a fuzzy roller, the paint mixes with the fuzz and creates small bumps on the wall. One way to remove the fuzz is to wrap masking tape all the way around the roller cover. When you pull the tape off, the excess fuzz will be pulled off along with it.

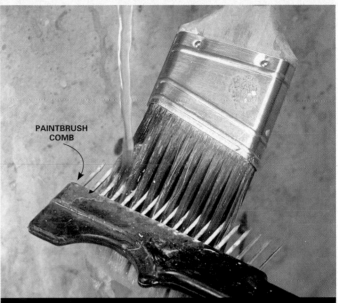

PAINTBRUSH COMB

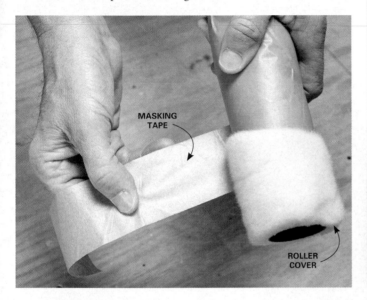

MASKING TAPE

ROLLER COVER

Comb the brush

A paintbrush comb is the best tool for cleaning a brush. Unlike other brush cleaning tools, a comb penetrates and cleans deep between the bristles. It also prevents the bristles from sticking together, which helps your brush stay soft and retain its shape longer.

Run water down into the bristles

After a few hours of painting, paint can work its way up into the bristles covered by the steel ferrule. If you don't clean the paint out of there, it will build up and cause your brush to get stiff and misshapen. After you comb all the paint out of the bristles, run water down into the brush. Finally, straighten out the bristles with a comb before you put the brush away. Protect the bristles by storing the brush in the package it came in.

Wear a rag

Before the first can of paint is cracked open, attach a rag to your belt so when you unconsciously wipe your hand on your pant leg, you're protected. Use a large rag and unfold it a bit, so the messy side stays facing out.

Keep leftover paint from hardening

Open up a can of paint from a job several years ago, and it's usually skinned over and hardened. To avoid this problem, keep leftover primers and paints in near-full cans. Paint stores, and many home centers, sell empty quart paint cans and covers for a dollar or two. Pour off your partial gallon leftovers into the quart cans to keep them from drying out. Then brush a sample of the color on the side of the can so you can identify it easily. Even better, include the paint color code so you can buy an exact match years later.

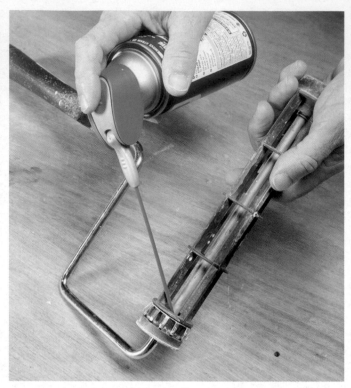

Lube the roller

Metal rusts, and the metal bushings or bearings in your paint roller are no exception. Do yourself a favor, and spray a little lubricant on your paint roller before you store it. A rusty paint roller can squeak. Pushing a roller back and forth for several hours is monotonous enough; adding a few thousand squeaks might drive you completely insane.

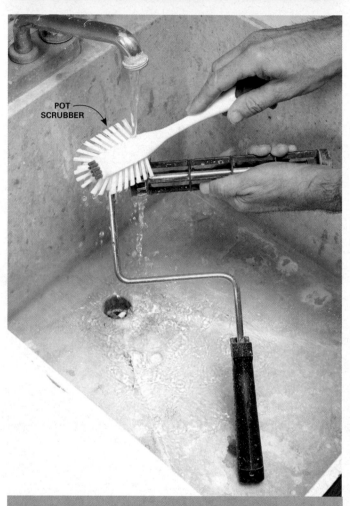

POT SCRUBBER

Scrub your roller

Don't neglect your roller. If you don't rinse off the roller, you'll end up with hardened paint inside the bushings or bearings, and that will ultimately result in a paint roller that doesn't roll. Keeping your tools clean doesn't have to be expensive. A cheap pot scrubber from a discount store works fine.

Keep a garbage bag close at hand

Never underestimate how much trash a painting job creates. And running around the house with big wads of plastic and tape covered in wet paint is not a good idea. Before you start, grab a trashbag and hang it on a doorknob or set it in a portable bag holder or trash can.

Paintbrush holder

Soak oil brushes in cleaning solvent without bending the bristles and ruining the brush! Clip a medium or large binder clip around the handle of a brush and spread the arms to span a cleaning container so the brush bristles don't touch the bottom.

BINDER CLIP

Give it the brush-off

Cleaning brushes is about as much fun as cleaning the outdoor grill. Here's a trick that makes the job a lot more palatable. If you run the brush under water before you start painting, the cleanup is a snap. Of course, this works only for latex paints, primers and finishes.

Overnight storage

If that "quick" painting project didn't go as fast as you'd hoped and you need an extra day, seal your brushes in a freezer bag. As long as it's airtight, you can store brushes for up to a week without cleaning. But don't push it; any longer and they'll dry out and stiffen up, making cleanup that much harder.

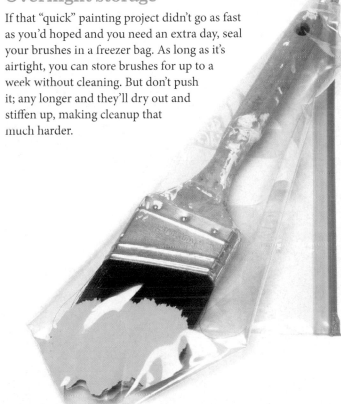

Clean up your mistakes

No matter how careful you are, you're bound to get paint on something you didn't mean to. Keep a can of paint remover on hand.

Paint remover works great for removing dried latex paint from trim, countertops, door hinges, vinyl floors or whatever it is you spilled on.

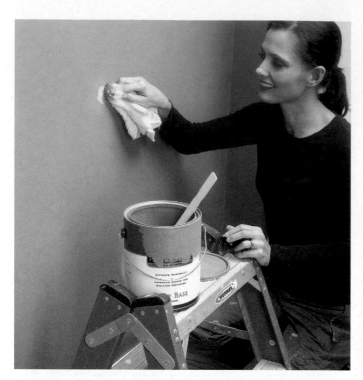

This rack is a great place to let paintbrushes drip dry after washing. Just notch a couple of pieces of 1-by material and attach them to a cross support. Pound in some nails and set the rack on top of your sink edge.

No-hassle paint touch-ups

No sooner do you finish painting a wall and cleaning up the rollers and brushes than you find some spots that need touching up. Don't bother getting the tools dirty again. Use an old washcloth or chunk of towel to do the job. Just ball up the washcloth, dip it in the paint can and bounce it over the spot a few times. The washcloth leaves the same kind of texture as a roller sleeve and you can throw it away when you're done. Zero cleanup!

Let the paint dry, then cut the tape loose for a perfect edge

If you're going to tape off your trim, you can't just pull off the tape once the paint is dry. Paint forms a film between the wall and the tape, and removing the tape tears pieces of dried paint off the wall. So before pulling off the tape, cut it loose.

Wait for the paint to completely dry, at least 24 hours, then use a sharp utility knife or box cutter knife to slice through the film. Start in an inconspicuous area to make sure the paint is hard enough to slice cleanly. If you cut the paint while it's still gummy, you'll make a mess. As you cut the paint, pull up the tape at a 45-degree angle.

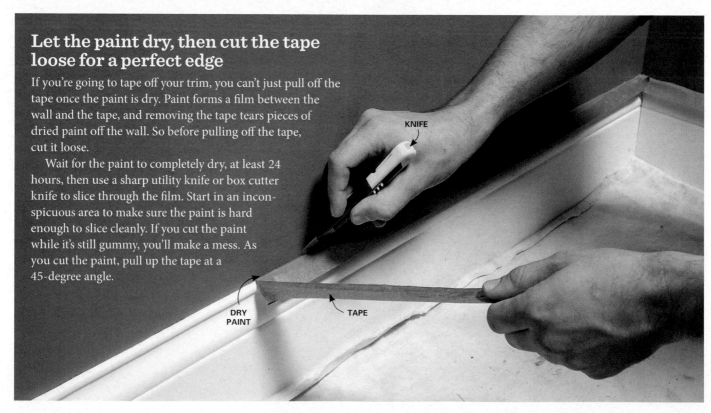

KNIFE

DRY
PAINT

TAPE

Three-stage brush-cleaning system

Save time and mineral spirits with this three-container brush-cleaning method. Partially fill three containers with mineral spirits. When you're done working for the day, swish your brush around in the first container. Wipe it along the edge of the container to remove as much finish as you can. Then repeat the process in the second container. By now the brush will be pretty clean.

Suspend the brush in the third container. Drill a hole in the handle and suspend it from a wire or dowel so that the bristles aren't resting on the bottom of the container. Put a lid on the first two containers, and wrap plastic wrap or aluminum foil around the brush handle on the third container. You can use the same mineral spirits for several brush cleanings.

When the first container gets too full of old finish, dump it into a fourth container labeled "used mineral spirits." Shift the second and third containers to positions one and two, and pour clean mineral spirits into the one you emptied and place it at the end of the line. You can reuse the mineral spirits from the "used" container after the finish settles. Decant it carefully to avoid stirring up the gunk on the bottom.

Using frozen paint

Freezing can ruin latex paint, but it may survive a few mild freeze/thaw cycles. Allow the paint to slowly warm up to room temperature, then stir it well. If the paint color and consistency appear normal, then it should be all right to use. If it looks like cottage cheese, it was frozen too long and you should let it dry on newspaper in a safe place, then put it in the trash.

WHOA...
KEEP THE DOG
AWAY

UNUSABLE
PAINT

Release masking tape with heat

If masking tape tears as you remove it or pulls off flakes of finish, heat it with a hair dryer. Heat softens the adhesive. Then pull the tape off at a 90-degree angle.

Chapter Eleven

WORKSHOP

Workbenches

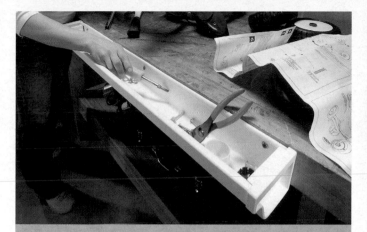

Vinyl gutter tool tray

What can you do with a leftover length of gutter? You can screw it to the edge of your workbench and use it to keep tools and fasteners out of your way but still handy for assembly work.

Drill holster

Avoid the sickening crunch—and possible damage—that happens when your cordless drill falls off a crowded workbench. Screw a 3-in. plastic adapter to the side or back edge of your workbench, and holster that tippy drill. Three-inch drainage adapters hold cordless and corded drills, so buy as many adapters as you have drills to keep them topple-proof and easy to grab.

LAWN DRAINAGE ADAPTER

Workbench power strip

Screw a power strip to the side of your workbench and you won't have to monkey with extension cords anymore when using power tools for bench work.

Laminate flooring benchtop

Leftover scraps of laminate flooring make a great workbench surface. Laminate is tough and easy to clean—dried glue or paint scrapes right off. If you fasten the laminate with small nails, you can easily pry it off and replace it every few years.

Rosin paper workbench cover

Here's instant protection for any kind of messy job. Before you start, just unroll enough rosin paper from this jumbo paper towel holder to protect your workbench. The thick paper absorbs all the glue or finish. When the paper gets too dirty, tear it off and throw it away. A roll of rosin paper is 170 ft. long, so one will last a long time. Here's how to build your paper holder:

Buy a roll of rosin paper and a length of 1-1/2-in. pipe at a home center. Round up some scrap lumber and get ready to do a little bit of head scratching to customize a bracket arrangement that works with your bench design. Our setup should give you the general idea. Bore 1-7/8-in. holes in the scrap wood brackets. Screw keeper strips over the holes to keep the pipe from falling out as you unroll the paper. Use a handsaw to cut the paper roll and a hacksaw to cut the pipe to match the width of your bench. Then load the roll and start dripping stuff all over it.

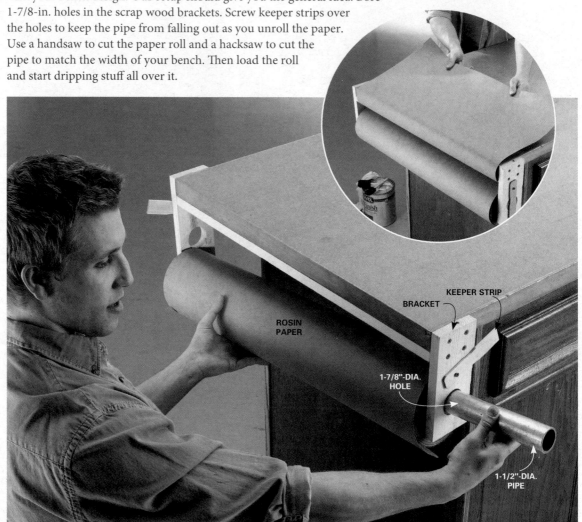

ROSIN PAPER

KEEPER STRIP

BRACKET

1-7/8"-DIA. HOLE

1-1/2"-DIA. PIPE

Upcycled miter saw stand

An old gas grill can provide the perfect base for a miter saw. Just remove the grill housing from the frame and build center framework that allows the saw to sit flush with the wings of the grill. You can remove your saw and store it underneath, giving you a mobile workbench as well.

Organizing tools and supplies

MESSY DRAWER

TIDY DRAWER

CUTLERY TRAY

Use single socks you find in the dryer

Protect safety glasses by storing them in a cotton sock. Hang the sock on the wall in your workshop and they'll remain scratch-free, dust-free and easy to find.

Cutlery tray tool chest

Be honest! Somewhere you have a tool drawer bursting with a combination of screwdrivers, nail sets, tape rolls, utility knives, scissors, scrapers, measuring tapes, files and knives. And often you have to dump everything out to find one tool. Here is a solution. Fit a large cutlery tray in the drawer to organize the tools so you can see and grab the one you want in a second. The tray is easy to lift out and carry to a job, and if you use a metal mesh tray, dust can't build up between the tools.

Handy razor blade storage

It's convenient to keep extra utility and straight box cutter blades near your workbench, in the kitchen and in the garage. But the question is how to store them when they're not in use. The solution is to glue a magnetic business card (a refrigerator magnet) to the inside of a cupboard door and to your workbench with the magnetic side out. The magnet is strong enough to hold the blades in place even if you slam the cupboard door.

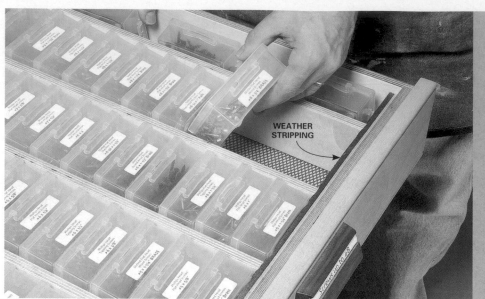

Find-anything hardware drawer

Tired of wondering where to find a 1-in. drywall screw or a 3/8-in. washer? Take a look at this setup.

In the drawer shown, movable partitions are held in place by strips of foam weather stripping at the front and back. The 44-plus boxes rest on edge, labels up, for easy grabbing and stowing. If you want, you can key the labels in on the computer and print them out on sticky labels.

Shop for boxes at craft, tackle, office or dollar stores. Or check online for wholesalers.

WEATHER STRIPPING

Quick-draw drill bit gauge

Ever strain your eyes trying to read drill diameters etched on the drill bit? They're hard enough to see when the bit is brand new. Give the bits a few years of hard use and they're virtually impossible to read. Stop the squinting and buy a drill bit gauge. Keep the bit gauge close at hand by applying a couple of adhesive-backed magnetic strips to a convenient spot on the drill press. Then store the gauge right on board.

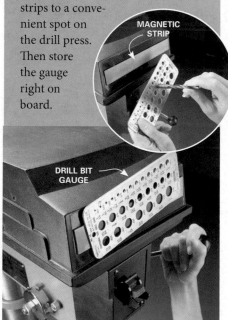

MAGNETIC STRIP

DRILL BIT GAUGE

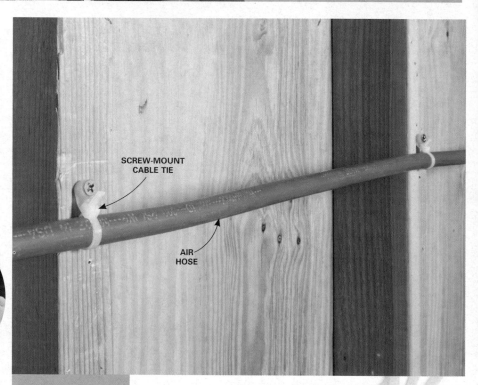

SCREW-MOUNT CABLE TIE

AIR HOSE

Pro Tip: To cut down on the noise in your shop, put your compressor in a closet or storage room and run a fixed air hose into your shop.

Cable ties for compressor hose

Instead of running an expensive copper air line from your compressor to the work area in your shop, just hang a regular air hose on the wall with screw-mount cable ties.

Woodworking skills

PIVOT POINT

TRAMMEL

BASE PLATE

Connect your router to a trammel and screw the trammel to a block. Cut the arc by making repeated shallow passes with a straight or spiral bit.

SPIRAL BIT

Cut perfect arcs and circles

Often, you can create a curve that's "good enough" using a jigsaw followed by a belt sander. But when an arc or a circle has to be flawless, a router is the perfect tool. Some careful setup is required, but the results are worth it. Mount an oversized base plate on your router so you can screw it to a 1x4 trammel. Before you start cutting the arc, raise the bit just above the wood. Then position it at the top of the arc and at both ends to make sure the cutting path is correct. When you cut, make shallow passes no more than 1/4 in. deep. Keep the router moving to avoid burn marks. You can use a 1/2-in. or smaller straight bit or a spiral bit to cut arcs. Spiral bits cut faster with less chipping, but they cost about twice as much as standard straight bits. Don't use a spiral bit that's smaller than 3/8 in. diameter. Small spiral bits break easily when you're making deep cuts.

Using biscuit joiners

A biscuit joiner is a superb tool for joining wood where it would be difficult to use nails or screws. The joint is strong, invisible and easy to create. The compressed wood biscuits expand on contact with moisture in the glue. Since the biscuits are placed in slots that are wider than the biscuit, you can adjust the joint a little after butting the two pieces together. Biscuits come in three common sizes: No. 0, No. 10 and No. 20. Here are some of our favorite biscuit tips:

CLIP BISCUITS FOR NARROW STOCK
The smallest common biscuits (No. 0) are almost 1-7/8 In. long. That's too long for 1-1/2-in. wide stock. But there's an easy solution: Just clip about 1/4 in. off both ends of each biscuit. Your slots will still be too long and visible at inside corners, but a little filler and finish will hide them.

BILL ZUEHLKE

NUMBER THE JOINTS
While you're marking the center lines of each biscuit slot, also number each joint. That will eliminate confusion and misalignments during assembly.

MAKE A GLUE INJECTOR
Spreading a neat, even bead of glue inside a biscuit slot isn't easy. You can buy special injectors online, or make your own using the cap from a marker and a fine-tooth saw.

BILL ZUEHLKE

ALWAYS DO A DRY RUN
Biscuits grab fast. During glue-up, you don't have time to correct mistakes or dig up a longer set of clamps. So always test the whole assembly—Including clamps—before you get out the glue. For complicated assemblies, give yourself more working time by using slow-setting wood glue.

Cutting edges with a router

It's almost magical the way you can transform a square-edged board into a wooden masterpiece with just a router and bit. Modern router bits with carbide cutters and guide bearings make the task almost foolproof. But there are a few tips and tricks that'll simplify the job and give you the best results. Here you'll learn these tips, as well as ways to secure small pieces of wood while you rout them.

Edge-forming router bits range from simple round-over or bevel bits to intricate cove, ogee and classical bits. You'll find a selection of common profiles at home centers and hardware stores, but to see the wide range of profiles available, search online for "router bits." Carbide edge-forming bits cost about $20 and up depending on the size and shape.

DON'T ROUT THE SIDES BEFORE THE ENDS
If you're planning to rout the ends as well as one or both sides of a board, rout the two ends first. Here's why. End grain has a tendency to split out as the bit exits the end of the cut.

ROUT THE ENDS FIRST
If you rout the sides first, the split-out will occur on the previously shaped edge. But if you rout the ends first, you'll cut off any damaged areas when you rout the sides.

MOVE THE ROUTER IN THE RIGHT DIRECTION
Router bits spin clockwise as you look down on the router, so moving the router counterclockwise tends to pull the pilot bearing tight against the wood and allows easy control of the router. When you're routing the outside perimeter of a board, move the router counterclockwise. However, when you're routing the inside of something like a picture frame, move the router in a clockwise direction.

TIPS FOR TIGHTER MITERS

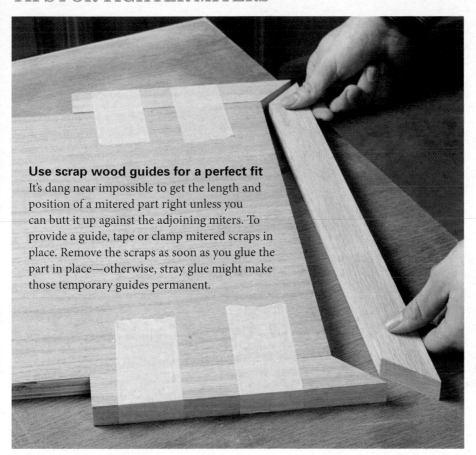

Use scrap wood guides for a perfect fit

It's dang near impossible to get the length and position of a mitered part right unless you can butt it up against the adjoining miters. To provide a guide, tape or clamp mitered scraps in place. Remove the scraps as soon as you glue the part in place—otherwise, stray glue might make those temporary guides permanent.

Match wood grain

Whether you're banding a tabletop or making a picture frame, make sure the wood color and the grain pattern match at the miters. Selecting matching wood at the lumberyard takes only a few extra seconds and gives you much better-looking miters.

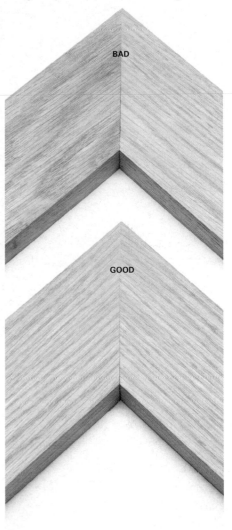

BAD

GOOD

Align with biscuits

It's not easy to align and clamp miters, especially when they're lubricated with a coat of slippery glue. That's why woodworkers often use biscuits on miter joints even where extra strength isn't needed. Cutting biscuit slots is a minor job that provides major help at glue-up time.

Square up with corner clamps

With some miter-clamping methods, you need to grab a square and make sure the corner is exactly 90 degrees. Not so with corner clamps; they automatically hold parts perfectly square. They're available at home centers or online.

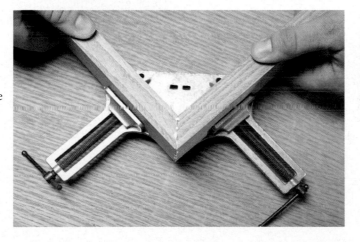

Rehearse before you glue

A dry run—complete assembly with clamps but without glue—is the best way to ensure a smooth, successful glue-up, whether you're assembling miters or anything else.

Miter, assemble then rout

Shaped moldings can be tough to miter, align and clamp. So make life easier by starting with plain square stock. Then, after assembly, grab your router and shape the edges. The risk with this method is that you'll gouge or splinter parts that are already in place. The best way to avoid disaster is to make a series of shallow passes instead of one full-depth cut.

Slow down your glue

It's hard enough to align and clamp miters without rushing to get it done before the glue begins to set (in five to 10 minutes, and even faster in warm, dry conditions). That's why there are slow-setting wood glues, which give you an extra 10 minutes or so.

If you can't find a slow version at your favorite home center, make your own. If you add one part water to 20 parts wood glue, you'll gain about five minutes of working time. The water will also weaken the bond very slightly. So if strength is critical, order slow-setting glue online.

'Lengthen' a board

Ever cut that last part just a bit too short? There's a solution for that: First, trim off the inside edge of the too-short part. By cutting off the short edge, you effectively make the mitered part longer. Then trim the same amount off the outer edges of the other three sides. Your edging will be a little thinner than you had planned, but nobody will notice.

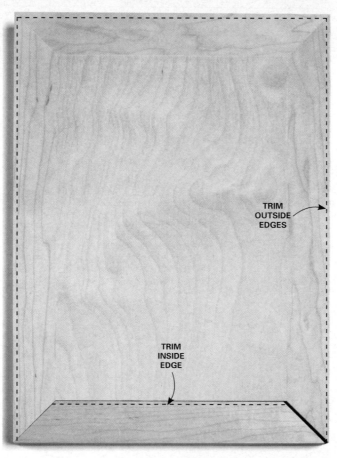

TRIM OUTSIDE EDGES

TRIM INSIDE EDGE

Clamp with your hands

When you're dealing with small or other hard-to-clamp parts, your hands make the best clamps. Simply rub the glued surfaces together and hold them tightly on a flat surface for about a minute. Let go and allow the joint to set for 30 minutes before handling it.

Micro-adjust with paper shims

If you've ever tried to adjust the angle of your miter saw by one-tenth of a degree, you already know how hard micro-adjustments are. Here's an easier way: Slap a few sticky notes on the fence, make test cuts and add or remove sheets until you get exactly the angle you want.

Feel the difference

When you're building a box or frame, the opposite sides have to be *exactly* the same length. To make sure they are, do the touch test: Set the parts side by side and run your finger over the mitered ends. You may not be able to see a slight length difference, but you'll feel it.

Bond joints instantly

Trim carpenters have used this system for years: Apply a few dabs of cyanoacrylate adhesive (aka "superglue") to one surface and apply activator (or "accelerator") to the other. Immediately press the parts together and they'll bond in seconds. No waiting, no complicated clamping setup. Activator is sometimes sold separately, sometimes with the glue. Look for it at home centers or shop online at woodworking suppliers.

Make your own corner clamps

This is an old favorite among woodworkers: Clamp on notched blocks, then add a bar clamp or two to squeeze the joint. This allows you to put a lot of pressure on the joint without buying any special clamps. If you're assembling a four-sided project such as a picture frame, join two corners first. Then, after the glue has set, join the two halves of the frame.

Handy jigs and shortcuts

Build a cutting grid

You can lay a few 2x4s across a pair of horses, but that's not as good as a grid, especially if you're cutting flimsy or small stuff.

For this version, you'll need five knot-free oak or pine 1x4s, 8 ft. long. The secret to building it: Clamp the crosspieces together and "gang-cut" the notches (photo below left). Do the same for the stretchers. Don't fasten the grid parts with glue or screws. Slip them together so they can be disassembled for easy storage.

SIMPLE 1x4 CUTTING GRID
Notched 1x4s create a solid "knockdown" cutting grid.

40"

3/4" x 1-3/4" NOTCHES

NOTCH FOR SAWHORSE

1x4s

96"

1x4 CROSSPIECES

A bigger top is better

Instead of using a 2x4 for the top of your sawhourses, try a 2x6. A 2x6 cut a few inches longer than the horse provides a surface for clamping. There's a storage benefit too: You can drill a hole in one end of the 2x6 and hang the horse on a nail or screw.

Perfect angle glue-ups

Octagonal, hexagonal and even square pedestal bases for tables can be aligned perfectly for gluing with heavy-duty plastic sealing tape. Cut your bevels on the workpiece edge and lay them with the inside face down and one end butted to a straightedge. Align the bevels so they touch along their entire length and tape them securely. Next, carefully flip them over and apply glue to the joints. Then stand them up, fold them together, tape the final joint and pull the shape together with belt clamps. Tip: To get the angles for your shape, divide 360 by the number of sides you want, then divide this number by 2 to get the bevel angle for each side.

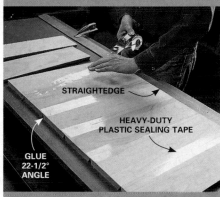

STRAIGHTEDGE

HEAVY-DUTY PLASTIC SEALING TAPE

GLUE 22-1/2° ANGLE

BELT CLAMPS

Build a dentil jig for a router table

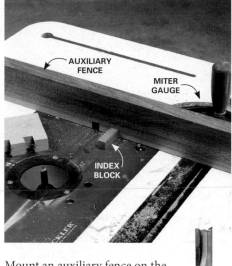

AUXILIARY FENCE

MITER GAUGE

INDEX BLOCK

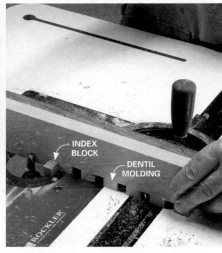

INDEX BLOCK

DENTIL MOLDING

Mount an auxiliary fence on the miter gauge. Run the fence across the straight bit to cut two notches 3/4 in. apart. Glue an index block into one notch and you're ready to make dentil molding.

1/2" STRAIGHT BIT

Cut the first notch with the stock against the index block. Fit that first notch over the index block and make the second cut. Continue repositioning the stock—notch by notch—until all the notches are cut.

Lathe tool rest—plus a ruler

Speed up layouts for any kind of lathe project. With a dry-erase marker, trace gradations right on the tool rest for specific distances for tenons, coves or beads. Now you won't have to hold a "story stick" to transfer layouts alongside the blank while the lathe is running. In the photo, we're preparing a stool leg blank for tapering. Using the ruled tool rest, we cut the tenon length first, lining up the parting tool with the marked line. Then we "part" a series of cuts to establish the leg's taper. The preliminary layout is finished in seconds, and we're ready to taper the leg by using the indexed cuts.

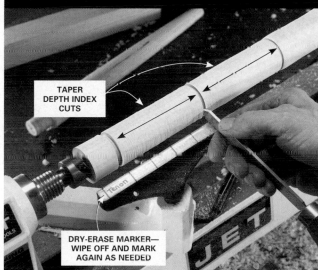

TAPER DEPTH INDEX CUTS

DRY-ERASE MARKER— WIPE OFF AND MARK AGAIN AS NEEDED

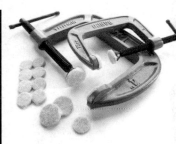

Gentle jaws for C-clamps

Are your C-clamp jaws leaving dents in projects or the furniture you're repairing? Press adhesive-backed felt pads for table and chair legs on the jaw faces (you'll get a better bond if you lightly sand the faces with fine sandpaper). Look for larger precut rectangular shapes that you can trim to fit your bar clamp faces as well.

Sanding tips

Vibration mitigation

If vibrating tools leave you with aching joints, try on a pair of cycling gloves. The gel-filled palms are designed to absorb vibration. They're sold at bike shops and discount stores.

Replacement sander pad

Can't find a replacement rubber cushion for your old palm sander? Make your own from a foam can cover. Just cut the foam to fit the sander and glue it on. Peel off the old pad, clean the metal base and attach the foam with contact cement. Works for clamp-on as well as stick-on sanding squares! You can find can covers at discount and convenience stores.

4" HANDLE

LABEL GRITS

BEGIN WITH COARSE PAPER AND ROTATE THROUGH FINER GRITS

Sharpening club

Using spray adhesive, apply sandpaper—medium to finer grits—on all four sides of a 12-in. piece of 2x2 hardwood. First cut or sand a 4-in. long handle on one end so you can move through the grits by spinning the handle. You'll grab the club whenever dull utility knives and chisels need resharpening, and it's also handy as a file sander for wood or metalworking. When the sandpaper is used up, just peel it off, respray and apply fresh sandpaper.

Sand faster with suction

Connecting to a vacuum doesn't just cut down on dust. It actually allows your random orbit sander to work faster. Even with the sander's built-in dust collection system, the sander rides on a thin cushion of dust that prevents full contact between the grit and the wood. So, by increasing dust removal, a vacuum improves sander efficiency. On some sanders, hooking up to a vacuum doubles the sanding speed.

Drum sander table

If you don't want to pop for a dedicated oscillating drum sander, a sanding drum chucked into a drill press is a quick way to sand contours. But unlike the real deal, there's no dust collection, and since the drum doesn't oscillate up and down, only the lower edge of the sanding surface gets used. It also means there's always a little gap where the drum is slightly above the drill press table. This simple sander table solves all these problems automatically.

Use 1/4-in. or any other thickness plywood for the base, and size it slightly smaller than the drill press table so you can clamp it down. Build a 1x4 frame, a few inches smaller than the base, so there's room for the clamps, and glue and pin it to the frame. Then glue and nail 3/4-in. material to the frame for the top. This one is 16 in. square. Build it longer or deeper if you want to sand wider or longer stuff. Cover the top with plastic laminate if you wish. It's worth the trouble because using a drum sander is tricky, and the slippery surface makes it much easier to control sanding.

Finally, drill a hole slightly larger than the drum in the center of the top and a dust-port hole in the frame sized to fit your shop vacuum hose. Move the drill press table up and down to use the entire sanding surface as it wears.

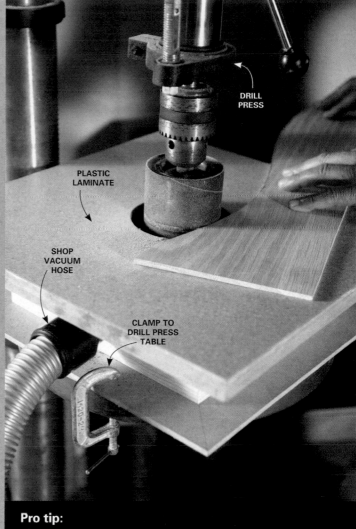

DRILL PRESS

PLASTIC LAMINATE

SHOP VACUUM HOSE

CLAMP TO DRILL PRESS TABLE

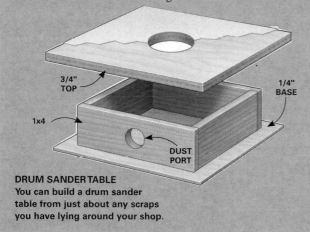

3/4" TOP

1/4" BASE

1x4

DUST PORT

DRUM SANDER TABLE
You can build a drum sander table from just about any scraps you have lying around your shop.

Pro tip:
The biggest mistake drum-sander neophytes make is to remove too much material on each pass. Don't be overly aggressive: Use coarse grits only when necessary, and use very light pressure on each pass. Feel for imperfections with your fingertips, and mark the high spots with a pencil.

Clog-free belt sanding

To keep the sanding belt clean and make it last longer when you're sanding gunky wood, screw a wire brush to the sawhorse and every so often touch the running belt to the brush. It will clean the belt up nicely.

Staining and finishing

Stain-saving spray applicator

Save your empty pump-type sprayers that have an adjustable-spray tip and use them to apply stain. Spray a small section at a time, then wipe it. You'll be surprised how little stain you use to complete the job this way compared with brushing. This technique is especially helpful for applying stain to intricate parts like spindles.

Renew woodwork without refinishing

If your stained and varnished woodwork is looking a little shabby, you can save time and money with this quick fix. You don't have to strip the finish from your dingy woodwork. Just head to the store and pick up some wood stain that's a close match. We like gel stain for this fix, but any wood stain will work.

Start your renewal project by washing the woodwork with soapy water. Rinse with clear water, then gently scrape off any paint spatters with a plastic putty knife. When the wood is dry, dip a rag into the stain and wipe it over the wood. Bare spots and scratches will pick up the stain. Finish by wiping the woodwork with a clean cloth to remove the excess stain. After the stain dries for a few days, you can add a coat of furniture wax or wipe-on poly to really liven up the old wood.

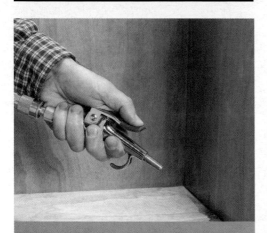

A blast of air

A great tip is to use your air nozzle to blow excess stain from tight corners and intricate moldings. A quick blast of the air nozzle cleans out the recesses, and then you can wipe up the stain with a cloth. You can also use the air hose before finishing to get rid of sawdust buildup in corners.

Work faster with pyramids

These handy plastic pyramids hold your project off the surface so you can paint the edges easily. Better yet, you can finish the front of doors (or the top of shelves) without waiting for the back to dry. Paint the back of the door and set it painted side down on the pyramids while you paint the front. The sharp points on the pyramids will leave only little spots on the wet paint, and they're easy to touch up later.

You'll find plastic pyramids at home centers, paint stores and hardware stores.

TEN TIPS FOR WATER-BASED FINISHES

(1) Raise the grain first

It's a good idea to raise the grain on raw wood before applying a water-based finish. Simply brush, sponge or spray on some distilled water and let it dry thoroughly (overnight is best). Then, resand with your final grit paper to break off the whiskers. Now when you apply the finish, the grain will stay down.

BEFORE ADDING WATER

AFTER WATER DRIES

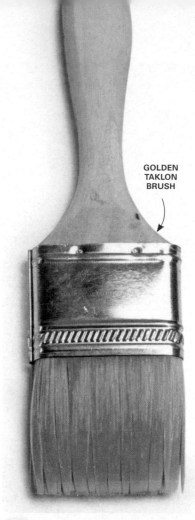

GOLDEN TAKLON BRUSH

(2) Seal oil-based stain

Oil and water don't mix. Water-based poly can have adhesion problems when applied over an oil-based stain that's not thoroughly cured. Always apply a barrier coat of dewaxed shellac to seal oil-based stain. After the shellac dries, a light scuff-sand will leave an excellent surface for the poly to grip.

The instructions on the can will indicate that you can apply a water-based clear coat right over an oil-based stain if the stain has thoroughly cured. However, the curing time can be several days, especially with an open-grain wood such as oak where the stain can sit uncured deep in the pores. Play it safe and seal the stain with a dewaxed shellac.

(4) Choose the right applicator

Buy a top-quality (i.e. expensive) fine-bristle nylon brush for spindle work, inside corners and narrow edges. The nylon bristles won't absorb water from the finish and become mushy like natural bristles will. Each nylon fiber is extruded to a point to resemble a natural bristle. The brush is very soft, and the variable fiber diameters create more space for holding material, meaning fewer dips in the can. Look for fine-bristle nylon brushes at woodworking stores, and expect to pay $20 to $30. (And for that kind of money, plan on taking care of it!)

For large, flat surfaces like tabletops, use a paint pad. It allows you to lay down an even coat in seconds and maintain a wet edge, even over a big area.

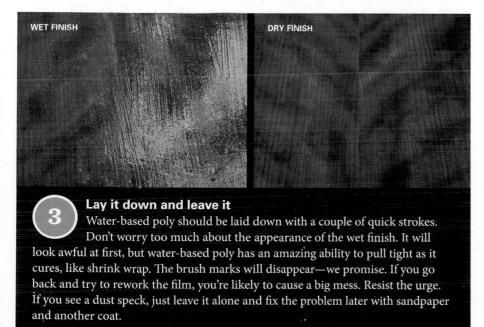

WET FINISH

DRY FINISH

(3) Lay it down and leave it

Water-based poly should be laid down with a couple of quick strokes. Don't worry too much about the appearance of the wet finish. It will look awful at first, but water-based poly has an amazing ability to pull tight as it cures, like shrink wrap. The brush marks will disappear—we promise. If you go back and try to rework the film, you're likely to cause a big mess. Resist the urge. If you see a dust speck, just leave it alone and fix the problem later with sandpaper and another coat.

PAINT PAD

5 Refinish kitchen cabinets with water-based poly

The low odor of water-based poly makes it an ideal choice for refinishing your existing kitchen cabinets in place. It doesn't matter what the old finish was, as long as you prep the surface properly before applying the water-based product. First use a degreaser cleaner to clean away any buildup of grease or cooking oil. Scuff-sand the old finish with fine synthetic wool, then seal with dewaxed shellac. Sand the seal coat with fine synthetic wool, then brush on two to three coats of water-based poly to complete the job.

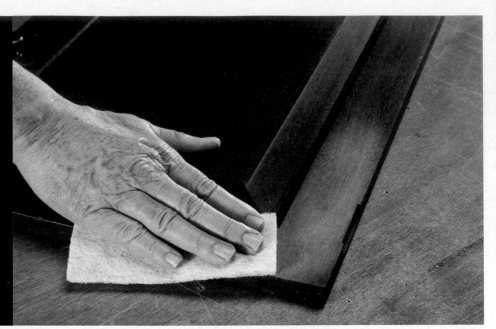

6 Use synthetic abrasives, not steel wool

Synthetic wool is a must-have product with water-based finishes. Traditional steel wool will leave behind bits of steel, which will react with the water and leave rust stains in the clear coat. Synthetic wool comes in various grades and is readily available where water-based finishes are sold. Use coarse to medium synthetic wool between coats. To rub out the last coat, use fine and extra fine. Synthetic wool is available at home centers, hardware stores and woodworking stores.

7 Strain your poly first

Unless you're using a brand new can of poly, always strain it with a medium-mesh strainer before applying it. Once the finish is used, it will be polluted with little bits of dried or semi-dried varnish, which will wreck your new finish. Stands and replacement meshes like the ones shown are available at woodworking stores and online.

9. Use an extender in hot, dry conditions

Water-based finishes are more sensitive to temperature and humidity than their oil cousins. It's best to apply your water-based poly when the air temperature is between 70 and 80 degrees F and the humidity is below 70 percent. If the air is both hot and dry, the poly may set so fast that it will be difficult to maintain a wet edge as you brush, or the film may not level properly before it sets.

The solution is to add an extender to slow the drying time. This is especially useful when you're coating a large piece like a dining table. Extenders are readily available at paint and woodworking stores.

8. Add color for the look of oil-based poly

Water-based poly dries water-clear and can leave wood with a cold look, especially on dark woods like walnut. To get the warm glow of oil-based poly, add a few drops of dye. Transtint Honey Amber is a great product (available at woodworking stores or online). Make a weak solution of dye and water, then stain the wood before you apply the poly. Believe it or not, you can also add dye directly to the poly before you brush it on.

A third coloring option is to seal the raw wood with wax-free shellac, then topcoat with water-based poly. Whichever method you choose, experiment on scrap wood to make sure you'll get the look you want.

10. Mist your wood before staining

Dry wood can aggressively suck up dye or stain, making it hard to control the color penetration. The result can be a dark, blotchy mess. For added control, try wetting the wood with distilled water right before you apply the dye or stain. (Be sure you've raised the grain first; see Tip 1.) The increased open time makes the color easier to control. A household pump sprayer or sponge works great.

Apply water-base finishes fast!

Water-base finishes have a lot of advantages. But because they dry quickly, they can be tricky on large surfaces: The first area you cover becomes tacky before you can smooth out the next, and you're left with brush marks that won't disappear.

Using a paint pad to apply the finish solves these problems because paint pads lay on the finish faster than a brush. Stir, don't shake, the finish and pour some into a paint tray. Dip the pad into the finish and apply it to the surface in long, even strokes. You'll be amazed at how quickly and smoothly you can cover even large areas.

If the project you're working on has some large surfaces and some smaller areas, pick up a few different sizes of paint pads. Large paint pads like the one here are available at any paint store or home center.

Spray on the final coat

Here's a trick for getting a glass-smooth finish on your next wood-working project. Start by brushing on a coat of gloss polyurethane. Let it dry overnight. Then lightly sand with 320-grit sandpaper to remove imperfections. Use a tack cloth or vacuum cleaner and soft brush attachment to remove the dust. Repeat this process for the second coat. Finish up by spraying on the final coat. You can buy aerosol cans of polyurethane in satin, semigloss and gloss finishes. Any of these can go over the gloss coats.

Brushing on the first two coats allows you to build up a thicker layer of finish with less cost and effort than spraying from cans. And using an aerosol can to apply the final coat produces a professional-looking finish, free of brush marks. We used Minwax polyurethane because we were able to buy the same finish in liquid and aerosol versions, and the aerosol can has a high-quality spray tip.

Repairing furniture and trim

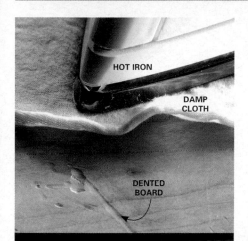

HOT IRON

DAMP CLOTH

DENTED BOARD

Iron out dents and scratches

Before final-sanding your next masterpiece, shine a bright flashlight across the surface to locate any dents. Lightly mark them with a pencil. Now lay a damp cloth over each bruise and press a hot iron down on the cloth. The steam causes the wood fibers to swell and fill the dent. Keep the iron pressed down until you hear steam and see it coming out of the cloth. After ironing, wait for the wood to dry before sanding. For deeper dents that don't disappear with the first ironing, push a pin into the area while it's still damp. This will allow steam to penetrate a little more during a second ironing and swell the crushed wood fibers.

Epoxy putty for wood repairs

This epoxy putty is perfect for small repairs to furniture or cabinets. It's easy to use and makes a strong repair. Just slice off a chunk and knead it until it's a uniform color. Then press the putty into the damaged spot. Let it harden a bit, usually about 15 minutes, until it's about the consistency of soap. Then carve or shape it with a knife, rasp or sandpaper.

After it fully hardens in about 60 minutes, you can sand the repair and finish it with paint or stain. You'll find this repair putty at home centers and hardware stores.

Get rid of dents

You can often get rid of small dents by wetting them. The moisture swells the crushed wood fibers back to their original shape. (You can't fix cuts or gouges this way, though.)

Moisture must penetrate the wood for this to work. Finishes prevent water from penetrating, so make a bunch of tiny slits with a razor blade to allow the water to penetrate. Use the corner of the blade, and keep the blade parallel to the grain direction. Next, fill the dent with water and wait until it dries. If the dent is less deep but still visible, you can repeat the process. The repaired surface may need a coat of wipe-on finish after it's dry to look its best.

Use a stain/poly combo to darken finished wood

A combination stain and polyurethane is convenient for saving time. But it's also a good choice when you want to touch up or darken a surface that's already finished. Stain alone won't penetrate a finished surface well, but a combination stain/polyurethane product will allow you to add one or two dark layers of polyurethane on top of the existing finish.

Fast fix for sticking drawers

To remedy sticking wood drawers, grab a wax candle and rub it along the bottom of the drawer and along the wood runner. The drawers will slide like new.

Touch up scratches

Furniture looking a little shabby with all those little scratches and dings? You know, the vacuum cleaner bumps here and there, and the Hot Wheels hit-and-runs? Not to worry. Here are several simple touch-up techniques that will make these minor eyesores disappear quickly and painlessly.

This is not furniture refinishing or even repairing, which are different games altogether. This is about hiding flaws so only you will know they're there.

1 Hide scratches with permanent-ink felt-tip markers. You can either use the furniture touch-up markers available at hardware stores and home centers, or, to get an exact match, buy markers at an art supply store that carries an array of colors. For thorough coverage, you may need to dab the ink onto the scratch, let it dry, then even out the color by stroking lightly across it with the tip. Keep in mind that colors tend to darken when they soak into wood fibers.

2 Touch up thin scratches with a fine-tip permanent marker. When filling in scratches, steady your hand against the furniture for accuracy; as much as possible, flow the ink only onto the scratch.

Glue a split rung

Split rungs can be repaired without disassembling the chair. Wedge open each split and apply ample glue to each split piece. Get glue as far down the split as possible without actually splitting the rung further.

Securely clamp the repair with padded clamps. Tighten until the glue oozes out and the split edges realign and pull tight. But don't crank down too hard and squeeze all the glue out of the joint. Clean up excess glue with a damp cloth but don't get moisture into joint. Wait about 20 minutes until the excess glue looks like soft licorice, then lift it off by gently scraping with a chisel or utility knife. For a completely invisible fix, you'll have to sand the area with fine sandpaper, color-match the stain and revarnish.

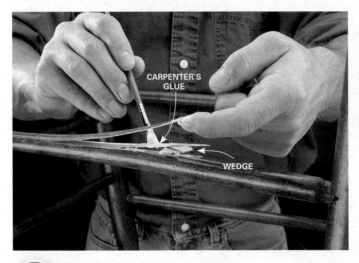

CARPENTER'S GLUE

WEDGE

PADDED CLAMPS

1 Wedge open a split ring with a wood wedge. Apply carpenter's glue to split pieces using a small brush.

2 Clamp the joint using padded clamps. Remove excess glue, first with a damp cloth and then with a sharp chisel 20 minutes later.

Gluing tips

Mask glue joints before prefinishing

Finishing the parts of your project before you assemble them can be a great time-saver and allow you to get a better-quality finish. But for a strong glue joint, you have to keep the joints free of finish (glue doesn't stick to varnish or stains very well). The solution is to apply masking tape to the surfaces that will be glued. Then remove it to expose raw wood when you glue up the project. Any good-quality masking tape will work. If you'll be using a water-based finish, you'll get the best results with a "no-bleed" tape.

GLUE GOES HERE

Apply wood glue with a flux brush

Flux brushes, available in the plumbing department of hardware stores and home centers, are just right for applying and spreading glue. They work especially well for gluing intricate joints like the ones in the coped door rail shown here. You can store a wet brush for a few days in water and then wash and use it over and over again.

CONTAINER WITH WATER

FLUX BRUSH

Cover bar clamps with wax paper

When you use steel bar clamps or pipe clamps, and wood glue comes in contact with the clamp, the moisture in the glue can cause the steel to leave a dark mark on your wood. Lay a sheet of wax paper over the clamps to prevent this "dark spot" problem. It will also catch glue drips that would otherwise get all over your clamps and workbench.

NEW GLUE JOINT

PREVIOUSLY GLUED JOINT

Add one board at a time

When you're gluing several boards together, it can be difficult to get all the top surfaces perfectly aligned. Here's a tip that solves the problem. Rather than glue and clamp all the boards at once, add one board at a time. Let the glue joint set up for about 20 to 30 minutes, then release the clamps and add another board. This method will take a little longer. But it makes it a lot easier to keep all of the boards' top surfaces flush, which makes for much easier flattening and sanding of the surface.

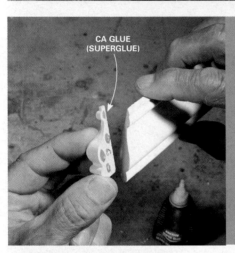

CA GLUE (SUPERGLUE)

Attach small pieces with superglue

Of course you reach for a superglue (cyanocrylate glue, or CA) to fix a broken teacup handle. But did you know that it works on wood, too? In fact, CA glue is really handy for attaching small trim pieces that would be hard to clamp. Just put three or four drops onto the parts and stick them together. We like the gel version of CA glue because it doesn't run off and make a mess.

SHARP CHISEL

PARTIALLY DRY GLUE

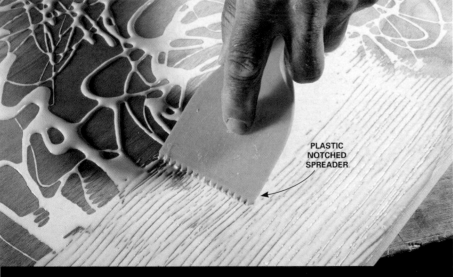

PLASTIC NOTCHED SPREADER

Spread glue with a notched trowel

When you're gluing large surfaces, an inexpensive notched plastic trowel works great for spreading the glue. To find one, look in the flooring or tile section of the hardware store or home center. If you're fortunate enough to have a "pinking" shears in the family sewing basket, you can make our own spreader from an expired credit card.

Let it jell, then shave it off

Look at any woodworkers' forum and you'll likely find a debate about the best way to remove glue squeeze-out. Some woodworkers insist that you should clean it up immediately with a damp rag. Others let it dry completely, then scrape it off. We think that in most cases the best method is to wait about 30 to 60 minutes—just until the glue turns a darker color and changes to a gel—and then shave it off with a sharp chisel. This will remove almost all of the glue without making a mess. You may still have a little cleanup to do (see p. 229), but it's a lot less work than cleaning up wet glue or removing hard glue.

Remove excess glue with an abrasive pad

It can be difficult to remove excess glue with a rag. And if you don't get it all off the surface when it's wet, the dried glue can show up as light spots when you finish your project. But a synthetic abrasive pad, dampened with water, works perfectly to remove the glue. Dip the pad in a container of water. Unlike a rag, which is hard to rinse glue from, the pad has a loose synthetic weave that releases glue easily. After rinsing out the pad, shake it to remove most of the water. Then use it to scrub off excess glue. When you're done, dry the surface with a clean rag. Green abrasive pads are found with the cleaning supplies at grocery stores, hardware stores and home centers.

HARDENED WOOD GLUE

Remove hardened glue with a paint scraper

We've all been there. You glue up your project and then quit for the night. The next day you discover the rock-hard glue and realize that you forgot to scrape off the glue squeeze-out. Don't despair. A sharp paint scraper makes fast work of hardened glue. Either a sharp steel scraper or, better yet, a carbide paint scraper will pop off all those glue beads in a heartbeat.

PERFECTLY ALIGNED

The right amount of glue

With a little experience, you'll develop a feel for how much glue is just enough. Too little glue creates a "starved joint," which will be weak. Too much glue makes a mess and wastes glue. With practice, you'll know just how much to apply. You should see a continuous line of small glue beads. When this perfect glue joint sets up a little, you'll find it easy to scrape off the jelled excess, and you'll have very little cleanup to do.

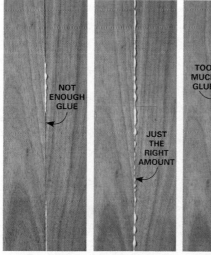

NOT ENOUGH GLUE

JUST THE RIGHT AMOUNT

TOO MUCH GLUE

Tack—then clamp

Wood glue makes boards slippery, so it can be hard to keep them lined up correctly while you apply clamps. An easy solution is to hold the parts in alignment with a few strategically placed brads before you apply the clamps. For leg glue-ups like we show here, cut your parts extra long and place the brads where they'll get cut off during the finishing process. Otherwise, just place brads where the filled holes won't be too visible.

Reminders for strong glue joints

■ **Make sure your gluing surfaces are clean and smooth** but not too glossy. Rough surfaces don't allow enough glue contact. Glossy surfaces prevent the glue from penetrating the fibers and getting a good grip. You can sand lightly to smooth roughness or remove gloss, but don't try to actually shape a joint by sanding; it's impossible to get a good mating fit that way. If you're sanding, use a block and be careful not to round over sharp edges.

■ **Clamp all glued joints.** Pressure is necessary to form a tight, gap-free bond, and to help force glue into the wood fibers. Clamping also prevents movement while the glue is hardening. In situations where you can't use clamps, use screws, elastic cords or weights.

■ **Do a dry run** with clamps before you apply any glue. This not only allows you to check for a good fit but also ensures that you will have your clamps adjusted to proper length, and all other necessary tools at the ready. It's important to complete a glue-up fairly quickly; even though it takes about an hour for most wood glues to set and 24 hours to cure, the initial "grab" takes place in two or three minutes, and clamping should be completed by then.

■ **Get a good fit** between the two glued surfaces. Wood glues (except for epoxy) won't bridge gaps, so any joint with gaps will be weak. The parts should fit together snugly. If you can't reshape the part with a router or table saw, try gluing thin wood curls in place to fill the gaps. (You can cut curls from a scrap board using a wood plane.)

Slow down

Glue-ups can be a frenzied, nerve-jangling activity. So why not slow things down a bit? Take the edge off your glue-ups with a slow-setting glue. The extra 10 minutes of open time can be a real lifesaver and nerve calmer.

Another fine mess

Wiping off wet construction glue can make a big, smeary mess. If you can't find the right solvent, spray some WD-40 on a rag and use it to clean the glue right off.

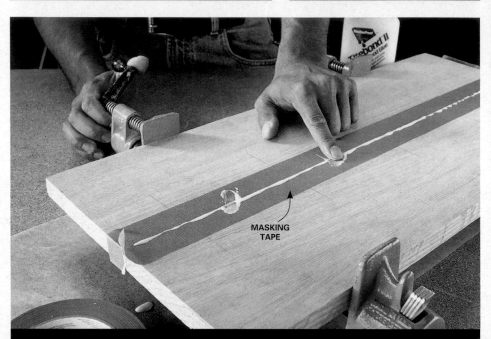

MASKING TAPE

Apply tape to control glue squeeze-out

Glue squeeze-out soaks into the fibers of raw wood, leaving blemishes when you later apply the finish. The usual solution for this is to clean it off with a wet rag or sponge. But too much water around the joint can weaken the bond. It's better to stick down masking tape along both edges of the joint before gluing. The excess glue will then squeeze out onto the tape instead of the wood, and you can just peel the glue away when it's dry.

Hot glue is hot stuff

If you think hot glue is just for holiday decorations and craft projects, think again.

You can also use it to fix knickknacks, temporary clamping, and countless other quick fixes. It's wonderful. Dab on a bit, hold the part for a few seconds to let it cool, and you're ready to go! It sticks to just about anything, and you can actually take stuff apart with some prying or heat (if you have to).

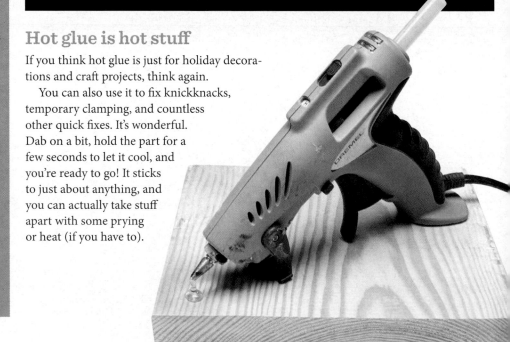

Fast and cheap glue roller

Here's a smooth tip for spreading carpenter's glue: Slide a piece of 1-in.-diameter pipe insulation onto a 4-in. paint roller frame and use it to evenly roll on the glue. When the job's done, just throw away the insulation. No more wasting store-bought rollers on a one-time job.

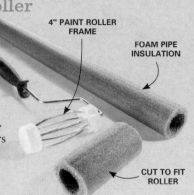

4" PAINT ROLLER FRAME

FOAM PIPE INSULATION

CUT TO FIT ROLLER

THROW AWAY AFTER GLUING

BOARDS TO BE FACE-GLUED

Choose the best type of glue

Yellow exterior glue (sometimes gray): Use it for outdoor projects, but not continuous submersion. Will be labeled "water resistant" or "exterior."

White and yellow interior glue: The most common "workhorse" wood glue. Not for outdoor use.

Liquid hide glue: Use it for furniture repair; very long open time for assembly—up to 30 minutes. Requires a long curing time.

Polyurethane glue: Use it when you need a completely water-proof glue. Also glues metal and some plastics. Long open time for assembly—up to 15 minutes; curing time: up to five hours.

Epoxy: Use it when you need to fill gaps and for great strength. Comes in two parts that must be mixed just before using. Epoxy will glue most materials, and it's waterproof. Won't wash off your skin—or anything else.

Use epoxy for tough-to-clamp joints

Sometimes you encounter wood joints that are very difficult to clamp—for example, the odd-angle miter shown, or very small pieces of trim. That's when fast-setting epoxy comes to the rescue. Mix it up, apply to both surfaces, and hold the parts together in exactly the position you want until the glue sets. You can use 90-second epoxy, or if you want more strength (and you have more patience), use the five-minute variety.

Chapter Twelve

CARS, RVs AND YARD MACHINES

Car maintenance

8 INTERIOR DETAILING TIPS

Unless you're fastidious about your car's interior, it's usually the last thing on your cleaning list. As the months roll by, grime, wrappers, dust and junk can just pile up. Unfortunately, most of us finally get around to the deep cleaning when we tape the "For Sale" sign on the windshield. So whether you're selling your car or just feeling ambitious, these tips from professional detailers will give you the most return for your energy. You'll feel like your car is brand new again.

ODOR
ELIMINATOR

1 Kill bad odors. Whether your vehicle smells like a Big Mac or cigarettes, one pump of an odor eliminator will solve the problem.

2 Slide the seat all the way forward and clean out all the junk underneath. You'll be surprised by what you find. We found a lost cell phone, enough pens and pencils to equip a small office, and enough change for several vending machine lunches. Vacuum the seats, remove the mats and vacuum the carpet. Use a brush attachment for the dash and door panels. Don't forget to clean out and vacuum those handy door pockets (another source of buried treasure) and the trunk.

PLASTIC
PUTTY
KNIFE

GOO
GONE

3 Scrape off those annoying stickers. While all of your national and state park stickers may call to mind great memories, they can be a visual hazard as they accumulate. The high-quality stickers will pull off if you can get under a corner and carefully pull them free at a 90-degree angle. Others will leave a gummy residue and require a bit more attention. Cover your dash with an old towel and dab on Goo Gone. Then scrape and wipe it off.

LONG-BRISTLED
ARTIST'S BRUSH

4 Brush out the air vents. These louvers are a real magnet for dust, and a vacuum with a brush attachment just won't get it all. Take an inexpensive paintbrush and give it a light shot of furniture polish. Work the brush into the crevices to collect the dust. Wipe the brush off with a rag and move on to the next one.

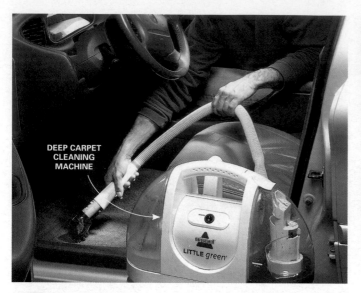

DEEP CARPET CLEANING MACHINE

LITTLE green

5 Deep-clean carpeting and upholstery. Use a carpet cleaning machine to get the deep dirt that settles into the fibers of the carpet. (Clean cloth seats this way as well.) It sprays the carpet with a solution of water and cleaner and then sucks the dirt and grime into a reservoir. A machine like this pays for itself after just a few uses. You can also rent one from a rental center or use a spray-on cleaner and a scrub brush instead.

little green

HAND METHOD

RESOLVE

6 Remember to get into the nooks and crannies. Detailing means just that—finding and dealing with all the trim lines and recesses that a quick once-over cleaning job misses. Wrap a cloth around an old, worn screwdriver (without sharp edges) and spray all-purpose cleaner on the cloth. Move it gently along the trim lines to pick up the gunk. Keep refreshing the surface of the cloth. Go around all the buttons and controls as well. Follow up with a rejuvenator.

simple green

Original

GRIME AT TOP OF WINDOW

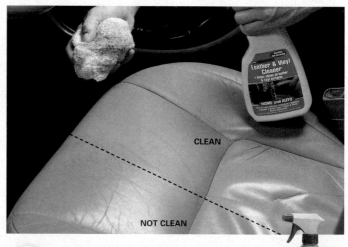

CLEAN

NOT CLEAN

Leather & Vinyl Cleaner

HOME and AUTO

7 Wash the windows, including the top edges. Ever notice that line of grime on the tops of windows when they're partially rolled down? Most people overlook this detail when giving their vehicle a quick wash. A few minutes with window cleaner and a clean rag is all it takes.

Windex Original

8 Clean and condition the leather or vinyl. After a couple of years, the color of leather seats no longer matches the rest of the interior. It's not enough just to condition the leather. First spray on leather cleaner and rub vigorously with a clean terry cloth towel. To avoid rubbing the grime back into the seats, keep flipping the cloth to expose a fresh surface. Let the seats dry for an hour and then rub in a leather conditioner to keep the leather supple.

Leather & Vinyl Cleaner

8 EXTERIOR DETAILING TIPS

Attention to detail when you're cleaning your vehicle's exterior can keep it looking new and prevent premature rust and a dull finish. In most cases, you can do a complete cleaning and detailing job in less than three hours. You'll not only enjoy driving a good-looking car but will also find that a well-detailed car can bring as much as $400 to $500 over book value when you decide to sell. Along with describing washing and waxing basics, we'll show you techniques that pros use to revive cars for resale.

1 Tired of your bumper stickers? Soak the sticker in warm soapy water for at least 10 minutes, then take a plastic putty knife and get under a corner and start working it loose. Never use a metal scraper or razor blade because they can scratch the finish. If the sticker still won't budge, wipe off the soap solution and give the sticker a spray of WD-40, let it absorb and start scraping again. The WD-40 will loosen the adhesive and act as a lubricant for the putty knife without harming your car's finish. Keep spraying as needed if you run into stubborn spots. Once the sticker is removed, you may have adhesive still stuck to the bumper. Dab rubbing alcohol onto a clean rag and scrub until it's gone. Wash and dry the area, then put on a coat of wax.

2 Wash the entire car one section at a time. Soak the entire car with your hose to get rid of loose dirt and dust, and use a heavy jet spray under the wheel wells where road dirt accumulates. Then fill a bucket with warm water and add car-washing soap. Dish soap is generally too harsh. Avoiding the direct sun, wash a section at a time and then rinse it immediately. Start from the top down: first the roof, then the hood, the trunk and finally the sides. Use a special wash mitt or a heavy terry cloth towel. Work the soapy water in a circular motion and get into corners and detail lines. Use a soft-bristled washing brush to get at areas where a rag or mitt can get caught (racks and license plate brackets, door handles, trim, etc.). Open the hood and trunk and wash the crevices where dirt gets trapped. When you've finished washing the last section, rinse the whole car again and then dry it with a chamois, starting from the top down. Wring out the chamois often to keep it absorbent. The idea is to avoid water spots and streaks.

3 Use a spray-on solution to clean doorjambs and weatherstripping. You can use a hose and bucket, but it's often tough to keep water from spraying into the interior. A spray-on wash is great for this because you'll have a lot more control and won't be flooding delicate door mechanisms with water. Get into all the nooks and crannies around the weatherstrip and hinges to make your car look showroom perfect.

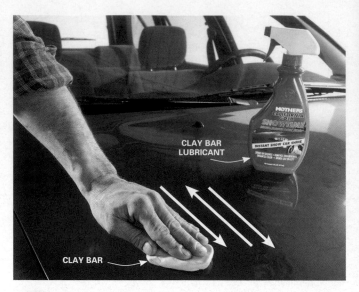

CLAY BAR LUBRICANT

CLAY BAR

4 Scrub the wheels and tires with a brush. Ordinary soap and water often aren't enough to get rid of caked-on brake dust and road grime, so buy a specialty cleaner for your type of wheels (painted, chrome, alloy or clear coat). Spray the wheel and let the solution work for about 30 seconds, then scrub with a soft-bristled brush to work the cleaner into all the small recesses. Flush with water and repeat the process if necessary. After you've dressed the tires to make them look showroom new (see next step), put a coat of wax on the wheels. Spray-on wax works best.

5 Wash the tires with soap and water, then rinse and dry. Next spray on a tire dressing and let it dry. The tires will look new and be protected for up to 30 washings.

6 Revive a dull paint finish. Contamination from brake dust and air pollution dulls painted finishes and eventually leads to surface rust. The best way to revive the finish is with a clay bar that actually absorbs these contaminants as you rub it back and forth across the paint. Professional detailers have been using this product for years. Now you can find it at auto supply stores. Spray the surface with either the lubricant that comes with your clay bar or liquid wax. Never use plain water. Rub the clay back and forth on the freshly lubricated section, overlapping each stroke and using light pressure. It will sound harsh at first, but as the clay bar absorbs contaminants, it will get quieter and smoother. Rework as needed until the finish feels as smooth as glass. Remove any residue by spraying on more lubricant and then buff with a clean terry cloth towel.

7 Wax your car at least twice a year. Very lightly mist a 2 x 2-ft. section with clean water, then apply a good-quality wax. Do a panel at a time, such as the hood or the roof, just as you do when you wash. Apply wax with an applicator or rag, rubbing in a circular motion. Let the wax dry to a haze and remove it with a lint-free, soft terry towel. Open the doors, the hood and the trunk to remove haze from the edges. Never wax in direct sun.

8 Give your weatherstripping renewed life. Dress door, trunk and hood weatherstripping with a silicone spray. Wash the weatherstrip first, then apply the spray to a rag (prepackaged wipes are available) and work it into the weatherstrip until it shines. You'll restore its suppleness, protect it from aging and keep it from freezing to the door in icy winter weather.

REPLACE THE 5 MOST NEGLECTED BULBS IN YOUR VEHICLE

The lightbulbs that burn out most often are the taillight, stop, turn signal, backup and headlight bulbs. But there are many other bulbs in a vehicle that could use your attention too. These are the five most commonly neglected bulbs that can affect your driving experience. Check yours to see if they work, and pick up replacements at any auto parts store.

MAP LIGHTBULB
Pry off the lens and pull the bulb out of the spring terminals. Snap in a new bulb.

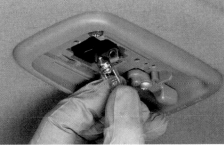

DOME LIGHTBULB
Pry off the dome light lens and spread the spring terminals. Drop one side of the "torpedo" shaped bulb out of the socket and lift the bulb out. Reverse to install.

HIGH-MOUNT STOP BULB
A burned-out high-mount stop lightbulb can also earn you a ticket. Pry off the interior trim cover. Then rotate the socket a quarter turn and swap out the bulb(s).

Bulb changing tips

We're not going to ask how many DIYers it takes to change a lightbulb. But did you know there are a few tricks to changing the bulbs in your vehicle? Read these and file them away in long-term memory.

■ Check the bulb for signs of tungsten filament deposits. The darker the buildup, the closer it is to burnout.

■ If you're replacing a bulb in an exterior socket, apply a very light coating of dielectric grease to the bulb's contacts. That'll prevent corrosion.

■ A long-life bulb is worth the price. It'll last at least twice as long as the original, so you'll most likely never have to replace it again.

■ A "blue" bulb gives off whiter light, making it easier to see in the dark. Use them for dome, map, fog and backup lights.

LICENSE PLATE BULB
Since a burned-out license plate bulb can get you a ticket, replace it if needed. Unscrew the lens or release the locking tab. Twist the bulb socket a quarter turn and pull it out. Snap in a new bulb and reinstall.

■ Skin oils can cause bulbs to swell and fail. It's especially important to prevent swelling on headlight and fog light bulbs.

FOG LIGHTBULBS
Most drivers don't realize their fog lights are burned out until they're needed most. If one is burned out, replace them both. Reach behind the fog light assembly to access the bulb. If you can't gain access, remove the entire assembly and then replace the bulb.

But skin oils can also cause miniature bulbs to swell and fail. Always wear gloves when you handle bulbs.

Replace your thermostat and radiator cap when you change the coolant

The thermostat is the single most important component in your vehicle's cooling system because it regulates engine temperature. Yet most owners don't replace it when they change their coolant. That's a mistake: A failed thermostat is the second most common cause of engine overheating and engine failure (a failed radiator fan is No. 1). And a worn radiator cap (sometimes it's on the overflow tank) can also contribute to engine overheating. Both parts are inexpensive and are cheap insurance against overheating.

A radiator cap is a snap to change (photo right). It's just a matter of unscrewing it and replacing it with a new one. Changing a thermostat yourself takes less than an hour (unless it's buried). To find out how to replace yours, see "Replace a Thermostat" on p. 242. But if yours is inaccessible, pay a shop to replace it.

RADIATOR NECK

Oil changes

Oil for high-mileage cars

High-mileage (HM) oil contains seal conditioners that rejuvenate brittle aged seals. And it contains additives to improve film strength when the oil is hot. Depending on the brand, HM oil may also include more anticorrosive, acid-neutralizing and antiwear additives. If you have a high-mileage engine and want to keep it running, HM oil is worth the higher price.

Always follow viscosity recommendations

Aside from neglect, using the wrong oil viscosity is the single most common cause of premature engine wear. And most of that wear occurs during cold starts. What's considered a cold start? If your vehicle hasn't run for three or more hours, it's cold—even if you live in Arizona!

The carmaker's recommendations are in your owner's manual or right on the oil filler cap. Never second-guess the carmaker's recommendations, even if your know-it-all buddy says a different viscosity oil will work better. Ignore the carmaker's recommendations at your own risk.

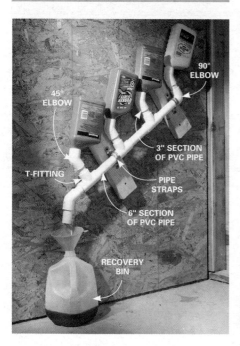

45° ELBOW

90° ELBOW

T-FITTING

3" SECTION OF PVC PIPE

PIPE STRAPS

6" SECTION OF PVC PIPE

RECOVERY BIN

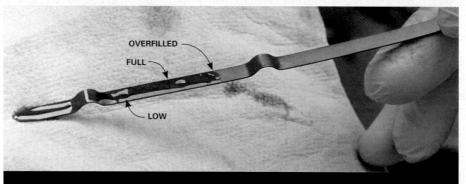

OVERFILLED

FULL

LOW

Fill only to the top line on the dipstick

Overfilling the crankcase is really bad for your engine. Even if your engine leaks or burns oil and you're tired of topping it off, overfilling isn't the answer. Running an overfilled engine actually causes excessive oil consumption that can destroy your catalytic converter (about $1,000 to repair). And, when the oil level is too high, rotating engine parts whip air into it, turning it into foam. Foam doesn't lubricate or cool, so engine parts overheat, wear and fail.

Get the last drops

If you service your own vehicles and other equipment, you can help save the environment and save a few bucks to boot with this oil recovery gizmo. Cut a 1-in. PVC pipe into 3-in. and 6-in. lengths and glue everything together using the fittings as shown. Mount the contraption to the wall with pipe clamps and use a gallon jug with a funnel for catching those last drops of oil. You can easily adapt the design to make it larger or smaller.

Buy a good filter for synthetic oil

Filter manufacturers usually make several grades of filters—good, better, best. If you use a mineral oil and change it and your filter on schedule, you don't need to spend more for a better filter. But if you use a synthetic oil or intend to go longer between oil changes, buy a top-of-the-line name-brand filter.

Get rid of old oil

Oil has a shelf life of about five years. So if you bought a truckload of oil on sale 20 years ago, don't think you can pour it in your 2013 truck. Oil degrades in the can or bottle just from sitting in your garage.

FIRST CONTAINER

SECOND CONTAINER

NO MESS

Instant oil funnel

Don't have a funnel handy? An empty plastic oil container will do the job. Cut the bottom out of the empty container with a sharp utility knife. This funnel can hold an oil container snugly, so you don't have to stand around waiting for the last drop to drain.

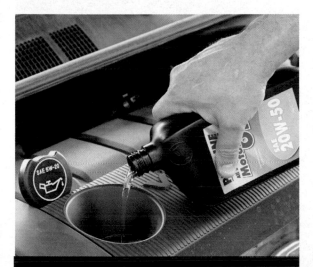

Adding the wrong oil is better than driving with no oil

You're supposed to check your oil level regularly. But most of us don't. If you're driving a leaker or an oil burner and find yourself critically low on oil, you've got to act fast or you'll destroy the engine. If you can't find the correct oil at the nearest convenience store, it's better to add the wrong oil than to continue driving on oil vapor. Grab a bottle of multi-viscosity oil that's the closest to the manufacturer's recommendation and pour in enough to restore the oil level. If you only added 1 qt., you can wait until your next oil change. But if you've added 2 or more quarts of the wrong oil, get your vehicle in for an oil change soon. Oh, and fix the leak that caused the low oil condition.

Q&A

Q. My car has high miles and my buddy told me to switch from 5W-30 to 20W-50 oil to get better piston sealing.
A. A 20W-50 oil does provide better piston-to-cylinder film strength. But it'll cause more engine wear at cold startup. Use a high-mileage (HM) 5W-30 oil instead and get the same protection at start-up and better film strength when hot.

Q. If I switch to synthetic oil, can I extend the drain intervals?
A. If your vehicle is covered by a warranty (factory or extended), you MUST follow the vehicle manufacturer's recommended oil-change intervals even with synthetic oil. If you're not covered by a warranty, consult the oil manufacturer for its recommended drain intervals.

Q. I'd like to switch to synthetic and read that because synthetics have better detergents, I need to flush my engine with solvents first.
A. Just make the switch—don't ever flush your engine with solvents.

Q. My engine needs oil. I have a bottle with the correct viscosity and the current "SN" rating, but it's a different brand. Can I use it to top off my engine?
A. Mixing different brands is fine.

A drip pan saves time

Car repair is a messy business, and if you don't use a drip pan or a large piece of cardboard, you'll wind up with an oily mess on your garage floor. If you're the kind of cheapskate who saves appliance boxes just for this purpose, more power to you. But the rest of you can easily afford to buy a real drip pan with a lip all around the edge. When you're done, just pour the oil into your recycling bottle and put the pan back under your car to catch any remaining drips.

Installing a cartridge filter

Many newer engines use a cartridge filter instead of a spin-on design. Always note the location of the O-ring as you remove the cap and replace it with the new O-ring in the filter box. Lube the O-ring with oil, and use a torque wrench set to the manufacturer's specifications to tighten the cap.

Mark the contact position

Loose filters are the No. 1 cause of oil leaks. Follow the tightening instructions on the box. Spin it on until the gasket contacts the mounting surface. Draw a line on the filter in the 12 o'clock position. Hand-tighten the recommended number of turns and then stop.

Car repairs

Online repair manuals

The inexpensive printed manuals that you find in bookstores and auto parts stores often cram many model years into the same book. To keep the price low, they often leave out exactly the kind of detailed repair instructions you may need—for example, to remove components like door trim panels, which have hidden fasteners.

But the Internet has revolutionized car manuals. Now you can download make, model and year-specific repair information for just about any repair job on any car. Simply find the pages that apply to your repair, print them out and haul them out to the garage.

In addition to full repair procedures, online services also provide the most up-to-date technical service bulletins and recalls for your vehicle. All the services charge a small subscription fee.

Best avoidable "oopses"

Mixing different types of coolant. Green, yellow, red, orange and blue coolants create cool "mud" when mixed. Cost of a new heater core: $400 to $1,000.

Putting E-85 in a "non-flex-fuel" car. This little mistake will cost you the price of a tow, a fuel tank and fuel line flush, a new fuel filter and a new tank of gas. Expect to pay about $400 for this "oops."

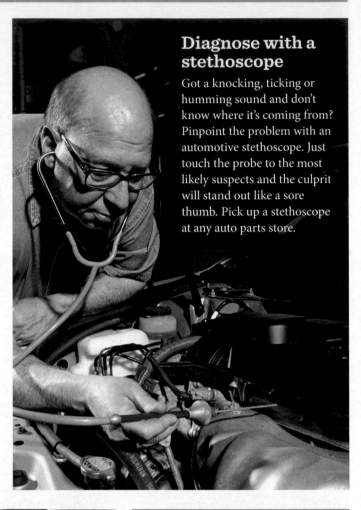

Diagnose with a stethoscope

Got a knocking, ticking or humming sound and don't know where it's coming from? Pinpoint the problem with an automotive stethoscope. Just touch the probe to the most likely suspects and the culprit will stand out like a sore thumb. Pick up a stethoscope at any auto parts store.

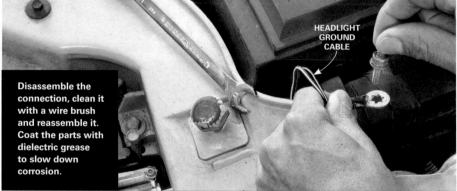

HEADLIGHT GROUND CABLE

Disassemble the connection, clean it with a wire brush and reassemble it. Coat the parts with dielectric grease to slow down corrosion.

Repair a dim headlight

If your car has a headlight that puts out about as much light as a flashlight with weak batteries, we've got a fix for you. Most DIYers think they've got a bad headlight switch or a bad connection in the power feed. But most dim headlights are caused by a corroded ground wire. Just trace the wiring harness from the back of each headlight assembly and see where it connects to the vehicle body. Clean it as described above.

When should I change the plugs?

Not all spark plugs are rated for 100,000 miles. In fact, some carmakers recommend replacement at 30,000-mile intervals. So always follow the spark plug service intervals shown in your owner's manual. But if you can't remember when you last changed your spark plugs, you can pull them and check the gap and their condition. Once you've put in the labor to do that, however, you may as well change them and establish a new baseline for the future.

Replace a skipping wiper arm

All wiper arms have a hinge at the base that allows the arm to flex as it follows the curvature of the window. If the wiper skips over certain spots, even with a new blade, chances are the hinge is binding from corrosion. It's most common on rear window wipers since they're used less often.

You can oil the hinge, but that's just a temporary fix—the corrosion and binding usually return. To fix the problem permanently, replace the wiper arm.

All wiper arms fit onto a splined shaft. Some are held in place with a nut. To replace that type, just lift the protective cap, remove the nut and pull off the arm.

The other type is held in place with a locking clip. Unlock it as shown in the bottom photo and install the new arm.

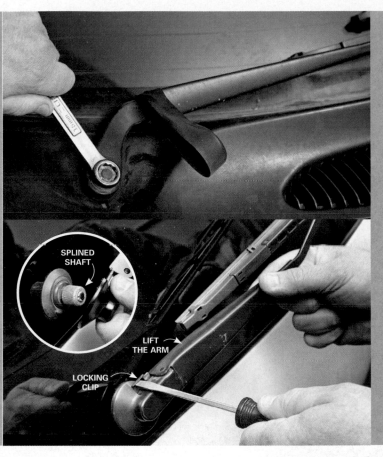

SPLINED SHAFT

LIFT THE ARM

LOCKING CLIP

SOME WIPERS ARE HELD WITH A RETAINING NUT. Lift the plastic cover and remove the retaining nut. Then pull the arm off the splined shaft.

OTHERS HAVE A LOCKING CLIP. Lift the wiper arm a few inches off the glass and slide the locking clip out. Then lower the arm and pull it off the splined shaft.

Chemicals to keep on hand

If you're going to do repair work, you simply have to keep some basic lubricants and special chemicals on hand. Here's what every shop should have.

- **LITHIUM GREASE** for latches and hinges.
- **BRAKE CLEANER** for removing oil and grease from metal parts.
- **RUST PENETRANT** for removing rusted fasteners.
- **DRY LUBRICANT** for lubricating metal to metal, and metal to plastic or rubber.
- **ELECTRONIC PARTS CLEANER** for dissolving corrosion on electrical connectors.
- **ANTI-SEIZE LUBRICANT** to prevent nuts and bolts from seizing in place.
- **DIELECTRIC GREASE** to repel water in electrical connections and prevent corrosion.
- **SILICONE SPRAY** to lubricate windows and weather stripping.

Why is my tire pressure light on?

The batteries in a TPS (tire pressure sensor) last five to seven years. But they're not serviceable. When they fail, you have to replace the entire sensor.

But before you run your vehicle into the shop, check the pressure on your spare tire. Some manufacturers install sensors on those tires as well, and they lose air just like your regular tires. Low pressure in that tire could be lighting up your TPS.

Troubleshoot windshield washers

If you press the button for windshield juice and nothing comes out, you probably have a clogged nozzle. Start your diagnosis by making sure there's fluid in the reservoir. If so, check for fluid flow at the tee near the cowl (Photo 1). If that checks out, leave the tubing off the tee and clear out the nozzle with a compressed air gun (Photo 2). However, if you couldn't get fluid flow at the tee, you probably need a new pump.

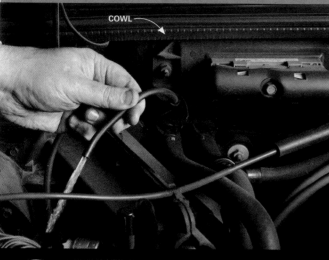

COWL

1 CHECK PUMP OPERATION. Follow the washer tubing from the reservoir to the tee. Disconnect the tubing and have a friend press the washer button. A strong stream of washer fluid indicates a good pump but a clogged nozzle.

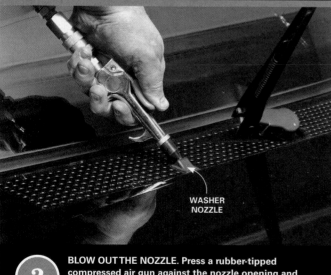

WASHER NOZZLE

2 BLOW OUT THE NOZZLE. Press a rubber-tipped compressed air gun against the nozzle opening and blow air backward through the nozzle (tubing still disconnected at the cowl). Then reconnect the tubing and try the washers again.

Replace a thermostat

In most cases, the cause of an overheating or no-heat condition in your vehicle is a faulty thermostat. And since a new "T-stat" costs only about $10, it makes more sense to replace it than to spend hours diagnosing the problem. If that doesn't fix it, at least you're only out about two hours.

Pick up a new T-stat and gasket, as well as RTV sealant, fresh coolant (to top off the system) and hose clamping pliers at an auto parts store. And while you're there, ask the clerk for the torque specs for the gooseneck bolts. Then gather up your metric sockets, a plastic scraper and a drip pan. Slide the drip pan under the engine to catch the spilled coolant.

The T-stat is usually located near the top of the engine under a "gooseneck" housing attached to the upper radiator hose. If yours isn't there, consult a shop manual to locate it. Remove the two or three bolts that hold the gooseneck in place and remove the T-stat (Photo 1). Next, clean both the engine and the gooseneck sealing surfaces (Photo 2). If the parts store gave you a plain gasket, coat one side with RTV sealant (self-adhesive gaskets don't need sealant). Then install the T-stat and gasket (Photo 3). If the old T-stat used a rubber O-ring instead of a gasket, lubricate the new one with fresh coolant before you insert it. Reinstall the gooseneck and top off the coolant.

REMOVE THE OLD THERMOSTAT. Pry off the gooseneck. Then remove the thermostat from the engine or the inside of the gooseneck.

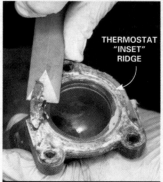

THERMOSTAT "INSET" RIDGE

CLEAN BOTH MATING SURFACES. Use a plastic scraper to remove the old gasket and any sealing compound. Then dry the surfaces with a rag.

RTV ON THIS SIDE

SELF-ADHESIVE SIDE DOWN

INSTALL THE NEW THERMOSTAT AND GASKET. Place the new thermostat in the recessed groove in either the engine or gooseneck (air bleed toward the top). Hold it in place with a self-adhesive gasket. Then apply a bead of RTV sealant.

Motorcycles and RVs

MODULAR FULL-FACE HELMET

REINFORCED SHOULDER PADS

LIGHTWEIGHT BALLISTIC FABRIC

CHEST IMPACT PAD

REINFORCED AND PADDED ELBOW AREAS

GLOVES WITH VISOR SQUEEGEE

REINFORCED AND PADDED KNEE AND ANKLE AREAS

MOTORCYCLE-SPECIFIC BOOTS

LIGHTWEIGHT KEVLAR

BELL RS-1

AERODYNAMIC DESIGN

BELL

Ride with the right gear

Let's get this straight right from the get-go: If you wear tennis shoes, shorts and a T-shirt and get into a crash, you'll be ground up like a piece of balsa wood on a belt sander. That's not opinion: It's fact. The proper safety gear includes gloves, boots, helmet and motorcycle outerwear with body armor. It's simple. Riders who dress in safety gear survive crashes with fewer injuries than those who don't.

Regardless of helmet laws, all the experts recommend donning a full-face, DOT-certified helmet before you get on a bike. Studies prove that motorcyclists who wear safety-certified helmets are far more likely to survive a crash. Helmet wearers also suffer fewer injuries and are less likely to incur long-term or permanent disabilities from head or neck injuries. You can buy a helmet certified by the Department of Transportation for as little as $99, or spend upward of $900 for an ultralight carbon fiber unit. Spending more usually gets you a lighter helmet that fits better, is more comfortable and offers more features.

Maintain your tires

Tire pressure and good tread are critical to proper handling, especially during crash avoidance maneuvers. Even a small change in pressure can dramatically affect how the bike handles during braking and turns. So experts recommend checking pressure every time you go out for a ride. Consult the owner's manual or the tire pressure decal on the bike. Also, adjust tire pressure accordingly if you're riding with a passenger.

Pay attention to the condition of the tires. Check the wear bar depth and check for age/heat-related cracks.

FLAT WEAR

WEAR BAR

Change the differential oil in your ATV

This simple drain-and-refill procedure should be done regularly. But many owners neglect it, resulting in huge repair bills. Refer to your owner's manual for recommended change intervals and the proper type of lube oil.

2 TO 3 LBS.

Fill your tires to the ATV manufacturer's recommended pressure (it's printed on a label stuck to the machine and in your owner's manual), never to the maximum pressure shown on the tire sidewall.

Tire pressure matters!

Many ATV owners have lost their low-pressure tire gauge and use an auto tire gauge instead. Big mistake! It won't give you an accurate reading. And according to experts, most owners overfill their tires, sometimes by as much as 20 to 30 lbs. That reduces traction and increases the "bounce" factor that could throw you from the machine. In 2006, ATV accidents in the United States resulted in an estimated 882 deaths and 146,600 visits to the emergency room. Don't be the next statistic. Inflate your tires to the proper pressure.

Lube clutch and brake cables

Repair shops replace a lot of cables that could last much longer with periodic lubrication. And, with replacements costing $20 and up, regular lubrication is just plain smart. Lubricate the cables twice per season. It's easy to do, but you'll need this special lubrication tool for an effective job. Buy it (and a can of spray cable lube) at your dealer or online.

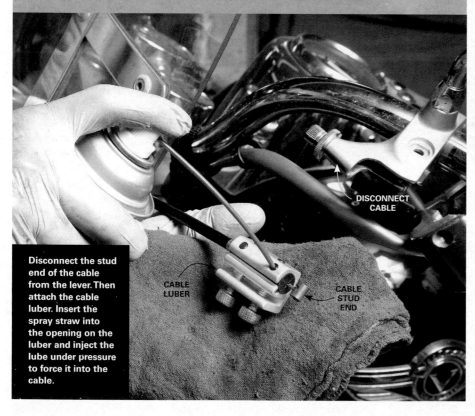

DISCONNECT CABLE

Disconnect the stud end of the cable from the lever. Then attach the cable luber. Insert the spray straw into the opening on the luber and inject the lube under pressure to force it into the cable.

CABLE LUBER

CABLE STUD END

Clean and maintain your ATV air filter

Most of you operate your ATVs in dirty conditions. That's fine; they're designed for that. But you have to keep the air filter clean. According to one local repair shop, just about every machine they work on has a seriously clogged filter. A dirty filter lowers your gas mileage and causes poor engine performance. Cleaning the filter is messy, but anybody can do it.

Buy an air filter cleaning kit from your dealer. It contains a bottle of cleaning solution and a spray can of filter oil. You'll also need a plastic cleaning tub, rags, a bucket of soapy water and chemical-resistant gloves.

Remove the foam filter and wipe any debris from the outside. Then dunk the filter in the cleaning solution for the recommended time. Squeeze out the excess solution. Rinse the filter with water and let it dry.

Pour fresh oil on the cleaned filter element. Then squeeze the foam to spread the oil into the pores. Reinstall it on the carburetor.

Trailers

High-visibility trailer

Paint the top of your trailer's loading ramp white and you'll be able to see it better. It makes a huge difference when you're backing up, especially on rainy days. At night, the back-up lights reflect off the white paint, and you can maneuver the trailer much more easily.

Yard tool holders

To make it easier to carry yard tools like rakes and shovels, build tool holders from PVC pipe for your tractor cart. Glue on end caps and attach the holders to the cart with U-brackets. Drill a hole in each end cap so water can drain out.

5-1/4" DROP, OR RISE

3-1/4"

2"

Selecting the right ball mount

Buying the right ball mount for receiver hitches is critical to the safe operation of your trailer. If you install the wrong mount, the weight imbalance may break either the ball mount or the trailer coupling, causing a huge accident that could easily kill people. Follow the measuring instructions below to find the right "drop" or "rise" height.

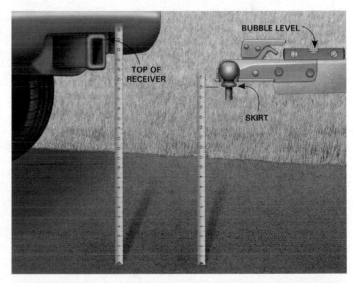

TOP OF RECEIVER

BUBBLE LEVEL

SKIRT

Park the vehicle and the trailer on level ground. Drop the trailer jack and level the tongue with a bubble level. Then lock the proper-size trailer ball into the trailer coupling. Measure from the ground to the skirt of the ball. Then measure from the ground to the top of the vehicle hitch receiver. The difference between the two measurements is the "drop," or "rise." Find the ball mount that's closest.

Loosen stubborn fasteners

Use an impact driver when you can

An impact driver and a set of high-end hex-shaft nut drivers are all you need to loosen small nuts and bolts. For larger nuts and bolts, you'll need an impact gun and a set of six-point, impact-rated (black finish) sockets. Ordinary chrome sockets can't handle impact work and may crack or shatter under the stress. And because impact-rated sockets have six points instead of 12, they're less likely to round over bolt and nut heads.

Cheater bar

Tool purists (and tool manufacturers) hate this tip because they think it's both dangerous and an abuse of tools. It is. But sometimes it's the only way to get the job done, especially if you're removing large nuts and bolts. Slide a metal pipe over the handle of a pipe wrench, a combination wrench or a socket wrench. The pipe will add tremendous leverage. It may be hard on tools and might even break them, but on the bright side, you'll most likely break the fastener loose and have fewer strained muscles and/or bruised knuckles.

Stuck fasteners can bite you

When it comes to causing pain, stuck fasteners can get the job done. Right when you're giving a stuck bolt all your muscle, wrenches will slip, bolt heads will snap off and your hands will get smashed against something sharp. So always wear gloves and try to orient tool handles so your hands will be clear if a tool slips.

Needless to say, pounding on stubborn fasteners with hammers, mallets and sledgehammers poses similar dangers. Never use a regular hammer for metal-on-metal impact. Bits of the hardened metal can break off and become embedded in your flesh. Safety glasses are a must, as well as hearing protection when you're running some of these very power noisy tools.

LOCKING PLIERS

ROUNDED JAWS

Lock on to wrecked heads

These pliers are best known by the brand name Vise-Grip. Whatever brand you have, they'll get you out of a jam when bolt and nut shoulders are rounded, or when screw slots or Phillips crosses are stripped out. Rounded jaws work best. Make sure the jaws are seated on the flats of the nut/bolt or around the screw head, and tighten the handle as much as you possibly can before turning the fastener.

Pound a combo wrench

Box-end wrenches work better than sockets on stuck heads because they twist in the same plane as the head, rather than being offset by an inch or more. That offset means sockets are likelier to slip off heads and round over shoulders. Fit the closed end of the wrench over the bolt head and try tugging in short pulses, instead of a full-throttle pull. That'll help loosen rust-bonded surfaces. If that doesn't do it, tap on the wrench with a plastic, brass or wooden mallet. It's a good way to loosen the bones in your hand, too, so wear leather gloves and keep your fingers well away from the impact zone!

The two most important weapons

If you're dealing with stuck metal-to-metal fasteners, there are two things you always need to do. First, soak the culprits in rust-penetrating oil—not an all-purpose spray lube. The sooner you start that, the better. Really rusty connections may need several hours of coating and recoating.

Second, you have to "shock" the fastener to crack the rust and allow the penetrant to soak in even further. That can mean "chattering" fasteners with an impact wrench, tapping with a ball-peen hammer, or even pounding on the handle of a screwdriver head or the side of a combination wrench while loosening. If there's one thing you can take away from this story, it's the importance of combining a rust-penetrating oil AND vibration.

Be gentle with spark plugs

If you snap off a spark plug or strip the threads, you'll have a real nightmare on your hands. So if a plug shows any sign of seizing, stop and spray on rust penetrant. Let it sit for at least 30 minutes and try to loosen it just a one-eighth turn. Don't get greedy and keep turning. Add more penetrant and turn the plug in and out slightly to work penetrant down into the threads. Saturate with penetrant and tighten/loosen only an eighth of a turn at a time. Eventually, it'll start turning freely and you'll be able to back it out.

Pipe wrenches aren't just for pipes

When you're dealing with really big stuck bolts, a pipe wrench might be your best option, especially if you don't own a giant set of wrenches or sockets. The long handle and aggressive jaw teeth will loosen the most stubborn bolts. Just make sure you get the jaws tight against the shoulders. Pipe wrenches are also a go-to tool when bolt shoulders have been rounded over.

Sacrificing a tool

It might seem sacrilegious to destroy a tool, but sometimes working in narrow or confined spaces makes it necessary. That's where your grinder comes in. Use it to make wrenches thinner and screwdrivers skinnier and to add tapers to sockets so they fit into tight recesses. But this technique comes with a warning. Grinding a tool compromises its integrity, so take extra precautions when using it (wear goggles and gloves). When you're done, toss the modified tool and get a new one—it's no longer safe for use on other jobs.

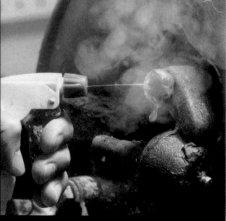

Heat is the last resort

Applying heat with a propane torch can expand a nut (or threaded opening) and loosen it. If you've tried everything and still can't free a bolt or nut, try heat. But first make sure the fastener is a good distance away from hoses, belts, gas tanks or anything else that might burn up your car or kill you in an explosion.

If the area is soaked with penetrant, spray it with nonflammable brake cleaner to remove it before you apply heat. Keep a fire extinguisher nearby. Once you've established that it's safe, aim the flame at the bolt head or nut, not the surrounding metal. Heat for about 15 seconds, but don't get it cherry red. Then spray the bolt head with water to cool it quickly. Continue spraying until it no longer steams. The expansion/contraction cracks the rust, so add more rust penetrant, let it soak and then add vibration. Then try to loosen it.

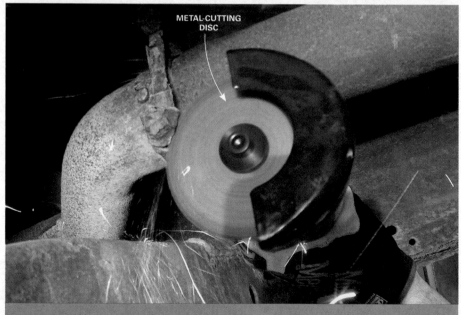

METAL-CUTTING DISC

Don't mess around—cut it off!

If you have a stuck nut/bolt that can be replaced, don't beat yourself up trying to unscrew the rusty one. Just cut off the stuck fasteners (or the parts around it if they're getting replaced) and buy new ones. Use a reciprocating saw with a hacksaw blade or, better yet, a cutoff tool. (You can get a cutoff tool for as little as $30 at any home center or hardware store.) Then take the leftovers to the store to match them up with new ones.

Whack stuck wheels

If your wheels are fused to the rotors and simply won't bust free, try this. Grab the biggest sledgehammer you have and pound on the bottom of the tire.

To avoid accidentally wrecking the sidewall or rim, jack up the truck, loosen the lugs and prop a 2x10 against the tire. Then pound away. The wheel will pop right off after a few swings. But if you wait until you have a flat on the side of the road, you won't have a sledge to free up a stuck wheel. So before you head out on that road trip, maybe you should rotate those tires and make sure your wheels aren't stuck, especially if you have an older car with some rust.

Stuck receiver hitches

A ball mount that's been in the receiver hitch too long can rust in place. Here's the trick for freeing it up. Use an air chisel (sold at any home center or auto parts store) and a special 1-in. hammer impact chisel.

After saturating the receiver hitch with penetrant, hold the hammer alongside the receiver tube and pull the trigger. Let the air chisel chatter away at the hitch for a minute or so. Then repeat on the other side of the hitch and try sliding the shaft out. You may have to try a few times and give the hitch a few whacks with a maul, but eventually it'll come out. Before slipping it back in, coat the shaft with water-resistant marine grease so it won't get stuck again.

HAMMER IMPACT CHISEL

AIR CHISEL

Poor man's impact driver

When you need to tackle stuck slotted or Phillips screws, buy a hammer-style impact driver. Apply rust penetrant and allow it to soak in. Then fit the right driver bit in the end, and pound on the end with a ball-peen hammer. This shocks the fastener, cracks the rust and twists the bit, all at the same time. The hammer blow keeps the bit in the screw head, preventing further damage to the slots.

Drill out rivets

Removing rivets is easier than you think. Just pick a drill bit that's a tad larger than the hole in the top of the rivet. Run the drill until the washer head is loose. Then poke the rest of the rivet out of the hole.

RIVET

Lawn mowers and other yard machines

Easier lawn mower oil draining

Here's a trick to make lawn mower oil changes a lot easier. Older gas mowers had a drain plug to remove used oil. But with many newer mowers, you have to turn the mower on its side to drain the oil, which is awkward. Instead, try clamping plastic tubing to a turkey baster and using it to drain the oil. Stick the end of the tubing into the oil fill hole and suck out the oil, then squirt the used oil into an oil pan and repeat as many times as it takes to empty the oil.

PLUMBING CLAMP

Nonstick lawn mower

To keep grass clippings from sticking to the underside of your mower, clean the underside and spray it with a nonstick cooking spray.

Easy-to-check dipstick

When you change the oil on your lawn mower, the oil and the dipstick are often so clean that it's hard to check the level. Mark the low line of the dipstick with a Sharpie marker to make it much easier to read.

No excuses!

To get in the habit of keeping your blade sharp, dedicate a set of tools for sharpening only. Hang them nearby so they're ready to go. And keep a second, sharp blade handy too. You can slip it on and sharpen the dull one later.

Lube up weed trimmer

If the self-feeding mechanism on your line trimmer sticks and binds, spray lubricant on the mechanism and spool. Use a dry PTFE lubricant that won't harm plastics. You'll get smooth, trouble-free operation.

Do you need a new blade?

Examine your blade when you remove it and look for the problems shown. If you're unsure of the condition of the blade, take it to a hardware store or home center and compare it with a new one.

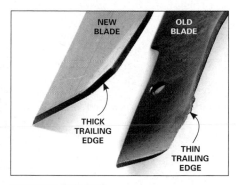

THIN TRAILING EDGE
The trailing edge, or fin, is the edge opposite the cutting edge. This fin is often slanted upward, which creates an updraft to lift the grass and grass clippings. Dust and sand will wear this fin down. When it's thin, replace the blade.

BENT
Set your old blade on your workbench and check for bends. If you're unsure, compare it with a new blade.

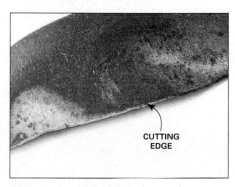

DENTS IN CUTTING EDGE
Replace blades that have deep dents that you can't file out and erosion from wear and sharpening. Also replace any blade that has cracked.

4 easy winterization steps for a lawn tractor

Before you put your tractor away for the winter, take a few minutes to prevent springtime troubles.

■ Moisture inside an unused engine leads to corrosion. "Fogging" the engine—spraying an oily mist into each cylinder—prevents this. All you have to do is remove the spark plugs and blast in some aerosol fogging spray (sold at auto parts stores). Then reinstall the spark plugs.

■ Storing a battery that isn't fully charged can lead to permanent damage, especially in cold weather. Connect the battery to a battery charger and charge it until you get a reading of 12.7 volts.

■ Stored gas will slowly gum up the whole fuel system, and the repairs can be expensive. So add a fuel stabilizer such as STA-BIL or Sea Foam to the gas tank before winter. (Adding stabilizer to your gas can year-round is also a good idea.) But remember that stabilizers aren't effective in gas that contains ethanol. If you don't know whether the gas contains ethanol, run the engine until the tank is empty.

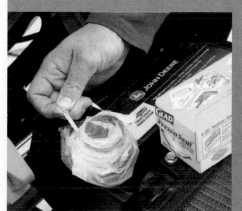

Cover the air intake and exhaust openings with plastic wrap or aluminum foil to keep critters from homesteading in your engine over winter.

Snow blower smarts

Don't wait for it to stop

If you're in for a huge snowfall, start clearing the snow before it reaches 6 in. Sure, you'll spend more time snow-blowing, but your machine won't have to work as hard, and it'll throw the snow farther. That'll reduce the height of the snowbanks flanking your driveway.

Get your property ready for snow

Before the snow flies, take a few minutes to inspect your property. Remove rocks, dog tie-out cable, extension cords, holiday light cords and garden hoses. Then stake out paths that run near gardens so you don't accidentally suck up rocks and garden edging. Mark your walk and driveway perimeters by pounding in driveway markers. If the ground is frozen, just drill a hole using a masonry bit and your battery-powered drill.

Start with fresh fuel

Stale gas is the No. 1 cause of hard starting. So don't use what's left in the lawn mower can. It's better to dump that summer blend into your car's tank, then refill the can with winter blend, which is more volatile and provides better starting.

Throw it far

Avoid throwing snow only partway off the driveway and then throwing it a second time. That just creates a heavier load for the blower. There are four ways to get the maximum throw: Take smaller bites of snow (see p. 253), run the blower at full rpm but at a slower ground speed, adjust the chute diverter to its full raised position and blow with the wind.

Don't swallow the newspaper

A frozen newspaper is the leading cause of machine jams. It can break shear pins or belts and damage expensive auger and impeller components. A fresh layer of snow over newspapers makes them hard to see, and they're easy to forget. So protect your machine by scouting the area before you hit it. If you do suck up a newspaper, shut down the engine and remove it with a broom or shovel handle—never with your hands. If you can't remove the paper, take your machine to a pro, who will charge a whole lot less than even the cheapest surgeon.

HALF WIDTH

Cool off, then gas up

If your snow blower runs out of gas halfway through a tough job, you'll be tempted to refill it right away. But think about this: The engine is hot and the gas tank sits right on top of that hot engine. Even worse, you're standing right over the machine holding a gallon of gas. If you spilled gas on the engine or overfilled the tank, you could instantly turn your snow-blowing adventure into a painful burn-unit experience. Even if you managed to escape injury, you could still wind up with a freshly toasted snow blower.

Snow-blower fires happen often enough that the manufacturers strongly recommend that you let the engine cool for at least 10 minutes before refilling. Take that opportunity to grab a cuppa joe or hot chocolate and warm up your fingers and toes. Then, once your personal tank is refilled, refill your snow blower and carry on.

Add stabilizer to the fresh fuel

Follow the stabilizer dosing recommendations on the bottle label. Add the stabilizer to the gas can right at the gas station so it'll mix up on the way home. Or, add a premeasured packet to the gas can before filling it with gas.

Take smaller bites to prevent clogs

When you get blasted with wet, heavy snow and you're in a hurry, it's tempting to crank up the speed and plow right through it. That's the single best way to clog your machine and wear out (or break) the drive belts. And when you consider how long it takes to constantly stop and unclog the chute, ramming at full speed doesn't actually save any time.

Worse yet, improperly clearing a clogged chute is dangerous, and the most common cause of snow blower–related injuries. Instead of making a full-width pass through the snow, manufacturers recommend taking smaller bites; about one-third to one-half the width of the machine. It's faster than slogging through a full path of heavy snow and it's easier on the machine. Another reason it's a better snow-blowing technique is that it allows the machine to throw the snow farther.

Switch to synthetic oil for easier starting

Small engines typically have to reach at least 400 rpm before they'll fire up. But traditional motor oil thickens when cold, making it much harder to reach that 400-rpm threshold. Synthetic oil allows the engine to spin faster when you yank the cord, so it starts with fewer pulls.

USE THE RIGHT LUBRICANT

Chain lube

Chain lube penetrates deep into roller chain links and doesn't fly off when the chain is in motion. To use it, clean off the old lube with spray solvent and a brush. Apply the chain lube and slowly rotate the chain to allow it to work into the links. Then leave it alone until the solvent evaporates. Chain lube resists water, dust and dirt better than ordinary oil. Use it for chains on bicycles, motorcycles, scooters, garage door openers and outdoor power equipment. But never use aerosol chain lube in place of a bar chain oil on chain saws.

Garage door lube

Garage door hardware operates in an environment that's often dirty and damp, sometimes hot and sometimes cold. That's why there's a special lube for it. Garage door

lubes are formulated to penetrate deep into hinges, rollers and springs but dry to a fairly tack-free finish to resist dust and dirt buildup. Many brands also contain anticorrosive additives to protect against rust.

White lithium grease

Grease is the lube of choice for higher-load items like bearings and axles because it cushions parts. And unlike oil, which tends to seep away, grease stays in place and lasts much longer. White lithium is a great all-around grease for lubricating light- to medium-load items like tools and garden equipment. It comes in aerosol cans and in tubes. Aerosols are easier to use because the solvent helps the grease seep into tight spaces. That can save you the trouble of disassembling components to grease them.

Dry PTFE lubricant

"Dry" lubricant actually goes on wet. But once the solvent dries, the product leaves a thin film of dry polytetrafluoroethylene (PTFE)—the same product used to make nonstick frying pans. The main advantage of dry PTFE is that dust doesn't stick to it. That makes it a great lube for dirty environments like your garage or shop. PTFE bonds to metal, wood, rubber and plastic—so it stays put. It's a light-load lubricant, so it's not the best lube for equipment that carries a heavy load or transmits high torque. And it doesn't have any anticorrosive properties (although some manufacturers spike theirs with an antirust additive), so don't use it on outdoor metal. Dry PTFE lube is available in both aerosols and squeeze bottles. Check the label to make sure the solvent won't harm the material you're lubricating. Note: Not all "dry" lubes are PTFE. Some are silicone, which is a different ball game.

Silicone lubricant

Silicone is the slipperiest of all lubricants, so it's a great choice for items that slide against one another. Silicone repels water, but not water vapor, so you can use it to dry out electrical connectors. But don't rely on it as a sealant in humid conditions. Use silicone to lubricate metal, wood, rubber and plastic. However, dust and dirt stick to silicone, so use it sparingly or use a "dry" version in dirty environments.

The biggest downside to silicone lubricant is that once you apply it to an object, you can never paint or stain it. And, since the spray drifts, it can contaminate nearby walls and floors. If you ever plan to paint anything in the surrounding area, mask off the spray zone before you spray.

Marine grease

Like lithium grease, marine grease is formulated to lubricate high-load items. But it's thicker and far more water resistant than lithium grease, so it does a fantastic job of inhibiting rust and preventing metal parts from "welding" themselves together with rust. Use marine grease to lubricate items that are directly immersed in water or constantly exposed to the elements. Like any grease, it's a tacky magnet for dust and dirt.

Synthetic grease

Synthetic grease is the best choice for gears, axles and bearings that carry

heavy loads, transmit high torque, operate at high temperatures or are subject to shear stress. Synthetic grease has less rolling friction than the petroleum-based grease you'll see next to it on store shelves. It resists thermal breakdown and shear, too, so it lasts much longer than other types of grease.

Rust-penetrating oil

Other products will free up stubborn nuts and bolts— eventually. But they won't do it nearly as fast or as well as oil formulated just for that job. Rust-penetrating oil contains an aggressive solvent to penetrate the rust. And it contains a special low-viscosity, low-surface-tension lubricating oil that flows into micro-cracks in the rust to get lube deep into the threads. But don't use it for purposes other than stuck stuff; it does a poor job of keeping things slippery.

LUBRICATION TIPS

Avoid the off-brands

Cheap brands cost less for a reason—they contain less of what matters. These two beakers show how much silicone was left after the solvents and propellants evaporated from a name-brand product and a cheaper "no-name" brand. The cheaper stuff cost 79¢ less—and contained far less lubricant.

Clean out the old lube

Adding fresh lube to old, degraded oil and grease is a prescription for equipment failure. To get the full advantage of fresh lube, always clean out the old lube with spray solvent and a rag (aerosol brake cleaner works well).

SOLVENT

PTFE LUBRICANT

Shake before using

All spray and squeeze bottle lubes contain solvents along with the actual lubricant. If you don't shake the product before application, you'll get a lot of solvent and very little lube.

Prevent seizing

Apply a thin coat of marine grease to a trailer hitch ball mount to prevent it from rusting and "welding" itself to the receiver.

Don't forget plain old motor oil

That leftover can of 30-weight motor oil isn't the very best lube for all jobs, but it's a handy and acceptable friction fighter for most. Heavyweight motor oil is thicker than most spray oils, so it provides a stronger film cushion. And motor oil has built-in anticorrosive additives to resist rust. Since it doesn't have any solvents, a full drop is really a full drop of lube. And it's cheap—a quart should last a lifetime.

DRY PTFE SPRAY

Choose dry lube for dusty situations

Dusty and dirty conditions call for a lube that isn't tacky. Dry PTFE is a good choice for this vacuum cleaner. It dries tack-free and bonds well to surfaces, so the spinning parts won't throw off lubricant.

Lithium grease for garden equipment

Lubricate heavy garden equipment wheels with spray lithium grease. It'll stand up to the load better than oil, silicone or PTFE. Take the wheel off and spread grease on by hand or shoot it with aerosol white lithium grease. Spin the wheel to work the lube into the axle before the solvent evaporates.

SYNTHETIC GREASE

Grease, not oil, for high loads

Reduce wear on gears and bearings with a heavy-duty synthetic grease. Spread it on all surfaces and rotate the parts by hand to distribute the grease. Never pack the gear case completely full unless directed by the manufacturer.

Chapter Thirteen

LAWN AND GARDEN

Lawn care

Perfect lawn patch

Here's how to cut out damaged grass and cut a sod patch that fits perfectly in its place: Lay a piece of sod over the bad spot and slice through both the sod and the damaged turf below with a sharp spade. Then dig out the bad spot and plug in the new sod. Water it daily for a couple of weeks and it will blend invisibly into your lawn.

CARDBOARD TUBE

Weedy tip

When you sow seeds, it can be hard to tell little weeds from the young sprouts. Cut cardboard tubes from toilet paper into one-third sections to encircle the seed and keep you from plucking out your young plants.

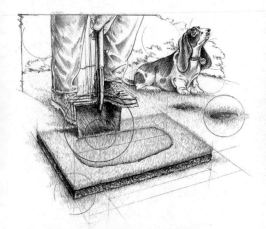

Water break on the go

If you don't want to stop mowing the lawn just to run into the house for a drink of water, attach a bicycle water bottle holder to the mower arm. Just fill up the bottle at the start and take your water breaks without breaking stride.

7 tips on fertilizing

1. Select fertilizers that are a combination of "slow" and "fast" release. They give the grass both immediate and longer-term nutrients.

2. Never fertilize wet or damp grass; wait until it's completely dry. Otherwise, the fertilizer will stick to the blades and could damage them. An exception to this rule is combination fertilizer/herbicides. They should be applied to damp grass, when no rain is forecast (and no watering) for 48 hours. Water after that.

3. Use a "broadcast" spreader to distribute the fertilizer because it spews out the granules, distributing them faster and more evenly than a "drop" spreader.

4. Fill the spreader on a hard surface like a driveway, patio or sidewalk—never on the grass. You'll be able to reclaim any spills and keep them from damaging the grass. Use a shop vacuum to pick up spills. You'll never be able to sweep up fine granules.

5. Water thoroughly after fertilizing to dissolve and drive the fertilizer into the soil.

6. If you aerate in the fall, apply the fertilizer afterward so the fertilizer will drop into the aeration holes for better soil penetration.

7. Never apply fertilizer when the ground is frozen because it won't penetrate the soil. Instead the fertilizer will run off and find its way into streams and waterways.

7 tips on weed-killing

1. Don't waste your money or time applying herbicides (except preemergence treatments) when there aren't any weeds. Fertilize instead.
2. Use a pump-up type sprayer to spot-treat weeds that are limited to specific areas. Only mix the amount of liquid herbicides you need that day. They have a very short shelf life once mixed with water.
3. The soil should be moist and the grass growing before you apply any herbicides.
4. Water your lawn thoroughly before applying any weed treatment.

5. Apply liquid herbicides only on calm, windless mornings. When the wind's blowing, you'll not only waste material but also possibly kill nearby shrubs and flowers.
6. Granular herbicides work poorly on viny broadleafs like clover or creeping charlie. Use liquid herbicides on those. Some work better on hard-to-kill broadleaf weeds. Ask for advice at the garden center.
7. Buy concentrated liquid herbicides; they're cheaper than premixed solutions.

CHEESECLOTH

BAMBOO STAKES

POWER CORE AERATOR

PULLED SOIL PLUGS

AERATION HOLES

Protect a newly seeded lawn

Protect a newly seeded small lawn or bare spots from hungry birds by laying strips of cheesecloth over the seedbed and securing the corners with small stakes. (Buy cheesecloth at hardware stores and home centers.) It holds the seed and soil in place during waterings and hard rains, especially on slopes. The cheesecloth also warns people to keep off your new grass. The grass grows through the cloth, which will disappear under the thickening grass and eventually decompose (inset photo).

GRASS GROWING THROUGH CHEESECLOTH

5 tips on aerating

1. Aerate only during cool weather. The exposed roots surrounding holes will dry out on hot summer days.
2. Wait two years before aerating newly seeded yards and one year before aerating newly sodded yards.
3. Make two passes at 90-degree angles. In heavily compacted soils, make a third diagonal pass for thorough aeration or before seeding.
4. Don't bother aerating lawns growing in sand unless there is a buildup of thatch.
5. The soil should be moist 3 to 4 in. deep before aerating. Otherwise the tines won't penetrate and extract the necessary 1- to 1-1/2-in. plugs.

YANK 'EM WHILE THEY'RE YOUNG!

OK, your lawn has been growing for a couple of months and you notice light green blades thickening up your Kentucky Blue. Before you think your lawn is having an exceptional season, think again: It's likely to be young crabgrass (see Photo 1).

Pulling, at this early stage, is a surprisingly effective way to get rid of crabgrass. But if the weed has pushed up three or four rows of leaves, inspect it carefully before you snatch it. If you spot a slender, green seed head that is still closed and folded up against the leaves of the plant, go ahead and pull it, too (Photo 3). However, after the seed head tines have spread out like a fork, leave it alone (Photo 4). Otherwise you'll scatter scads of seeds right over that nice big hole you've just created by removing the mature weed. You might as well be trying to cultivate new crabgrass!

Come fall, seed bare and patchy areas. With good lawn care practices, you'll soon crowd out those fallen crabgrass seeds.

1 Pull out crabgrass as soon as you spot it. Young plants leave only a small hole in your turf, which desirable grass types will quickly fill.

2 Young crabgrass plants perfect for pulling have two to four sets of leaves but no splayed seed heads.

3 Immature crabgrass plants have tight, green seed heads. They're more difficult to remove, but it's still OK to pull them.

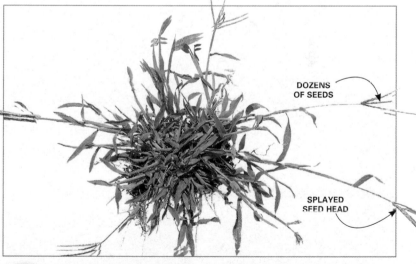

4 Fully mature crabgrass has splayed seed heads. It's best to leave it alone. Pulling will leave a big hole in the lawn and spread up to 5,000 seeds per plant. The plant will die in the fall. Then hit the area next spring with pre-emergence granules to keep the seeds from sprouting.

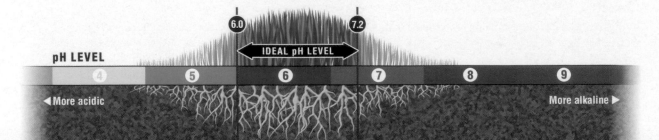

pH LEVEL

6.0   7.2

IDEAL pH LEVEL

4   5   6   7   8   9

◄ More acidic   More alkaline ►

THE BEST pH LEVEL FOR GRASS
The acidity level is gauged on the pH scale. A pH of 7 is neutral. Below that is acidic and above it is alkaline. Soil that has a pH of between 6 and 7.2 is best for grass. Above or below that range can be highly detrimental to root development and leaves grass susceptible to heat stress and disease.

Tips on pH

■ Once you adjust your lawn's pH, test it again in four months to see if it has maintained the correct pH range. Treat it again if necessary. Once you've established a consistent level, retest and adjust it (if necessary) every three years.

■ Inexpensive, do-it-yourself test kits for pH testing are available at garden centers but aren't very accurate. For reliable results, get a professional analysis.

■ Don't mix the front and back yard samples. The whole idea is to tell which areas need treatment. Pay to have each area tested separately.

■ Pelletized limestone is the best way to raise pH levels. Iron sulphate or sulphur is generally used to lower pH. Applied incorrectly, however, this treatment is potentially damaging to your lawn, so be sure to follow the directions.

■ Grasses in soils with high or low pH values won't make the best use of naturally occurring or added fertilizers.

Test the soil pH and adjust if necessary

Soil pH is often overlooked but is one of the key ingredients to a healthy lawn. If you've watered, mowed and fertilized properly and still have a sickly lawn, overly acidic or alkaline soil could well be the problem. Grass is most content in a soil that's slightly acidic. If you've never checked your lawn's soil pH, it's a great idea to take soil samples and have them tested. Don't be intimidated; it's a simple process both to test and to correct any problems.

Check your soil pH by calling a garden center or a university or county extension service that tests soil samples. They'll tell you how to collect and submit samples. Different parts of the yard can vary significantly. The best way to collect samples is to follow the grid shown.

Once you know the pH, the garden center will help you determine the best treatment to achieve a more grass-friendly pH. It's inexpensive and just a matter of applying the proper amounts of nutrients with a spreader.

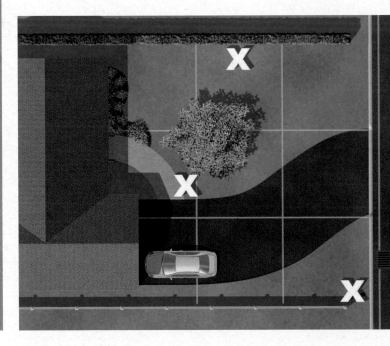

Mix together samples from the center of the yard near the house and at spots at opposite sides of the yard. Use the same sampling pattern for the back yard and have the two mixed samples tested separately.

Controlling pests

Burrowing chipmunks

Chipmunks typically start their tunnels next to something solid, such as front steps or sidewalks, and burrow under it for protection.

To keep the critters out, bury a strip of hardware cloth 2 ft. deep in the ground around the steps and along the sidewalk. Chipmunks won't be able to get through it and they won't dig down far enough to get under it. You can buy 2-ft.-wide strips of hardware cloth at home centers, so you won't have to cut it.

If your chipmunk problem persists and they start to dig somewhere else on your property, simply catch them in live traps and relocate them away from residential areas.

Suffocate ants with soap and orange oil

Drenching ant mounds with dish soap alone can be effective. But according to the Penn State Cooperative Extension service, a method showing even more promise for a wider variety of ants (including fire ants!) is drenching ant mounds with a mixture of dish-washing liquid and orange oil.

Orange and other citrus oils contain d-limonene (citrus peel extract), which destroys the wax coating of an ant's respiratory system. A Texas A&M extension study had success drenching fire ant mounds with 1-1/2 oz. of orange oil and 3 oz. of liquid dish soap per gallon of water. You can buy orange and other citrus oils at farm supply stores and online.

Cedar oil repels ticks, fleas and mosquitoes

Plant oils such as cedar oil, lemongrass oil and others evolved to protect plants from insect damage. The EPA considers cedar oil a safe pesticide in low concentrations (higher concentrations can irritate the skin and be toxic if ingested). Cedar oils are also often used in flea sprays for pets.

Spraying cedar oil diluted with water on your lawn and shrubs can repel insects. However, the Colorado State University extension cautions that spraying horticultural oils might damage certain sensitive plants or trees or those under drought stress.

Kill slugs with corn meal

Cornmeal is one of many pet- and kid-friendly slug remedies. Slugs love it, but can't digest it and die. Others include:
- Crushed eggshells, pine needles, diatomaceous earth and other abrasive materials sprinkled around plants.
- Tin cans filled with a few inches of beer sunk into the ground, which attracts slugs and drowns them.
- Slugs will also shelter beneath a board or an upside-down pail. Set one out each evening and you can kill a bunch of slugs each morning.

Trees and bushes

Don't plant too close to a building

Plant a tree with its mature size in mind. Many arborists suggest planting a tree no closer to a structure than one half of its expected mature canopy spread. Tree roots and branches need space. Pruning a tree planted too close to a structure to keep it from damaging your roof, foundation or siding can damage or disfigure the tree.

Also, some trees develop large surface roots that can crack or lift driveways, patios and sidewalks. If that's a concern, plant well away from these surfaces or choose a tree less likely to produce above-ground roots. Also, watch out for overhead power lines—most shade trees will grow at least to the height of residential power lines. Choose shorter, ornamental trees for these areas.

Tree trunk protector

Protect the trunks of young trees and bushes from lawn trimmers and critters by using 6-in. flexible plastic drainage pipe. Cut a short piece of pipe, split it along its length, and wrap it around the young tree.

3 tips for pruning roses

Keeping your favorite roses in shape is easier than most gardeners think. In fact, it can be done in three simple steps.
1. Remove dead and damaged stems. It's easy to tell which stems to clip—these are the ones that are dull brown or gray with no new growth. Cut near the base of the plant.
2. Remove crossing or rubbing branches. Also take out stems that are growing toward the center of the bush or trailing on the ground.
3. Take a step back and look at the shape. Trim branches that don't follow the shape you're looking for. The goal is to have evenly spaced stems on all sides of the bush with the center somewhat open.

ELLEN THOMSON

Don't add soil amendments

For years, experts recommended adding compost, peat moss or fertilizer to the planting hole. However, most now agree that you shouldn't backfill with anything other than the original soil from the planting hole. Soil amendments in the planting hole can discourage the tree roots from spreading into the surrounding soil and can cause poor water drainage. Also, in some instances, fertilizers can kill young roots.

Plant in fall or early spring

The ideal time to plant a tree is in early spring before "bud break" or in the fall before the tree goes dormant. Cool weather allows the tree to establish roots in its new location before new top growth puts too much demand on it. Some trees establish better if planted in early spring. These include oaks, pines, dogwoods, American holly, willows and black gum. Avoid planting trees during the summer when they're in full leaf and susceptible to heat stress.

Don't plant too deep

If you plant the root-ball of a tree too deep, new roots can girdle the trunk and may also suffer from a lack of oxygen. Plant a tree so the root collar—where the uppermost roots attach to the trunk—is about an inch above the soil level.

In many cases, containerized trees from nurseries are planted too deep. Don't go by the soil level in the container. Dig down into the planting medium to find the root collar so you know how deep to plant the tree.

If you're planting a bare-root tree, leave a cone of soil at the bottom of the planting hole and set the root system on top. Place the handle of your shovel flat across the hole from one side to the other to make sure the crown is level with the surrounding soil. You should be able to partially see the root collar, or trunk flare, after the tree is planted.

Dig a shallow, broad hole

Dig a saucer-shape hole three to five times the diameter of the root-ball (or the spread of the roots for a bare-root tree). This allows the roots to easily penetrate the softened backfill and properly anchor the tree.

If you're planting in clay or wet soil, use a garden fork or your spade to roughen the bottom and sides of the planting hole to avoid "glazing." Glazing happens when the sides and bottom of a hole become so smooth and compacted that water can't pass easily through the soil. In extreme situations, it could block roots from penetrating the sides of the planting hole.

Caution: A few days before you dig, call 811 to have your underground utilities marked. Learn more at call811.com.

BILL ZUEHLKE

Mulch wide, but not deep

Mulch holds moisture, moderates soil temperatures, reduces competition from grass and weeds, and prevents lawn mowers and trimmers from nicking the trunk. Make a 3-ft. (or larger) circle of mulch 2 to 4 in. deep around the trunk. But don't mulch too deep. This can create surface drainage problems and deprive roots of oxygen. Keep the mulch 3 or 4 in. from the trunk to avoid disease, rot and pest problems.

Some good mulch choices are shredded bark or composted wood chips. Don't use woven or plastic landscape fabric or other weed barriers underneath the mulch. These can cause major problems later on as seeds grow roots down through these materials and anchor themselves into the barriers.

Water carefully

You'll need to water your new tree until the root system is well established. Don't rely on a "rule of thumb" for watering. The right amount of water depends on the weather conditions, your soil and the planting site. The most reliable method for knowing when to water is to stick your finger 2 to 3 in. into the ground. You want to keep the soil at the level of the root-ball moist but not wet. Allow the soil's surface to begin to dry out between waterings.

For the first few weeks, you may have to water every few days depending on the weather. After that, longer (deeper), less frequent watering is much better than shorter (quicker), frequent watering. To help the tree create deep roots to resist drought and wind, encircle it with a soaker hose a few feet out from the trunk and run it a trickle for an hour.

Overwatering can be as bad or worse than underwatering. If you're watering more than twice a week, there's a good chance you're overwatering.

Set the roots free

Cut away all rope, twine, wire, staples and burlap before backfilling (you can leave natural burlap underneath the root-ball if you can't cut it all away). If the roots circle the root-ball, but none are thicker than a pencil, use your fingers to tease the root-ball apart. But if the tree is severely root-bound and has circling roots larger than a pencil in diameter, use a newer method called box cutting. To box-cut a root-ball, use a pruning saw to shave off all four sides, creating a square root-ball.

JEFF GILLMAN

Root-cutting shovel

For digging in root-filled soil, make a small "V" in the tip of your shovel or trowel with a file or grinder. Keep it sharp with a file. The "V" will trap and slice the roots as you dig.

Gardening

25 TIPS FOR PLANNING THE PERFECT GARDEN

Die-hard gardeners will tell you that a garden is a work in progress. Even established gardens require a little tweaking from season to season. But if you thoughtfully plan before you plant, your landscape will beautifully endure for years to come without costly and time-consuming alterations or additions.

Search online or spend a few hours at the library flipping through gardening books and magazines in search of garden designs that appeal to your personal tastes. Then follow these 25 tips to sketch out landscapes that are sure to flourish with minimal upkeep and without pricey do-overs.

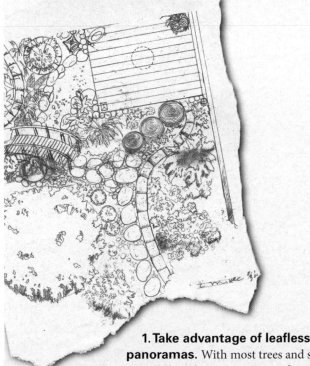

1. Take advantage of leafless panoramas. With most trees and shrubs showing only bare bones, winter is a fine time for spotting ho-hum holes in your landscape. Check for areas that could use a punch of winter interest—consider adding evergreens, berry-bearing shrubs and trees with interesting forms or bark to boost four-season appeal.

2. Know your site. Spend a day or two checking how many hours of sun your gardens receive each day to ensure you incorporate light-appropriate plants into your design. Keep in mind that full-sun plants require at least 6 hours of sun, partial-shade plants need between 3 and 6 hours and shade-tolerant plants benefit from 2 or 3 hours of direct light or from receiving indirect or filtered light all day.

3. Consider the big picture. Sketch out an overall picture of your yard, including entertainment areas, your house and other buildings. Enlarge the sketch and mark off existing landscape features like trees, shrubs and gardens. Pencil in proposed plantings to see how they fit within the existing landscape.

4. Allow plenty of room. Design extra-deep borders large enough to house an array of low, medium and tall plants and that allow you extra space to add more plants as the mood strikes.

5. Pace off measurements. Before you sketch, estimate the amount of space you wish to dedicate to a planting bed. Use the measurements to draw a blueprint to scale on graph paper. Keeping in mind plants' mature sizes, pencil in desired plants to get a realistic idea of how many you can fit into the space.

6. Color in the lines. On your plan, use markers, watercolors or colored pencils to color in existing plantings. Then color in your planned additions to make certain that the old and new hues complement each other.

7. Make like a landscape pro. Design gardens that carry the eye from earth to sky. Anchor borders and beds with structural plants, such as trees or tall shrubs, and then layer in climbing vines, smaller shrubs, varying-height perennials and sprawling ground covers.

8. Settle on a style. Determine whether you're going for a clipped formal look, casual cottage appeal, a native prairie or a combination of styles.

9. Pick a palette. Are you partial to pastels? Do red-hot hues get your creative juices flowing? Working within a color scheme will help you set a cohesive scene and prevent you from buying unsuitable plants in weaker moments.

10. Lay the groundwork. When planning your design, include pathways, arbors, ponds, large containers, fountains, statuary and garden benches that draw both foot traffic and attention through the garden.

11. Cultivate perennials for pennies. Designate a sunny corner for growing perennials from seed. Sow the seeds in early spring, and by mid- to late summer, you'll have loads of plants to fill out your borders.

12. Add raised beds for vegetable, herb and cutting gardens. Growing your own produce and easy-care annual flowers for summer arrangements saves money. Plus, raised beds take less time to weed.

13. Create a budget. Determine how much you want to spend for this year's plantings, mulch and soil amendments. Plan on putting in paths and buying the larger, structural plants first. When budgets are tight, think about filling in your design over the course of several years.

14. Reiterate a scheme. Plan on replicating plant forms, colors and textures to easily fashion flow, a sense of movement and a harmonious whole garden.

Tips continued on next page.

15. Forget the finicky. Opt to include native plants or ones that are hardy and reliable in your planting zone—you won't have to replace them down the road.

16. Look for deals. Many spring garden catalogs offer bare-root forsythia, hydrangea and red-twig dogwood saplings for a couple of bucks or less. The stick-like, rooted saplings take a few years to fill out and flower, but their bargain-basement prices allow you to mass their forms inexpensively or to add them throughout the landscape as a repeating element.

17. Invest in gardener's gold. Incorporate plants—such as daylily, hosta, bearded iris, bee balm, purple coneflower and yarrow—that you can divide in a few years for more (free!) plants.

18. Think foliage, not flowers. Sketch in plants with silver, gray, chartreuse, variegated and bright-colored foliage for gardens that remain colorful as flowers fade.

19. Consider every season. Slot in plants with different bloom times to ensure a succession of blossoms throughout the year.

20. Plant a living wall. Pencil in trellises, hedges and plant groupings to camouflage unattractive views, define garden rooms and buffer traffic noise.

21. Supersize it. You'll fill a lot of space without spending big bucks if you include large, quick-growing plants, such as Russian sage, fountain grasses, Autumn Joy sedum, hydrangea and shrub roses like Carefree Delight, Knock Out and Magic Carpet.

22. Contemplate companions. Peruse garden books, plant catalogs and Web sites for garden images that showcase appealing plant combinations that you can duplicate in your design.

23. Pair like-minded plants. Group those with similar light, water and soil requirements together—if you plant water-thirsty cultivars with drought-tolerant plants, you're sure to lose one or both to either too-dry conditions or root rot.

24. Enhance the wow factor. Add one or two plant groupings or shrubs that are sure to stop passersby in their tracks.

25. Vary forms and textures. Incorporate plants with ferny fronds, grassy spires, coarse spikes, fuzzy foliage, waxy surfaces and broad leaves in varying mounded, cascading and upright forms.

5 secrets to hillside gardening

- Use dampened soil as if it were mortar to help secure rocks.
- Install drainpipes to keep water from puddling and saturating the soil.
- When taking on a hillside gardening project, account for how much time it'll take. Sometimes, it takes two or three times to get a wall right.
- Make sure you have enough rock on hand. It's easy to underestimate how much you'll need.
- Cover plants with mulch to protect them in the winter months.

TERRACE GARDEN

Sump pump garden watering

Tired of your sump pump pumping all of its water into the yard and leaving it a swampy mess? Put the water to good use. Dry-fit some PVC pipe to where the sump exits the house and run a length of tubing out to your flower bed. Now when the pump comes on, the water is directed to where it will do some good!

Be sure to disconnect the setup in the fall to prevent the discharge line from freezing in the winter.

POSTHOLE DIGGER

Posthole planter

Save your back and knees with a posthole digger. It works great to dig holes for all size plants, the depth is consistent, and you get a perfect-shaped hole every time. Best of all, it eliminates a lot of kneeling and bending.

Tarp trailer

With a big plastic tarp, you can easily drag leaves, branches or mulch around your yard to wherever you need it. A 9 x 12-ft. tarp is about the right size.

POULTRY NETTING

TENT STAKES

Munch-proof your flower bulbs

Keep hungry critters from snacking on your freshly planted flower bulbs by staking poultry netting over the bed. You can either remove the cloth in the early spring or let plants grow through the holes and leave it throughout the growing season.

Simple veggie washer

We all love growing fresh vegetables in the garden, but all the dirt that comes along with them is a pain. Make cleaning easier with this great veggie washer. Drill holes in the bottom and sides of a 5-gallon bucket with a 5/8-in. spade bit. Place your fresh-picked veggies in the bucket and hose them off before you bring them inside. The dirt and sand stay out in the garden, and only the veggies end up in your kitchen.

5/8" HOLES

Rein in an invasive plant

Plants like gooseneck loosestrife have underground rhizomes (roots) that can spread to all corners of your garden before you know it. To contain them, slice out the bottom of a plastic container with a utility knife (Photo 1) and push this "collar" into the soil (or drive it down with a mallet) to encircle the plant and its invasive root system (Photo 2). If the soil has become compacted, cut around the plant with a spade first. Note: This technique won't contain plants that spread above ground like strawberries and mint.

5 tips for pet-friendly gardens

■ Include sweeps of lawn where dogs can wander aimlessly, roll about or frolic freely.

■ Guide pets through your gardens by laying clearly defined pathways that are easy on their feet.

■ Keep dogs safely contained, and keep unwanted visitors out, by fencing in your yard.

■ Run lattice around the bases of porches and decks to prevent pets from burrowing into these spaces and getting stuck beneath the floorboards.

■ When buying products to treat lawns or gardens, read the labels to ensure the products are pet-safe.

Portable potting

Cut a piece of plywood roughly to the shape of your wheelbarrow's back end and screw a few wood cleats along the sides to keep it from slipping off while you wheel. Now you'll have both soil and a potting surface right at hand when you take the wheelbarrow to the garden.

STAY-PUT CLEAT

Grow tulips to bloom in the middle of winter

How about tulips under the Christmas tree this year? You don't have to wait until spring to enjoy the refreshing color of hardy bulbs like tulips, daffodils and crocuses. By "forcing" bulbs, you can have them bloom at any time during the year. Here's how.

Fill clay pots with a light soil mix and plant the bulbs so the tip is just above the soil surface. Mix in a tablespoon of bonemeal in each pot as a fertilizer and lightly water. Set the pots in a place that's dark and cool, approximately 40 degrees F, for 12 to 14 weeks. Once small shoots start to emerge, bring the pots out to a shaded spot for a day or two. Gradually give the plants more light and warmth. First keep them in a location where the temperature is 55 to 60 degrees F and the light is bright but indirect. Once the plants are green and about 5 in. tall, move them to a sunny window to start their bloom.

The temperature, amount of light and type of bulb will affect how long it takes for the bulbs to bloom. But it usually takes three to five weeks for the plants to show their color once they're brought out into the light.

6 tips for perfect soil in raised garden beds

Perhaps the biggest advantage to growing plants in raised beds is the promise of perfect soil. Here are some tips to help ensure that you achieve success!

■ Before you even think about putting up bed walls, you must thoroughly work up the existing soil.

■ Adding soil to a raised bed is a lot like making cake batter—the more it's mixed, the better the results. So as you add new soil, keep tilling and working the existing and new soil together. Failure to do this will hamper drainage.

■ A good general soil mix is one-third topsoil, one-third composted manure and one-third sand. Mix these together first with a shovel, then fill the raised bed.

■ Maintain the soil's fertility with mulch, organic material, such as compost, leaf mold (a compost produced by tree leaves that break down) or composted manure and/or chemical fertilizers.

■ Be sure to use composted manure, not fresh manure, or you'll end up with too much nitrogen in the soil, which can burn plant root systems.

■ Potting mix is also acceptable for raised beds, as it contains more perlite and peat, both of which provide better drainage.

Easy-read rain gauge

Drip food coloring into the bottom of your rain gauge the next time you empty it out. When it showers, the coloring will reconstitute and tint the water to make the gauge easier to read.

MOSS MILKSHAKE

50/50 MOSS AND BUTTERMILK

CONCRETE POT

Paint-on moss

If you like the soft, weathered look of moss-covered pots but don't feel like leaving the process to the whims of nature, try this trick. Search cool, shady spots for moss and gather two or three cups. Put equal parts moss and buttermilk in your blender and mix it up to make a moss milkshake. Paint the moss solution onto any porous, unglazed masonry pot or planter. Place the pot in a shady spot and keep it moist by misting once or twice a day. Depending on the temperature and humidity, you'll start to see moss growing in a month or two. You don't have to wait to add a shade-loving plant to the pot.

Outdoor living

How much gas is left?

Grab the bathroom scale and weigh your propane tank to calculate how much cooking time remains. A normal-size tank with a 20-lb. capacity weights about 17 to 18 lbs. empty and about 37 to 38 lbs. when full of propane. A full-size grill (35,000 Btu) will cook for 30 minutes per pound of propane. The tank shown tipped the scale at 21 lbs., so it contains about 4 lbs. or approximately two hours of grilling time (4 lbs. x 30 min.)

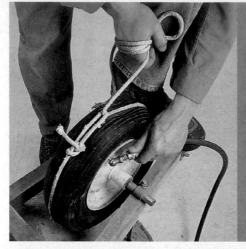

Fix for a flat

Ever had a flat tire on your wheelbarrow where the rim became separated from the tubeless tire? When you try to refill the tire, the air just leaks out along the rim. Here's an old trick that should fix it. Make a loop in a rope, place the rope around the middle of the tire and through the loop, and pull back on the rope. The pressure will cause the sides of the tire to squish out and make contact with the rim. Then the tire will be sealed enough to hold air.

3 easy ideas for clean birdbaths

■ To clean your birdbath, put two cups of vinegar in the bath and fill it to the brim with water. Cover with a trash-can lid, and let the bath soak overnight. Scrub and rinse well.

■ To attract butterflies to your birdbath and avoid algae, put a layer of builder's sand in the bottom of the birdbath.

■ Add a pantyhose leg stuffed with oat straw inside to your water for an algae-free birdbath.

Fish for leaves in your pond

If you have trees growing over your pond, falling leaves and seed pods will make a mess of your crystal clear water. Just use a fish landing net to catch that debris (leave your koi where they are!). The water drains right through the loosely woven netting, and the leaves are ready to dump.

Tippy baths aren't for the birds

Leveling a paver stone under your bird feeder is a slick way to keep your birdbath from tipping over and the water in the bowl level. Round or square paving stones like the one we're using are readily available at garden centers.

Dig a hole about 2 in. deeper than the thickness of the paver. Spread and roughly level a 2-in. layer of sand in the hole. Set the paver on the sand and check it with a short carpenter's level. Lift one edge of the paver and add or remove sand to level it.

The super-simple water garden

If you want an instant water garden, simply slip a plastic barrel liner into a decorative wooden barrel, set some pavers of various heights in place to act as pedestals and then perch a few potted aquatic plants on top. Just make sure to position the plants at the depth indicated on the plant tag or information sheet. The only drawback to this approach is that the container won't look as natural close up—you can see the plastic pots below the surface. You can even add a spouter to the barrel; the pump can simply sit on a pedestal without a cup.

If you can't find a plastic barrel liner, you can make a watertight terra cotta container by plugging the drain hole with plumber's epoxy (shown) and applying two coats of polyurethane.

POLYURETHANE

PLUMBER'S EPOXY

LINER

PAVER PEDESTALS

Walkways and patios

Line a walkway with bricks or pavers

Is your concrete walkway in decent—but boring—shape? Adding color, texture and width to an existing walkway by lining it with pavers is a whole lot easier and cheaper than replacing it. Stone, clay and concrete pavers are all good choices. The basic procedure involves digging a trench one paver wide along the walkway, leveling in a bed of sand or pea gravel, then setting and tamping pavers so they're flush with the top of the walkway.

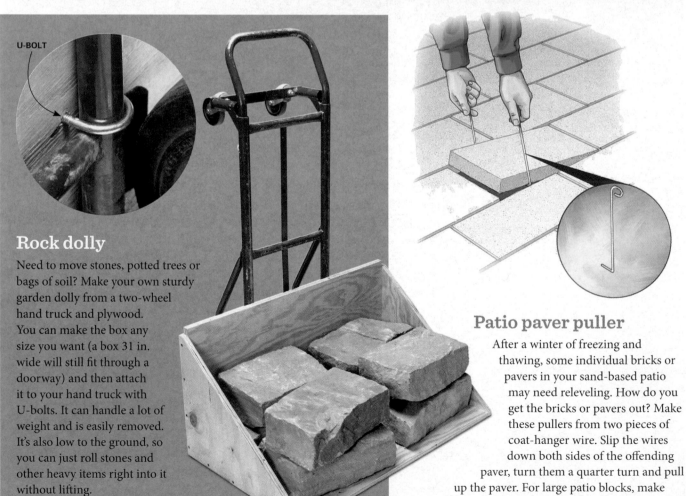

U-BOLT

Rock dolly

Need to move stones, potted trees or bags of soil? Make your own sturdy garden dolly from a two-wheel hand truck and plywood. You can make the box any size you want (a box 31 in. wide will still fit through a doorway) and then attach it to your hand truck with U-bolts. It can handle a lot of weight and is easily removed. It's also low to the ground, so you can just roll stones and other heavy items right into it without lifting.

Patio paver puller

After a winter of freezing and thawing, some individual bricks or pavers in your sand-based patio may need releveling. How do you get the bricks or pavers out? Make these pullers from two pieces of coat-hanger wire. Slip the wires down both sides of the offending paver, turn them a quarter turn and pull up the paver. For large patio blocks, make four pullers and get a second person to help.

THYME

TOUGH PLANTS FOR PATHS

Weeds growing in your path can be a real eyesore, especially if they spill over and start growing in your yard. To eliminate that problem, grow perennial plants between stones in a path. These plants can all tolerate some foot traffic: creeping thyme/mother-of-thyme, woolly thyme, carpet bugleweed/Ajuga reptans, creeping jenny/creeping charlie/moneywort, dead nettle/ creeping lamium, blue star creeper, brass buttons, Mazus reptans and sedum.

To help you select the best ground cover, consider:

■ The amount of sunlight reaching your path (full sun, partial shade, full shade), because different plants thrive under different conditions.

■ The amount of traffic the plants will need to endure. Light traffic means the plants will be stepped on once or twice a week. Moderate traffic is once a day. And heavy traffic is similar to walking on your lawn several times a day.

■ The type of soil (poor or rich) and moisture conditions (wet or dry).

■ Appearance—plant height, texture and color. If the path is heavily traveled, keep the plant height extremely low to prevent tripping.

Then take your list to a local nursery specialist to walk you through the options best suited for your area. Also note how the plants grow and spread—to determine plant spacing and the number of plants you need to buy. Be sure to avoid plants that are considered invasive species in your area, like creeping jenny (moneywort), which is listed as an

invasive species in Tennessee, Wisconsin and the Northeast. You can find this list by visiting plants.usda.gov, or ask your local nursery specialist.

It's difficult to grow anything in a trampled area. The soil gets so compacted that roots cannot deliver water and nutrients to the plant. Add good drainage as well as a layer of topsoil at least 1 in. deep around the stones so your ground cover can thrive.

Finally, help your new ground cover prosper with a weekly soaking (the plants need to stay moist) and a weekly hand weeding. And if you'd like to keep the plants short between the stones, consider varieties that tolerate mowing, such as thyme and ajuga.

Creeping Thyme
(Mother-of-Thyme)
Thymus serpyllum
Zones: 4 through 9
(most of U.S.)
Height: 2 to 4 in.
Plant spreads 12 in.
Full sun to shade
Withstands heavy traffic

Carpet Bugleweed
(Ajuga) *Ajuga reptans*
Zones: 3 through 9
Height: 4 to 6 in.
Plant spreads 12 to 18 in.
Full sun to partial shade
Withstands moderate traffic

Creeping Jenny
(Creeping Charlie, Moneywort)
Lysimachia nummularia
Zones: 4 through 8
Height: 2 to 4 in.
Plant spreads 18 to 23 in.
Partial shade
Withstands moderate traffic

Dead Nettle
(Creeping Lamium)
Lamium maculatum
Zones: 4 through 8
Height: 6 to 8 in.
Plant spreads 12 to 23 in.
Partial to full shade
Withstands moderate traffic

Chapter Fourteen

OUTDOOR REPAIRS AND IMPROVEMENTS

Siding and trim

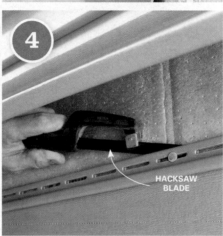

SIDING UNLOCKING TOOL

HACKSAW BLADE

The sound of mice— or popping siding?

If you're hearing the sound of mice in your vinyl siding, chances are that your vinyl siding was nailed too tightly. Vinyl siding tends to expand and contract considerably with temperature changes. For this reason, manufacturers design it to hang loosely on the nails rather than to be tightly nailed like wood siding.

Your problem should be easy to diagnose. Simply go outside, grab the lower edges of a siding course and try to slide it back and forth (Photo 1). Manufacturers require about 1/4-in. play at both ends, so if it's nailed properly (loosely), you should be able to slide it 1/4 to 1/2 in. If all the siding is tight, it was installed wrong and should be redone. If only a few pieces are tight and you can't find the contractor who installed it, buy an unlocking ("zip") tool and unfasten the section above, exposing the nails (Photos 2 and 3). Find the tight nails and cut them (Photo 4). Renail right next to the old nail, leaving at least a 1/16-in. gap between the nailhead and the vinyl to allow easy movement.

Can aluminum, vinyl and steel siding be painted?

They can be but there are a few rules you must follow. First, scrub the siding with cleaners to remove all the dirt, chalk and mildew. Rinse with clear water. Prime rusted areas on steel with exterior rust-inhibiting primer. Aluminum and steel siding can be painted with any color paint. But vinyl siding can only be painted with a light color. Darker colors will cause the vinyl siding to warp or deform from heat absorption.

30-LB. FELT

Flash the butt joints

Caulking butt joints for wood or fiber cement board is unnecessary, and some manufacturers prohibit it. However, you should flash behind the joints. You can use metal, house wrap or any other approved WRB (weather-resistant barrier), but ordinary 30-lb. felt paper works great. It's easy to work with and cheap, and it isn't noticeable if a seam happens to open up a little. Tack it to the wall so it doesn't get knocked out of place when you install the second piece of siding.

Clean vinyl siding

Vinyl siding usually cleans up easily with nothing more than soap and water, and a yearly scrubbing will keep it looking new.

For basic cleaning, use general-purpose cleaner mixed with warm water. Apply it with a soft-bristle cleaning brush, scrubbing the full length of each lap as shown. Start at the bottom to avoid streaking, and use your garden hose to rinse off each section before it dries.

For tough spots like paint drips, tar, and pencil and pen marks, use a non-abrasive bathtub cleaner or nylon scrub pad (inset photo). Use ammonia cleaners or a solution of 1 part bleach in 4 parts water to clean mold and mildew stains. (However, never mix ammonia and bleach.) Rinse thoroughly while the siding is still wet.

Pro tip: Don't use paint thinner, nail polish remover, spot removers, paint remover, straight chlorine bleach or furniture cleaner on vinyl. These types of cleaners can damage the surface of the siding.

Clean tough stains off with a nonabrasive cleaner that won't damage the surface of the vinyl.

Scrub siding from the bottom up with a soft-bristle brush.

Watertight cable

TV and Internet signals are the only things coaxial cables should be bringing into your house, but improperly installed cables can let in water, which can lead to rot and mold. So the next time you're trimming the bushes, take a quick look where the cable enters the house.

Cable should never run downward and directly into your house. Rainwater will adhere to the cable and follow it right into your home. Ideally, the cable should run upward and then in. If your cable was installed incorrectly, contact your service provider and voice your concerns. If the provider refuses to fix the problem, see if you can reroute the cable in order to gain a couple of feet. Try to avoid splices if you can. They can weaken your signal.

If you're installing new cable, loop the cable before it enters the building. The loop will not only help shed the water but also provide extra cable in case a mistake is made inside.

A properly sized feed-through bushing will allow you to drill a slightly larger hole so you can fish the cable in without damaging it. Dab silicone caulk behind the bushing before pushing it into its final resting place.

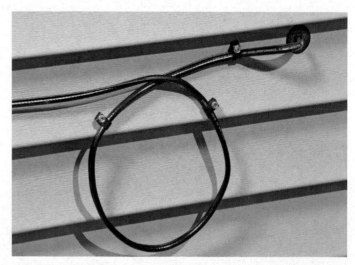

LOOP THE CABLE
A loop provides extra length for minor repairs or rerouting later. It also forces water to drip off the cable rather than follow the cable into the wall. A bushing seals around the cable and protects it from the sharp edges of the siding. Fasten the cable with clamps.

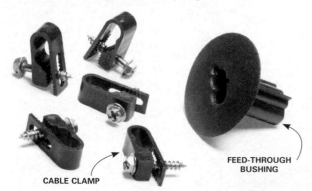

CABLE CLAMP

FEED-THROUGH BUSHING

Garages and driveways

SPRAY-PAINTED FOUL LINE

Garage door foul line

Here's the straight solution for keeping bikes, trikes, garden tools and car bumpers from being squashed by a descending garage door or triggering the electric eye. Close the garage door and press down a strip of 2-in. wide masking tape along the inside edge. Lay another strip of tape 1-1/2 in. to the outside of the first. Spray on the line, pull the tape and let dry. Now when you close the door, glance at the line to be sure the door will seal on concrete, not on a tool or the tail of your sleeping cat.

The best asphalt sealer for a driveway

Not all asphalt sealers are created equal. Thin sealers are mostly cosmetic. Heavy-duty sealers contain less water and more solids, which fill cracks and create a durable topcoat. They also come with longer protection claims (read the label) and are more expensive.

You'll find two different formulations. Coal tar emulsion sealers resist gas, oil and brake fluid better than asphalt emulsion sealers. But asphalt emulsion sealers are more "user friendly"—they're practically odorless, and they don't irritate or burn the skin (especially important for people with respiratory conditions or sensitive skin).

No matter which formulation you choose, buy the heavy-duty version and look for one labeled "easy stir." This means solids stay suspended longer, so you can apply a more uniform coat to your driveway.

Lock up the overhead door

Some people "lock" the door when they go on vacation by unplugging the opener. That's a good idea, but physically locking the door is even better. An unplugged opener won't prevent fishing, and—if you have an attached garage—it won't stop a burglar who has entered through the house from opening the garage door from inside, backing in a van and using the garage as a loading dock for his plunder. Make a burglar's job more difficult and time-consuming by locking the door itself.

LOCK THE TRACK
If your door doesn't have a lockable latch, drill a hole in the track just above one of the rollers and slip in a padlock.

Two types of garage flooring

There are two general types of garage flooring: coatings and coverings. If your garage floor is in good condition, you can pick either one. But if the floor has lots of cracks or pockmarks, a covering is better because it hides damage. A coating, even a low-sheen version, has a tendency to highlight blemishes. Coverings are also immune to moisture problems that can make coatings peel.

UCOAT IT EPOXY FLOOR PAINT

G-FLOOR ROLLOUT MATS

KIWI RIGID TILES

Permeable pavers promote percolation

Say that six times fast! Reducing storm water runoff to improve water quality is a key initiative across the United States, and many communities have issued guidelines encouraging homeowners and builders to use permeable construction materials for walkways, patios, sidewalks and driveways. If a new patio or driveway is on your to-do list this year, consider using permeable pavers like these. These permeable pavers are clay bricks designed to be strong enough to withstand foot and light vehicle traffic while allowing water to filter quickly into the soil through spaces between the pavers. Permeable pavers are available in various colors and costs depending on the region.

A typical city block can generate five times more runoff than a wooded area the same size.

Clean up rusty door track

Garage door tracks often rest directly on damp concrete floors, where they eventually rust. However, there's no reason they can't be slightly above the floor and stay dry: The garage rafters carry the weight of the track and the angle brackets hold the track in place.

Clean up the tracks and prevent rusting by simply cutting off the bottom 1/2 in. First make sure all the angle bracket bolts are tight, then cut the track bottoms off (Photo 1). Use a rag dipped in thinner to remove any lubricant on the first 6 in. of track, then scrape and brush off as much rust as you can. Finally, paint the bottom with a metal spray paint that's formulated to bond to rusted areas (Photo 2).

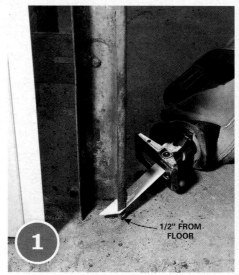

1

1/2" FROM FLOOR

Mark the bottom of the track, then cut the metal with a reciprocating saw or hacksaw.

2

Clean the bottom of the track with mineral spirits, wire-brush the rust and then paint the area.

Decks, fences and other structures

Tree house building tips

Site considerations

■ Choose a healthy, long-lived hardwood for maximum support, with load-bearing branches at least 8 in. in diameter (larger if the species is a softwood).

■ The best trees include maple, oak, fir, beech and hemlock.

■ You don't have to build it very high, just high enough so nobody gets a bump on the head when walking underneath it.

Keep weight and stability in mind

■ Build the platform as close to the trunk as possible and add diagonal bracing for extra strength to support uneven loads.

■ Put the load over the base of the tree, not on one side.

■ For heavy tree houses, consider spreading the weight among several trees.

■ A tree house will act as a sail in strong winds, which can add a large load to the tree's roots. In high-wind areas, build your tree house in the lower third of the tree.

Fence post footing

When building on one main trunk, level the main platform by cantilevering the beams and supporting them from below.

SETTING A FENCE POST
Pour concrete so it extends a few inches above the grass. Then taper the edges to drain water away from the wood post.

How to stop fence post rot

Concrete piers should always extend above the soil, and the top area should be sloped away from the post to provide drainage. Burying the concrete below the surface may look nicer, but it's a surefire way to accelerate wood rot.

Almost instant shade

Is your deck or patio delightful in spring and early summer but scorching by July? Create a mid-season awning by stringing twine or wire between 2x4s and planting fast-growing vines at the base. Given full sun and regular feedings, morning glories will cover the structure by midsummer.

Use water and the back of your shovel

If you're digging in sticky clay soil, dip your clamshell digger in a bucket of water so the soil won't stick. Knock off clumps on the back of the shovel. Spread a tarp to keep dirt off your grass.

Centered growth rings indicate the post is made from peeler core and won't accept pressure treatment well (right), while off-center rings mean the post is not the log's center (left).

Choosing 4x4s

Pressure-treated 8-ft. 4x4s are typically made from "peeler cores," which are the byproduct of plywood production. When a log is turned on a lathe to produce plywood veneer, the center that remains, called the peeler core, is used as a post. These cores often contain the pith, or center of the log, which doesn't accept pressure treatment as well. Peeler-core posts are more likely to warp and twist than posts cut farther away from a tree's center.

When shopping for 4x4 posts, look at the ends. If growth rings start near the center of the post and expand outward, it's almost certainly made from a peeler core (see photos). If the rings are off center, it's not the log's center. Buy 10-ft. posts instead of peeler-core 8-footers and trim them to fit.

Long-lasting outdoor furniture

Any wood resting on the ground will rot, especially if it's end grain. That's because water wicks up into the same channels the tree used to transport water. So whenever you build outdoor furniture, do two things: First seal the end grain with waterproof woodworking glue. And if the legs are resting on masonry, pound in plastic furniture buttons. That keeps the wood slightly elevated so it won't be sitting in puddles.

FURNITURE BUTTON

EXTERIOR WOOD GLUE

Gutters and downspouts

5 DOWNSPOUT UPGRADES

Water puddling around a foundation from an ineffective downspout can create major problems, ranging from damp basements to structural damage. It's worth finding a system that works for you. Here are the pros and cons of a variety of options.

1 Vinyl recoiling sleeves

These install with a simple strap and automatically unfurl as they fill with water.

■ *Pros:* They move water away from the foundation by dispersing it sprinkler-style, then recoil when it stops raining. They work well when you need to move water only 3 or 4 ft. away from the house to a slope where it will then run off naturally.

■ *Cons:* You need to remove the end clip to flush out built-up debris, and you should remove the entire sleeve in freezing temperatures to prevent damage.

RETRACTED

2 Flip-up/ swiveling/tele- scoping spouts

Some simply flip up and out of the way, while others telescope for extra length and swivel 180 degrees to direct water away from the building at any angle.

■ *Pros:* The open-top design makes them easy to maintain. Fully extended, some carry water up to 6 ft. away from the foundation.

■ *Cons:* The most expensive option, one vulnerable to damage in areas where there's lots of foot traffic.

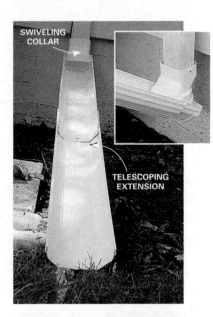

SWIVELING COLLAR

TELESCOPING EXTENSION

3 Flexible accordion spouts

Attaches to your downspout with two screws.

■ *Pros:* Can be easily twisted to go around corners, shrubs or other obstacles and are easily moved when mowing. Two or more segments can be snapped together, making them ideal for situations where you need to move water over longer distances.

■ *Cons:* They look a little industrial—but none of these products is going to win any beauty contests.

4 A below-grade extension

You'll need a downspout adapter and end cap, some 4-in. PVC pipe and adapters.

■ *Pros:* This is especially effective when the extension needs to cross a walkway or is in a "knock-off-prone" area.

■ *Cons:* Connecting and burying everything takes more time than other methods, but it's the most permanent solution. For this system to work, your lawn needs a little slope; make certain the pipe slants away from the house at least 1/4 in. per ft. If it clogs, clean it out with a plumbing snake.

OUTLET

5 Do-it-yourself flip-up spout

Create your own by removing a 2-in. section from the top of a standard extension, then use two screws to create a "hinge" when securing it to the downspout elbow.

■ *Pros:* When it's time to mow, simply flip the extension up. And the price is right.

■ *Cons:* They are subject to "operator malfunction"—if they're left in the "up" position, you'll get water around your foundation during a storm.

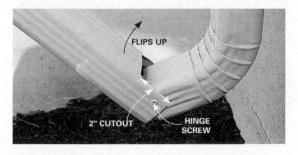

FLIPS UP

2" CUTOUT   HINGE SCREW

Easier gutter cleaning

An old plastic spatula makes a great tool for cleaning debris from gutters! It doesn't scratch up the gutter, and you can cut it to fit gutter contours with snips. Grime wipes right off the spatula too, making cleanup a breeze.

DIVERTER

Stop spills with a diverter

Some roofs have long sections of valley that carry a lot of rainwater at high velocity. When that water comes blasting out the end of the valley, it can shoot right over the gutter. A diverter will help direct the water back into the gutter where it belongs. Fasten a diverter with a couple of sheet metal screws to the top of the outside edge of the gutter.

Fix overflows with a larger downspout

If you have a 50-ft. gutter with one 2 x 3-in. downspout, your gutter probably overflows during heavier rainfalls. When installing an additional downspout isn't an option, install a 3 x 4-in. downspout in place of the smaller one.

Start by removing the old downspout. Use the new 3 x 4-in. drop outlet that you buy with your new downspout as a template to trace an outline for the larger hole. You can cut out the larger hole with a tin snips, or you could use an oscillating multi-tool equipped with a metal-cutting blade. Insert the drop outlet in the hole and fasten the new downspout with sheet metal screws. Make sure to seal the drop outlet to the gutter with seam sealer.

If you need a color other than white or brown, it will be a special order, but you should be able to get the color you need.

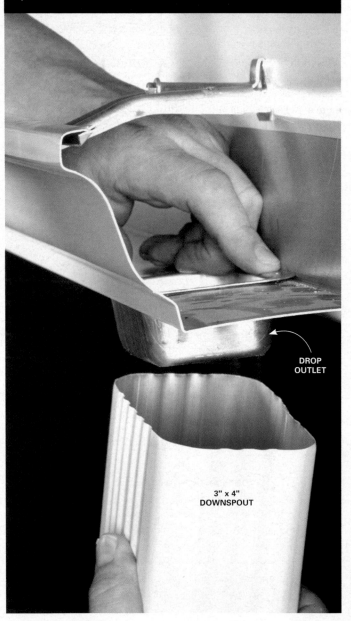

DROP OUTLET

3" x 4" DOWNSPOUT

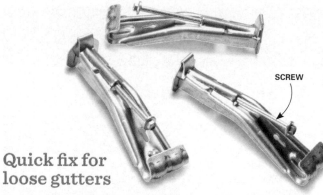

SCREW

Quick fix for loose gutters

Years ago, spikes and ferrules were a common method for hanging gutters. They do the job all right, but eventually the spikes work themselves loose. Pounding them back in is a temporary fix at best.

One way to make sure your gutter doesn't fall off the house is to install fascia hanger brackets. Installation is simple: Just hook the bracket under the front lip of the gutter, and then screw the other side of the bracket to the fascia. Leave the old spikes in place—a spike head looks better than a hole in the gutter.

If your shingles overhang your fascia by a few inches or you have steel roofing, buy the brackets with the screws built in (the type shown here). They cost more, but the head of the screw remains a couple of inches away from the fascia, making them a lot easier to install.

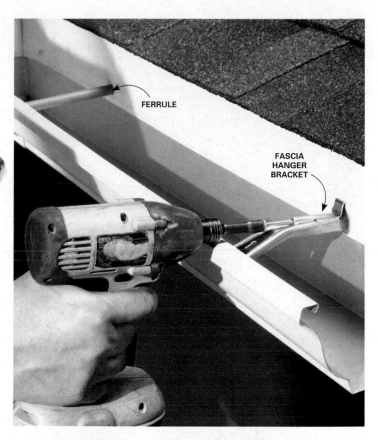

FERRULE

FASCIA HANGER BRACKET

Snake out spouts

Your plumber's snake is a great tool for pulling clumps of wet leaves out of clogged downspouts.

NEW END CAP

1 SCRUB AROUND THE LEAK
Scour off oxidation around the seam or end cap with a scrub brush or coarse steel wool. Rinse with water and let the area dry.

2 APPLY THE SEALER
Squirt a bead of sealer around the seam or end cap and work it in with a gloved finger. Let it dry.

Seal leaking end caps on gutters

To fix your gutter leak, start by scooping out all the crud. Clean the area with household spray cleaner, a scrub brush and rags to get it as clean as possible. If you have to, resort to a toothbrush for crevices. The cleaner it is, the better your patch will hold over time. Next, remove any oxidation and apply the seam sealer (Photos 1 and 2). Go back several days later and cover the entire area with a rubberized coating to prevent rust.

Concrete and masonry

Perfect crack filler

If you've ever tried to fill a crack in concrete with regular caulk, you know what a mess it can be. Self-leveling concrete crack filler solves this problem. Just fill the crack and a few minutes later the caulk settles to form a perfectly smooth joint. For wide cracks, insert lengths of foam caulk-backer first to create a better caulk joint and reduce the amount of caulk needed. Self-leveling caulk is available at home centers and hardware stores. Look for the words "self-leveling" on the tube.

Repairing a concrete sidewalk

For chips and rough areas, use vinyl concrete patch. It's available at home centers and hardware stores. It's a fine-powdered cement with vinyl fortifiers and it really sticks to old concrete that's been properly prepared. You can trowel it as thin as 1/16 in.

To prepare the concrete for repair, first remove all the loose material with a chisel and/or steel brush. Then rinse the area well with water. A spray nozzle on a garden hose works great. Make sure to sponge out puddles of water, but leave the area damp. Mix the concrete according to the label directions and apply it with a trowel or putty knife. As you work it, vinyl patching material becomes stickier and harder to smooth, so don't wait long to apply it after you've mixed it.

Caution: It might be hard to believe that concrete can be dangerous. But the strong alkalinity of cement can cause chemical burns just like a strong acid. By the time you realize you're being burned, you may already have skin damage. That's why it's essential to prevent prolonged skin exposure to wet concrete. And why you should be extra careful to keep wet concrete from getting in your eyes. Wear rubber gloves, a long-sleeve shirt, long pants and safety glasses. Wear rubber boots if you'll be wading in concrete. Rinse wet concrete from your skin immediately and remove clothes that have become saturated with concrete.

How to fix broken bricks

If the bricks in your wall are breaking apart, simple patching probably won't work. Any patch material you apply will just pop out again unless you solve the underlying expansion/contraction problem. The bricks in this photo, which are recycled Chicago-commons (a soft brick used at the turn of the last century) are cracking because they were set with a newer, nonflexing Portland cement mortar.

For a problem like this, you have two choices. Either reuse the old bricks but with the right mortar (lime mortar or lime putty), or rebuild with new bricks. Pick a brick that's harder and more weather resistant.

Eliminate efflorescence

Efflorescence, the result of leaching mineral salts such as calcium carbonate, is the powdery white discoloration that can appear on brick, concrete and other masonry. Although it is unsightly, it is not harmful to the brick. To remove it, mix a weak solution of muriatic acid and water, brush it on the wall, scrub and rinse with water. Wear goggles and rubber gloves.

Ordering concrete for a shed

Here's a brief rundown of what you need to know when placing an order.

■ **Amount.** Calculate the volume you need in cubic yards. Multiply the length (10 ft., for example) by the width (10 ft.) by the depth (.35 ft., or 4 in.) and divide it by 27 (the number of cubic feet in a cubic yard). You get 1.3 cu. yds. Then add 10 percent to allow for spillage and slab depth variations.

■ **Strength.** Call a local ready-mix company, tell the supplier what the concrete is for, and ask about the best mix (proportions of cement, gravel and sand). For a shed, the supplier will probably suggest a mix with a capacity of about 4,000 psi (pounds per square inch).

If you live in a region with freeze/thaw cycles in winter, ask for 5 percent air entrainment to help the concrete withstand freeze/thaw damage.

■ **Cost.** Concrete is sold by cubic yard, but the price will vary by region. Also, expect a fee for delivery. There could be other fees for such things as Saturday delivery and small loads. Ask about these fees so you know the total bill before the truck arrives.

■ **Unload time.** Ask about the normal unload time (usually 7 to 10 minutes per yard) and if there is a fee for overtime. If the truck can't reach the site, make sure you have two or three people with wheelbarrows ready to go.

Don't drill into brick

Whenever you install a lightweight item like a downspout on brick, always drill into the mortar joints instead of the brick face. The brick is more likely to crack, and if the downspout ever needs to be moved, patching a hole in gray mortar is a lot easier than trying to match the color of the brick. And always install plastic anchors because metal anchors more likely to crack the mortar when they expand.

CRACK-RESISTANT MIX

The best type of bagged concrete to use for a walkway

If you want to get your walkway back into service fast, your best choice is "high early strength" concrete. This type of concrete has a higher percentage of cement in the blend so it sets up faster than standard concrete mix. You can walk on it within 10 to 12 hours, compared with several days.

It also generates more heat than standard bagged concrete mix, which means you can tackle your walkway project earlier or later in the season, in temperatures as low as 35 degrees F, with less chance of setting and hardening problems.

However, if your walkway has many steps or landings with exposed edges, we recommend fiber-reinforced, crack-resistant concrete mix. It contains thousands of little plastic fibers to make it more resistant to shrinkage cracks, edge chipping, impact damage and scaling during freeze/thaw cycles. Crack-resistant concrete takes three days to set up, so your walkway will be out of commission that long, but it can make concrete steps more durable under harsh conditions.

The right concrete for a project is a matter of trade-offs. Consider setup speed, surface durability and the amount of weight the surface will bear. No matter which product you choose, use as little water as possible. The lower the water-to-cement ratio, the stronger the concrete and the better the shrinkage resistance.

HOLIDAY TIPS

ALARM

HEAT SENSOR
ANGEL

LOW-WATER
DETECTOR

Zip-tie your decorations

Zip ties are a simple way to string holiday lights on banisters and fences without marring the railing with nail marks. A pack of 20 zip ties costs a few dollars at home centers. You'll find them in the electrical supplies aisle. After the holidays, snip the ties off with scissors.

Christmas tree safety

First off, choose a recently cut, healthy tree. A fresh tree holds moisture better. Grab a tree branch and run your hand over it—no more than a few needles should fall off. As soon as you get the tree home, cut 1/2 in. off the trunk and place the tree in a bucket of water until you're ready to bring it into the house. When you set the tree up to decorate it, make sure it's stable in the stand and won't tip over, and water it frequently. A 6-ft. tree needs about 1 gallon of water every other day.

When decorating, use lights rated for indoor use that don't create heat (such as LED lights). And don't overload your electrical outlet. If you want to power dozens of strands of lights and other electric decorations, plug them into different circuits around the house. If you continually blow a circuit, it's probably overloaded.

Here are some other tips:

■ Don't use electric lights on a metal tree.
■ Unplug tree lights before leaving the house or going to bed.
■ Keep the tree at least 3 ft. from candles and fireplaces.

Christmas tree safety systems are available that will detect low water in the tree stand and send a warning if a fire starts (see photo). Place the system's low water detector in the tree stand. It'll send an audio alert and trigger flashing lights on the attached heat sensor if the water level gets too low.

The ornamental angel used for this device signals a remote alarm if it senses heat, warning you that a fire could start or has started. The alarm plugs into the wall. For more information, search "Christmas tree safety system" online.

Holiday light storage stands

If you use lots of holiday light strings each year, you know that storing that many without wrecking them is tough. Here's a solution: Just screw a dowel to each end of a wooden base cut to the size of a large plastic bin. Then wrap your lights around the dowels in a figure eight and place the stand in the bin. You'll be amazed how many light strings you can wrap around the stands without tangles or damage.

Ornaments by the cup

It's hard to store fragile ornaments without breaking them. That's the beauty of this solution: Use a plastic storage container and store each ornament in a separate plastic cup. By using cardboard to separate the layers, you can stack a lot of ornaments in one sturdy box without any tangling or breaking. You can reuse the same cups and cardboard year after year.

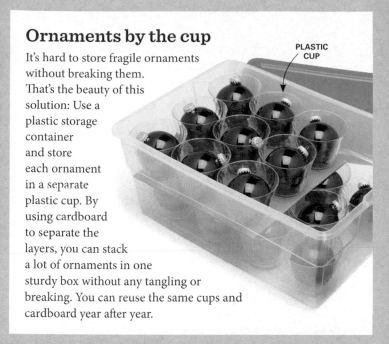

PLASTIC CUP

Easy outside light control

We all love the cheerful glow of outside holiday lights, but going out in the cold to plug them in and unplug them is a pain. Use an outdoor remote control switch that you can control from inside your home or car. You can buy these devices at home centers or online. All you do is plug the switch into any outdoor outlet and use the small transmitter to control it.

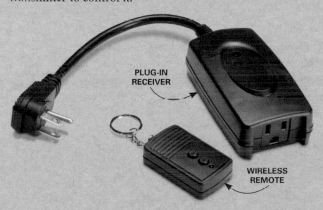

PLUG-IN RECEIVER

WIRELESS REMOTE

Lazy Susan tree stand for wood floors

Winding the lights around a Christmas tree is always a pain, but you can rotate the tree in its stand—without scratching up the floor. Put a bath rug underneath the tree stand, fabric side down, rubber side up. Now you can easily turn the tree to string your lights and place your ornaments just where you want them. It makes "undecorating" the tree a breeze too. Just fold the rug under the tree skirt to keep it hidden.